Spoken Discourse

BLOOMSBURY DISCOURSE

Series Editor: Professor Ken Hyland, University of Hong Kong

Discourse is one of the most significant concepts of contemporary thinking in the humanities and social sciences as it concerns the ways language mediates and shapes our interactions with each other and with the social, political and cultural formations of our society. The *Bloomsbury Discourse* aims to capture the fast-developing interest in discourse to provide students, new and experienced teachers and researchers in applied linguistics, ELT and English language with an essential bookshelf. Each book deals with a core topic in discourse studies to give an in-depth, structured and readable introduction to an aspect of the way language in used in real life.

Other titles in the series:

Academic Discourse, Ken Hyland

Corporate Discourse, Ruth Breeze

Discourse Analysis (2nd edition), Brian Paltridge

Discourse Studies Reader, Edited by Ken Hyland

The Discourse of Blogs and Wikis, Greg Myers

The Discourse of Online Consumer Reviews, Camilla Vasquez

The Discourse of Text Messaging, Caroline Tagg

Discourse of Twitter and Social Media, Michele Zappavigna

Historical Discourse, Caroline Coffin

Metadiscourse, Ken Hyland

News Discourse, Monika Bednarek and Helen Caple

Professional Discourse, Britt-Louise Gunnarsson

School Discourse, Frances Christie

Sports Discourse, Tony Schirato

Using Corpora in Discourse Analysis, Paul Baker

Workplace Discourse, Almut Koester

Spoken Discourse

RODNEY H. JONES

Bloomsbury Academic
An imprint of Bloomsbury Publishing Plc

BLOOMSBURY
LONDON · OXFORD · NEW YORK · NEW DELHI · SYDNEY

Bloomsbury Academic

An imprint of Bloomsbury Publishing Plc

50 Bedford Square
London
WC1B 3DP
UK

1385 Broadway
New York
NY 10018
USA

www.bloomsbury.com

BLOOMSBURY and the Diana logo are trademarks of Bloomsbury Publishing Plc

First published 2016

© Rodney H. Jones, 2016

Rodney H. Jones has asserted his right under the Copyright, Designs and
Patents Act, 1988, to be identified as the Author of this work.

British Library Cataloguing-in-Publication Data
A catalogue record for this book is available from the British Library.

ISBN: HB: 978-1-4725-8990-3
PB: 978-1-4725-8989-7
ePDF: 978-1-4725-8991-0
ePub: 978-1-4725-8992-7

Library of Congress Cataloging-in-Publication Data
A catalog record for this book is available from the Library of Congress

Series: Bloomsbury Discourse

Typeset by Deanta Global Publishing Services, Chennai, India
Printed and bound in India

Contents

Transcription conventions

(0.1)	pause (length in seconds indicated by number in parentheses)
(.)	pause of less than 0.1 seconds
[ ]	overlapping speech
=	latching
.	falling intonation
?	rising intonation in questions
^	rising intonation
↑↓	rising–falling intonation
↓↑	falling–rising intonation
<u>word</u>	stress/emphasis
WORD	shouting
$	'smile voice'
(gesture)	non-verbal behaviour

1

What is spoken discourse?

Coming out

This is a book about how people use conversations to manage their lives – to get things done, to form and maintain relationships with other people, to enact certain kinds of social identities and to participate in social groups. To illustrate some of the complexities involved in the study of spoken discourse, I would like to begin by considering the following conversation:

Son: Can I tell you something?
Dad: Yeah.
Son: Will you love me? Period?
Dad: Yes.
Son: Like you you'll always love me, as long as I'm ...
Dad: Don't worry.
Son: Dad I'm gay.
Dad: Gay?

Most readers will immediately be able to identify this conversation as a particular 'type' of conversation occurring between particular 'types' of people, a conversation with its own particular set of 'rules'. As soon as we read this conversation, we understand that this son and his father are not just chatting. They are *doing* something very specific: they are engaging in the practice of 'coming out', a practice that most readers will recognize: they may have read about it or seen it enacted in movies or on television, they may know people who have taken part in this practice, or they may have participated in it themselves. Therefore, most readers would have little trouble inferring all sorts of things about the relationship between these two speakers and imagining what might be going on inside their heads. More importantly, nearly everyone who reads this will have some idea about whether this is a 'successful' encounter of its kind or not, and whether or not the participants have performed their roles in the encounter appropriately.

When I refer to 'coming out' as a particular 'type' of conversation, what I mean is that it is governed by a particular set of discursive conventions. That is not to say that this type of conversation always occurs in the same way. Far from it. But people engaging in the *genre* of 'coming out' do have a rather well-defined set of actions that they need to accomplish if they are going to be recognized as 'pulling it off'. Minimally, the genre must consist of two actions (or 'speech acts'), what we can call a *revelation* and a *response*. For the revelation to count as such it must meet certain conditions: one being that it contains information that the other person is (at least to the knowledge of the person carrying out the revelation) not aware of, and for it to count as part of the genre of 'coming out' it should be about a particular topic, that is, the sexuality of the person carrying out the revelation (although nowadays people are appropriating the label 'coming out' to refer to all sorts of other revelations). It should also be, for the most part, a voluntary action – revealing that you are gay while being tortured doesn't really count as 'coming out'. The response part of this genre is also a matter of choice. In societies in which this practice is usually carried out, reactions to the revelation are usually seen as being situated somewhere between the two poles of acceptance and rejection, and acceptance or rejection of the revelation is usually taken to entail acceptance or rejection of the person who has made it and is seen to have important consequences for the future relationship of participants. It is for this reason that we find the response in the above conversation rather unsatisfying. The father's response ('Gay?') could be interpreted as a request for clarification or as an expression of surprise, but it could also imply a kind of rejection, simply due to the fact that it does not express the 'preferred response' (Pomerantz 1984) of acceptance. In any case, we cannot be sure yet about the nature of this response, and if our sympathies are with the son, we can't help but feel concerned.

Partly because of the 'high stakes' of this practice, there is usually another set of actions involved, which normally occur before the *revelation*, which we might label the *preparation*. Actions designed to set the scene or prepare people physically, mentally or emotionally for other actions occur in many different types of conversation such as the delivery of 'bad news' by physicians (see e.g., Maynard 2003). In this case the preparation is accomplished through the use of three questions ('Can I tell you something?', 'Will you love me?' 'Like, you'll always love me …?'). These questions perform multiple functions. First, they delay the revelation, signalling to the father that what is about to be said may be difficult for his son to say or for the father to accept. Second, they serve as a kind of *metadiscourse* – a way for the participants to make what they are doing explicit by talking about it. By asking 'Can I tell you something?'

the son frames the ensuing conversation as a certain kind of conversation, specifically one that will involve some kind of new information – something more than just 'small talk'. Finally, the questions serve the function of eliciting a kind of *promise* from the father as to the nature of his upcoming response. By eliciting an agreement to 'always love him', the son makes it more difficult for the father to choose a response involving rejection.

Just to say that this conversation is an example of coming out, then, ignores all of the other practices necessary for its accomplishment. As the analysis above reveals, 'coming out' also depends on many 'smaller' actions, actions of revealing and responding, and of asking and answering that are part of the 'technology of conversation' (Sacks 1992a: 339). In fact, this whole business of coming out would not really be possible without the 'equipment' that conversation provides, which enables people not just to form meaningful utterances like 'Daddy, I'm gay,' but also to perform actions like revealing and responding in an orderly way. Of course, it might be possible to accomplish the action of 'coming out' without uttering words – a child, for example, might display certain behaviours or leave certain objects to be found by the parent, allowing the parent to infer the information – and in some societies, these 'silent' acts of coming out seem to be preferred (see e.g., Liu and Ding 2005). Even such cases, however, still depend on the basic mechanisms of conversation – that is, they depend on the parties assuming that certain actions have meanings, and these meanings are arranged in an orderly sequence in which what one person says or does creates an invitation for the other person to respond in a particular way.

At the same time, this conversation represents only one moment in a long chain of actions and interactions that are necessary to understand the *social practice* of 'coming out'. From the perspective of the person doing the 'coming out', for instance, the conversation likely represents only a small part of a much longer process, a process that might include a whole host of other practices including discovering his sexuality, concealing this discovery, and finally working up the courage to reveal it (Liang 1997). And for the person on the receiving end of the revelation, it may be interpreted in the light of a long chain of practices involved in parenting, including observing the son's behaviour, asking if he has a girlfriend, etc.

So the first thing we can say about spoken discourse is that it always involves people *doing something*, whether that something is momentous like 'coming out' or less momentous like asking a question. We can also say that these 'doings' are usually not simple, but often involve not just multiple actions (such as revealing and reacting) but also multiple social practices. Finally, we can also conclude from this short transcript that although we can *infer* a lot about what is going on here, there is a lot more going on here that we cannot really be sure about given the limited information we have. This last point, as we will see, is one of the main challenges involved in studying spoken discourse, the fact that whatever we do, our knowledge about the social interactions that we study is always somehow incomplete. But, as we will also see, this is also one of the main challenges of *participating* in conversations, the fact that our knowledge about what the other person 'really means' by what they say is always also somehow incomplete. And so when somebody responds to our revelation that we are gay with the utterance 'Gay?', all we can do is do our best to *infer* what they mean by this.

Between the lines

Often when people transcribe conversations like the one above, they focus on what people say and don't give much information about how they say it, and they focus on the words rather than the pauses in between the words. By adding more information about how this exchange actually sounded, however, we may get a slightly different impression of how it went:

```
61   Son:   can I tell you somethin?
62          (0.8)
63   Dad:   yeah
64          (0.8)
65   Son:   willya love me? (.) period?
66          (1.1)
67   Dad:   yes.
68          (0.7)
69   Son:   like you you'll always love me^ (0.5)
70          As long as I'm [ah
71   Dad:                  [don't worry
72          (3.4)
73   Son:   Dad I'm gay.
74          (2.3)
75   Dad:   gay↓↑
```

As can be seen from this new version of the transcript, there are quite a lot of silences in this conversation (indicated by numbers in parenthesis which show the length of the pauses in seconds). In fact, the two parties are actually *not* talking more than they are talking. Most of the silences occur where you would expect pauses to occur in conversations: in between turns. One function of these kinds of silences, of course, is to help manage when each of the participants is supposed to speak. Generally, one person speaks, and then remains silent long enough for the other person to realize that it is their turn to talk. At the same time, the length of most of the pauses between turns in this conversation seem much longer than would normally be necessary for the next person to figure out that it is their turn to talk. Of course, the length of pauses between turns in conversations varies a lot across cultures and across contexts. Tanya Stivers and her colleagues at the Max Plank Institute in the Netherlands (2009) did a study of the average amount of time that occurs between conversational turns in ten languages and found that it varies from around 7 milliseconds for Japanese to around 469 milliseconds for Danish, with English falling in between with an average of 237 milliseconds between turns. Contrast this with the conversation above in which some pauses between turns last as long as two or three seconds. Two or three seconds is actually a very long time to pause between turns in a conversation.

How long people pause, of course, depends not just on the conventions of their culture, but on their relationship with the person whom they are talking to, the topic of their conversation, and most importantly, what they are *doing* in the conversation (e.g., revealing a secret or reacting to a surprising piece of news). So, just as the speakers in this conversation are doing things with their words, they are also doing things with their pauses.

As we saw above, what people are doing with their words is not always entirely clear from the words themselves. People often have to make inferences about what the other person means. This process of making inferences, of course, is, even more challenging with pauses, since pauses lack the kind of propositional content we find in utterances. On the other hand, given what we know about this social practice, we can quite comfortably infer the meanings of some of these pauses. We can assume, for example, that the 3.4-second pause that occurs before the son's turn in line 73 ('Dad, I'm gay') constitutes part of the preparation, signalling that the ensuing utterance will have particular significance. We might even take it to communicate something about the psychological state of the speaker. The 1.1-second pause after the question in line 65 ('willya love me?' (.) period?) might be more difficult to interpret. We might take it as the father hesitating to express unconditional love for his son, but we would more likely take it as a signal that the father finds the question unusual, and this interpretation would be confirmed in turn 71 when, in response to the son asking this question again the father not only does not pause, but doesn't even wait for his son to finish before giving his answer ('don't worry'). The most problematic pause, both for us, and probably for the son, is the 2.3-second pause in between the revelation and the reaction (line 74). Occurring where it does in the conversation, it is almost impossible for us (and, most importantly, for the son) not to assign to that silence some meaning, regardless of what the father actually meant by it.

When we start to look at the conversation in this way, we realize that there is a lot going on in spoken discourse apart from the words people speak, and, for that matter, a lot more going on that we as analysts *don't* have access to, even with this 'enhanced' transcript. While we now know, for example, that the son puts extra stress on certain words (like tell and gay), we don't know exactly how much stress. We also don't know what kinds of non-verbal behaviour accompanied these utterances. Knowing the sort of expression the father had on his face when he said 'gay↓↑' might, for example, help us interpret this utterance better.

So now there are a few other facts we can add to our understanding of spoken discourse, the first being that, spoken discourse is almost never a straightforward exchange of information; it always involves some degree of 'guessing' about what other people mean by what they say (or don't say). The second is that whether or not people are able to guess correctly often depends on more than just the words they say to each other. It also depends on who the people are, and where they are, and on their previous relationship and the store of knowledge they bring to the conversation, and on various non-verbal ways of communicating like pauses and facial expressions. Finally, we have learnt something about the way spoken discourse is represented and the consequences that it can have on the way we interpret it. Because the second example of this conversation contains information about pauses, intonation and pronunciation, we may interpret it slightly differently than we did the first version. At the same time, we become aware that there is still a lot of information missing from this transcript that may further change how we interpret it. In other words, our analysis of spoken discourse depends crucially on how we represent it, and any representation of spoken discourse is not just an incomplete representation of what actually happened, but is also potentially a kind of distortion, exaggerating the importance of some aspects of the interaction over others.

Mediation

As you might have noticed from the numbers assigned to the lines, the excerpt I gave above does not begin at the beginning of the conversation. As you might also have guessed, the conversation goes on for some time after the father has said 'Gay?'. Below is a longer excerpt:

    34   (phone ringing)
    35   Dad: hello? (0.4)
    36   Son: hey daddy↑↓

```
37        (1.0)
38  Dad:  hey bu::d↑↓ (0.2)
39  Son:  hey waddayu doin.
40        (1.1)
41  Dad:  waddum I doin?=
42  Son:                =$ye yeah.$
43        (0.6)
44  Dad:  I'm listenin t'my son thinkin (inaudible) cuz I ain't heard his voice
45        in a long ti:me
46        (0.7)
47  Son:  well wedup (.) waddayu doin right now.
48        (1.3)
49  Dad:  jus (inaudible) sittin upsta:irs^ (0.3)
50  Son:  oh who's with you.
51        (1.5)
52  Dad:  Sherry^ (0.5)
53  Son:  oh
54        (2.2)
55        ah::
56        (0.6)
57        hey canna tell you somethin?
58        (2.6)
59  Dad:  what?
60        (0.6)
61  Son:  can I tell you somethin?
62        (0.8)
63  Dad:  yeah.
64        (0.8)
65  Son:  willya love me? (.) period?
66        (1.1)
67  Dad:  yes.
68        (0.7)
69  Son:  like you you'll always love me. (0.5)
70        As long as I'm [ah
71  Dad:                 [don't worry
72        (3.4)
73  Son:  Dad I'm gay.
74        (2.3)
75  Dad:  gay↓↑
76        (1.8)
77  Son:  like always have been (0.6) I've known since (.) forever
78        (1.2)
```

79		and uh::
80		(1.2)
81		I know I haven't seen you in like a year↑↓ (0.2) and uh:
82		(1.0)
83		I I don't know when's the next time I'll be able t'seeya n
84		I didn't wanna doit over the pho:ne. (0.5)
85		and I wanted to tell you (0.9) in person but ah::^
86		(1.3)
87		I da I mean I didn't wantcha t'find out any other way.
88		(2.8)
89	Dad:	okay^
90		(2.6)
91	Son:	you still love me?
92		(0.5)
93	Dad:	ah still love ya son.
94		(4.1)
95		yes I still love ya. (0.4)
96	Son:	you okay? (0.2) Dad?
97		(1.7)
98	Dad:	doesn't change (0.4) our relationship.
99		(4.3)
100		hear me? (0.2)
101	Son:	yeah ↓↑
102		(4.3)
103	Dad:	doesn't change our relationship (0.3)
104	Son:	you're the first one I told I haven't told Mom. (0.9)
105		or (0.1) any of the gi:rls^
106		(1.6)
107	Dad:	°kay°
108		(1.9)
109	Son:	s:o::^
110		(2.0)
111		I d'know (0.2) do ya wanna tell Mom for me?
112		(1.2)
113	Dad:	he he he he he he he (1.3) I don't believe so.
114		(1.3)
115	Son:	duya think she'll know?
116		(4.9)
117	Dad:	I think it's gonna be a shock.
118		(2.9)
119		I had my suspicions there for a lil' while^
120		(4.2)

```
121  Son:   yeah?
122          (3.1)
123          well other than that every$thing's$ great. (0.7) so^
124          (3.8)
125          um:^
126          (2.2)
127          uh [huh^
```

We learn a lot more about the situation from this longer transcript. First, we find out how the son deals with his father's incomplete reaction by taking over the floor in turn 43 to further elaborate on his revelation, and then to offer various explanations as to why he is making his revelation at this particular time and in this particular way, periodically pausing to give his father a chance to elaborate on his reaction, which he finally does with an also vaguely unsatisfying 'okay^', until finally the son returns to his initial question to elicit the 'proper' reaction, 'you still love me?', to which the father finally replies, 'ah still love you son.' We also see how the father, perhaps realising the insufficiency of his initial reaction, attempts to repair this by repeating his acceptance of his son ('yes ah still love ya' ... 'doesn't change (0.4) our relationship' ... 'hear me?' ... 'doesn't change our relationship').

But perhaps the most important thing we learn from this longer excerpt is that this conversation is not occurring face-to-face but is *mediated* through the telephone, and the knowledge that this is a telephone conversation also changes how we interpret it. 'Coming out' over the phone has a slightly different meaning from 'coming out' in a face-to-face conversation, attested to in this particular example by the fact that the son finds it necessary to *account* for why he is using the phone ('I didn't wanna doit over the pho:ne (0.5) and I wanted to tell you (0.9) in person but ah::^ (1.3) I da I mean I didn't wantcha t'find out any other way.'). But the fact that this is a telephone conversation also changes the way we (and the son) might interpret specific utterances by the father and the pauses between these utterances. A long pause over the telephone – during which we have no access to the other person's facial expression and gaze – is experienced differently from the way it is in face-to-face communication. There are also certain utterances and exchanges that only make sense if we know this is a telephone conversation. Take, for example, the opening.

```
35  Dad:   hello? (0.4)
36  Son:   hey daddy↑↓
37          (1.0)
38  Dad:   hey bu::d↑↓ (0.2)
39  Son:   hey waddayu doin.
```

In a face-to-face conversation, the initial 'hello', which serves as a response to the son's 'summons' (coming in the form of a ringing phone) would, of course, not be necessary, unless the father was behind a closed door and the son needed to knock to gain access to him. Even the utterance in line 39 ('hey waddayu doin.'), a common question at the beginning of a phone conversation, would mean something slightly different if it occurred in a face-to-face conversation. One reason why the father's answer, 'I'm listenin t'my son ...' strikes us as slightly humorous is that, when delivered over the phone this question is usually meant to gain access to information that is not perceptible to the person who asks the question.

Most importantly, the fact that this conversation is mediated through the telephone makes certain things possible that would not be possible in a face-to-face conversation. For example, it makes it possible for the son to talk to his father even though they may be thousands of miles apart. We call a particular technology's ability to make certain things possible the *affordances* of that technology. But just as technologies have affordances, they also have *constraints*, that is, they can also prevent people from doing certain things. The telephone, for example, prevents the son from seeing his father's facial expressions, which, in these particular circumstances, might provide very useful information to him. Of course, nowadays with videoconferencing tools like Skype and 'FaceTime', all of that is changing (Sindoni 2013). The most interesting thing about affordances and constraints is that sometimes it's difficult to tell which is which, that is, often affordances are, at the same time, constraints, and constraints are, at the same time, affordances. For instance, although there are distinct disadvantages to the son not having access to his father's facial expressions, this might actually make it easier for him to deliver this delicate piece of news because of the 'emotional buffer' created by the technology's constraints. A similar example can be seen in the work of the conversation analyst Harvey Sacks, who studied suicide hotlines. One of the affordances of the telephone, he remarked, at least from the point of view of people who want to talk about their suicidal thoughts, is that it allows them to avoid identifying themselves if they don't want to (Sacks 1992a).

It would be a mistake, however, to think that, were this conversation taking place 'face-to-face' it would be *un*mediated. Face-to-face communication would give participants different tools with which to communicate, tools like facial expressions and gestures, but these tools themselves are also *mediational means*, with their own sets of affordances and constraints. It is a central claim of this book that *all* spoken discourse is mediated in some way. Minimally, all spoken discourse is mediated through the human voice and the biological apparatus that is used to produce it, which comes with its own affordances and constraints for the production of certain kinds of sounds and sound combinations. The body, with its various expressive parts – such as the face and hands – is also a tool through which our interaction with others is often mediated. Finally, face-to-face interactions are always mediated through various aspects of the physical setting, rooms, furniture, and other objects.

There are also technologies involved in spoken discourse that are less visible because they exist not as physical tools but more as sets of rules and expectations inside the heads of speakers. Most spoken interactions, for example, are mediated through some kind of language or 'code' with its particular ways of labelling things and phenomena, of dividing up and categorizing the world. Along with these codes, we bring to situations certain sets of rules for interacting and expectations regarding how different kinds of interactions are meant to unfold, which I referred to above as *genres*. These codes and sets of rules about using them are often part of larger *social practices*, which can be considered highly developed 'technologies' for getting things done in the societies in which we live. The practice I am focusing on here is the practice of 'coming out', but we can think of many other examples of social practices, practices such as attending lectures, eating at fast food restaurants, skateboarding, and giving testimony in a court of law, each with its own conventions regarding who is allowed to participate, what roles they are meant to take, and what they are supposed to say. In fact, even things like social roles or *identities* (like father, son, lawyer and skateboarder) can also be seen as tools, which we take up and use differently in different situations.

It may be strange at first to think of things like social practices and social identities and even languages as 'technologies' in the same way that we think of telephones and computers, but as much as telephones and computers, these things are cultural artefacts, invented by human beings for getting things done. In his 2012 book, *Language: The Cultural Tool*, anthropological linguist Daniel Everett makes a spirited and persuasive argument for treating language as a 'tool' whose invention was shaped by the practical needs of those who invented it rather than as a mental capacity or 'instinct' as some linguists would have it, and if language can be considered a tool, so then can any organized code of semiotic conduct.

Getting back to the conversation above, then, we can say that it is mediated not just through the telephone, but also through the voices of the participants, through a particular variety of the English language, through the sets of rules governing the conduct of this particular type of conversation, through the social identities of 'father' and 'son', the social categories of 'gay' and 'straight', and the social practice of 'coming out'.

And so, the main thing this longer excerpt teaches us about spoken discourse is that it is always *mediated* through certain 'technologies' or 'cultural tools', some of which are physical (like telephones) and others of which are symbolic, like the English language and the social practice of 'coming out'.

Widening the circumference

One thing that should be clear from our analysis so far is the fact that the more of this conversation we have access to, the better we can understand what's going on, Sometimes this involves 'zooming in', finding out something about the small details of the interaction like the length of pauses between turns, and sometimes it involves 'zooming out', seeing what people say and do as part of a larger conversation or activity, such as a telephone call. This process of 'zooming in and out' is called 'circumferencing' (Burke 1969; Scollon and Scollon 2004), and is an essential methodological procedure in the study of spoken discourse, because it allows us to gain new perspectives on what people are saying and doing by focusing on different 'scales' of action (Blommaert 2005, 2010; Lemke 2000).

While the transcript of the phone conversation I gave above can tell us a lot about who these people are and what they are doing and the different kinds of technologies they are appropriating to perform these actions, there is still some rather crucial information about the wider *context* of this 'coming out' that is not included. Below is what occurs just prior to the son placing the phone call:

(Start of video)
1   (The screen shows a room with a table and chair. There is a map of the
2   World hanging on the wall above the chair.)
3   (2.0)
4   (A young man enters the screen holding a mobile phone. He has short hair
5   and is dressed in fatigue trousers and a white tee-shirt.) (5.0)
6   Son: hey it's um (1.3) the morning of sep September twentieth^ (0.9)
7   I (.) could not sleep (.) it's uh two forty five^ (1.0) and I am (0.8)
8   uh probably as nervous as (.) as I can ever remember being (0.9)
9   ahm: (0.7) mm (0.8) I'm about to call my dad^ (0.8) in Alabama^
10   (0.3) umm (1.2) I think it's (.) I'm in Germany right now so I think
11   we're seven hours ahead^ (0.8) so it should be like (0.5) seven
12   forty five at night.
13   (drinking) (1.6) (swallowing sound) (0.7)
14   u:hm^ (1.2) so hopefully
15   I'll be able to (0.9) get holda him (0.8) uhm he has no clue (1.8) nor
16   do any members of my family. (1.0) a::m (2.6) really kind of
17   pa:nicing about this like all weekend^ (1.0) en I said (1.6) um that
18   wanna do it^
19   (3.9)
20   I wonder if I'm gonna be able t'get holda them

21		(3.5) .hhh
22		(9.4)
23		(phone ringing 2.0 secs)
24		(4.5)
25		(whispered) my heart (inaudible) beating
26		(20.01) (double beeping sound)
27		(0.8)
28		(single beeping sound)
29		(12.5)
30		(phone ringing 1.5 secs)
31		(2.5)
32		hh. (.) ahh.
33		(0.7)
34		(phone ringing 1.5 secs)
35		(1.8)
36	Dad:	he<u>ll</u>o? (0.4) (on speaker mode)
37	Son:	<u>hey</u> daddy↑↓

This short introduction by the son to the conversation he is about to have includes some information about the context of the situation that dramatically affects how we interpret what's going on here. We now know, for example, that the son is placing the phone call from Germany to his father in Alabama, nearly 5,000 miles and six time zones away. This helps to further explain why the son has chosen to deliver this news via the phone rather than face-to-face. From the information about the son's location, as well as his appearance, we may even be able to infer that he is a US serviceman from Alabama stationed at a US military base in Germany, a piece of contextual information which might be treated as highly significant if you know anything about the contentious debates surrounding gays and lesbians in the military that have been taking place in the United States over the past twenty years, culminating in the lifting of the ban on openly gay service members in 2011, or if you know anything about the culture of the military or the culture of Alabama. We also get to find out something about the history of the relationship between the father and the son, the fact that, as far as the son knows, neither the father nor any of his other family members know that he is gay. Finally, we learn something about the son's internal emotional state, how nervous he feels about going through with the social practice of 'coming out', which is also part of the context of the situation.

The most important thing we learn about the context of this 'coming out', however, is that it is being videoed, that it is actually part of a larger performance which the son has uploaded onto his YouTube channel with the title: 'Telling my dad that I am gay LIVE!'[1] This new piece of information completely changes the way we regard this interaction. What we had before imagined was a private conversation we now know is a kind of public performance. We know that the words spoken by the son were designed to be heard not just by his father but by the audience of his YouTube channel. At the same time, we may realize that the father was at the time probably not aware that his words were to be made public to an audience of millions of people. With this new information, we 'hear' the son's words and the father's words slightly differently.

All of this also puts *us* in a very odd position regarding this conversation. We have, in a way, suddenly become participants in it, but participants with ambiguous roles. On the one hand, we are positioned as outsiders listening in, as eavesdroppers, especially when it comes to what the father is saying. On the other hand, we have in some sense been invited by the son into the conversation as 'ratified' participants (Goffman 1966, see Chapter 5) with a legitimate role to play, first, as 'witnesses' to the conversation between the son and his father, and second as interlocutors with the ability to talk back to the son about his coming out via the 'comment' function on YouTube, which tens of thousands of the viewers have, leaving comments like:

> So proud of you. I'm glad your father understands. God bless you.
> (Aye, Dats Camo!)

and

> Absolutely disgraceful. If my son had come out as gay, I would have stoned him to death. Luckily, here in Texas, it's easier for us to ship away any unwanted sons or daughters we have. A gay son ain't no son of mine!
> (Liam C.)

In fact, from the time this video was posted in September of 2011 to the time I am writing this chapter, 73,092 comments had been posted underneath it. Many of these comments were direct responses to the video, but others were responses to other commenters. In other words, this video had become (before it was removed when the channel was 'hacked' in July of 2015) an occasion not just for a conversation between the poster and his viewers, but also for hundreds of side conversations among viewers. Of course, not all of the people who watched this video commented on it. In fact most of the over 7.5 million people who had watched this video at the time of writing did not respond at all, and others responded in less verbal ways by simply 'liking' it (76,882) or 'disliking' it (8,201).

---

[1] Available at https://www.youtube.com/watch?v=FszfGDVu2Vo.

Understanding the kinds of roles that viewers can take up in relation to the video becomes even more complicated when we consider the larger context of this poster's YouTube channel as a whole, a channel which he operated under the screen name AreYouSuprised, and which was almost totally devoted to videos documenting his 'journey' of coming out (to his friends, his comrades in the military, his parents, and to the general public).[2] So, while some viewers were encountering this person for the first time in this video, others were 'fans', and so were able to interpret this conversation in the context of other videos the poster had posted and the longer *process* of coming out that this video was part of.

We may regard these complex configurations of participation as rather unusual, something unique to internet communication and the age of YouTube, and it is true that technologies like digital video and the internet have had a significant impact on the ways we participate in conversations (Androstopholous and Tereick 2015). At the same time, many interactions which we consider quite normal have similarly complex overlapping and inter-nested forms of participation. Think of, for instance, the kinds of participation that often characterize university lectures, where the primary interaction, that between the lecturer and the students, is more often than not accompanied by side interactions between students and even interactions between students and non-co-present others via computers or mobile phones. Or recall the last time you witnessed a couple having an argument on a public bus or subway train, how they manage to carve out a zone of private space in public, at the same time maintaining some level of decorum that comes from an awareness that they have an audience. Even a typical conversation around a family dinner table can be incredibly complex, with multiple interactions often occurring simultaneously, and participants moving in and out of these different conversations and taking on different roles in them (see e.g., Erickson 1986, 2004).

Most models of spoken discourse see 'prototypical' conversations as bounded, private affairs involving usually just two participants who are often defined by roles such as 'speaker' and 'hearer'. Although some conversations are like this, most are more complicated, involving all sorts of participants who dynamically negotiate different types of 'speakership' and 'hearership' in relation to other participants.

And so what this version of the conversation teaches us about spoken discourse is that it often involves rather complex configurations of participation. As the sociologist Erving Goffman (1959) pointed out more than half a century ago, whenever we interact with others, we are always performing. But these

---

[2]Original url: https://www.youtube.com/user/AreYouSuprised. This channel has been removed. Videos currently available at: https://www.youtube.com/channel/UCsqGpoYl_MdQvLszlYVD3pw (I would like to thank Randy Phillips, the owner of this channel, for his kind permission to quote from and analyse this material).

performances are hardly ever simple; they often involve us performing multiple different roles for multiple different audiences at the same time.

Another point about spoken discourse that this version of the conversation highlights is the fact that the contexts in which interactions take place are also complex and layered, and different aspects of context become relevant to different participants at different moments. In discussing the context of this coming out, for example, we can speak of the context of the telephone conversation in which it occurs, or the physical context of the rooms in which the son and father are sitting, or the context of the son and father's relationship and the history of their interactions about this topic, or the context of the US military and its history of attitudes and policies towards homosexuality, or the context of Alabama where the son grew up perhaps surrounded by people who espoused rather traditional conservative values, or the context of the son's YouTube channel in which this private conversation is turned into a public display, linked to the other videos he (and other YouTubers) have posted about this topic. All of these aspects of context are important and relevant to different people at different moments in the interaction, and they all interact with and affect one another.

Finally, what this version of the conversation highlights is that spoken discourse, especially nowadays, is actually more 'permanent' and more 'portable' than we usually think. We often think of speech as ephemeral (at least in comparison to written discourse), believing that our words disappear into the air once they are uttered. But with the widespread use of portable audio and video recording devices (often embedded in our mobile phones), it is becoming easier and more common for people to record their utterances so that they can be replayed in physically and temporally remote contexts and even broadcast to large audiences. Even without such devices, however, our words are more durable than we usually imagine: what we say is constantly being remembered and repeated by others, and much of what we say consists of reporting words that we or others have uttered in the past. In fact, we might, following the Soviet literary scholar Mikhail Bakhtin (1981, 1986), go so far as to say that pretty much *all* that we say is a repetition of what others have said in the past, appropriated by us and adapted to our own specific purposes. The young man in this video is not the first to utter the words, 'Dad, I'm gay,' and he certainly won't be the last.

Talking heads

As I said above, this is a book about spoken discourse. It's not a book about coming out, or YouTube or the US military's now defunct 'Don't Ask, Don't

Tell' policy. But I will be drawing on the examples of Airman Randy Phillip's now famous 'coming out videos' because they illustrate so well both the practical and the ethical challenges of spoken discourse that I wish to explore in this book. I have also included examples from other contexts, graduation ceremonies, classrooms, service encounters, WhatsApp conversations, political protests, and police traffic stops. As with Randy's coming out videos on YouTube, these other examples also illustrate something about the *consequentiality* of spoken discourse, how what we say to each other (and how we say it) affects the kinds of social identities and social relationships that we are able to create for ourselves, and the kinds of societies we are able to create for one another. It is not hard to see in the example above how an intimate conversation between a son and his father can also have wider social and political implications. My argument in this book is that all of the conversations we have have wider social and political implications, because it is through these conversations that we work together to interpret, negotiate and construct our social worlds.

Many people when they think of 'spoken discourse' or 'conversation' get a picture in their minds that is not very different from Figure 1.1, a picture of two 'talking heads', each sending messages to the other, messages which begin in one person's brain, are encoded into speech and transmitted to the other person's ears and then sent to their brain for decoding.

Although this diagram seems to make intuitive sense, it doesn't much resemble the example I just analysed, nor any other 'real-life' conversation for that matter. First of all, it only assumes two participants, and, although this is sometimes the case, conversations often involve multiple participants (some of them co-present and some of them not). Second, it assumes a rather direct and unproblematic pathway from the brain of one participant to the brain of the other through the medium of spoken language, ignoring all of the other 'technologies' through which spoken discourse is *mediated*: including telephones and YouTube channels, gestures and facial expressions, social

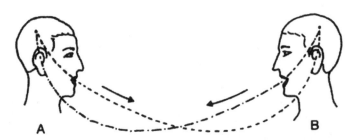

FIGURE 1.1 *Saussure's* 'le circuit de la parole' from Course in General Linguistics *(1916/59: 11).*

identities and social practices. Third, it presents communication as totally devoid of context: A and B in this diagram are floating in empty space; they are not *doing* anything other than transmitting information, and they have no identities like 'father' 'son', 'soldier' or 'YouTube celebrity' (they even look the same). Finally, it makes it all seem much easier than it is, that transmitting and receiving messages is simply a matter of encoding and decoding language; as long as you are familiar with the code that the other person is using, you will have no trouble understanding them. We know, of course, not just from analysing the conversation above but also from our own experiences of having conversations that this is not always the case.

The above diagram appeared in the book *Course in General Linguistics* (1916/59) by the famous French linguist Ferdinand de Saussure to illustrate what he referred to as *parole* or 'speech', and if it seems a bit incomplete or even distorted this may be because Saussure, like many linguists, was not particularly interested in 'speech'. He was much more interested in *langue* the 'system of language' which people make use of when they speak. In Saussure's view, real speech is too 'messy' to be worth studying. The idea of language gives us a way to focus on the one aspect of speech that is amiable to systematic analysis. He writes:

> Taken as a whole, speech is many-sided and heterogeneous; straddling several areas simultaneously – physical, physiological and psychological – it belongs both to the individual and to society; we cannot put it into any category of human facts, for we cannot discover its unity. Language, on the contrary, is a self-contained whole and a principle of classification. As soon as we give language first place among the facts of speech, we introduce a natural order into a mass that lends itself to no other classification. (Saussure 1916/59: 9)

In other words, in the diagram above, Saussure is not representing speech in all of its complexity, but a pared down version of speech which emphasizes the aspect of speech that he is interested in studying: language. This view of speech has been extremely influential in the past hundred years, and it has led to a rather distorted view of spoken discourse in which the primacy of language (as a kind of code) has been exaggerated. Many people who study spoken discourse focus almost exclusively on language, ignoring all of the other technologies people appropriate when engaging in social interaction. This overemphasis on language as 'code' also ends up creating a distorted view of participants in spoken discourse, who in this model tend to be defined according to the processes of encoding and decoding that they apparently engage in. They are seen as merely 'speakers' and 'listeners', abstract identities which, in the end of the day, as Bakhtin (1986: 68) observes, are essentially fictions. He writes:

> Still current in linguistics are such fictions as the 'listener' and 'understander' (partners of the 'speaker'), the 'unified speech flow,' and so on. These fictions produce a completely distorted idea of the complex and multifaceted process of active speech communication. Courses in general linguistics (even serious ones like Saussure's) frequently present graphic-schematic depictions of the two partners in speech communication – the speaker and the listener (who perceives the speech) – and provide diagrams of the active speech processes of the speaker and the corresponding passive processes of the listener's perception and understanding of the speech. One cannot say that these diagrams are false or that they do not correspond to certain aspects of reality. But when they are put forth as the actual whole of speech communication, they become a scientific fiction.

What I will be focusing on in this book is spoken discourse, not 'speech'. The problem with the term 'speech' is that it focuses us too narrowly on the act of encoding thoughts into language and articulating them through the articulatory organs. Sometimes, in fact, when people think of 'speech' they think exclusively of vocal articulation: we go to a 'speech therapist', for example, to remedy some problem we have with the pronunciation of speech sounds, not for more complex problems of spoken discourse such as how to tell your father you're gay.

So what do I mean by 'discourse' and what is the difference between 'spoken discourse' and 'speech'? Most people who work in the rather broad and fractious field of 'discourse analysis' acknowledge that the word discourse has three main meanings. The first meaning is 'language above the clause'. This meaning is designed to distinguish what discourse analysts study from what other people interested in language study. While many linguists are interested in rather small units of language like sounds (phonemes), words (morphemes) or clauses (the building blocks of 'sentences'), discourse analysts are interested in larger units like texts and conversations, and sometimes even larger units like collections of texts or conversations and how they might fit together in the context of social events, social relationships, or social institutions. The focus here is mainly on the *structure* of discourse, how sentences fit together to form cohesive and coherent texts, and how utterances fit together to form cohesive and coherent conversations. The discourse analyst James Paul Gee (2014b) says that, on this level of discourse, analysts are mainly interested in two things, the way we 'package' what we say (whether we say, for example, 'Dad, I'm gay', or 'Dad, I'm a homosexual', or 'Dad I really don't like girls'), and how we arrange these packages to create a logical 'flow' of communication (so that the 'package' that the father offers next is seen to be connected to the 'package' his son offers).

The second definition people usually give for the word 'discourse' is 'language in use'. What this means is that rather than studying language as an abstract system of meaning the way linguists like Saussure, whom I mentioned above, and Noam Chomsky, whom I will discuss at length later on, do, discourse analysts are interested in how people actually *use* language in real life, specifically, how they use language to engage in specific actions in the world with specific other people. As I said above, whenever we speak we are always *doing* something, and a key focus of the discourse analyst is on this *doing*. What this also means is that discourse analysts are not interested in analysing 'sentences', if what we mean by sentences are things made up by linguists to illustrate particular linguistic structures. Instead, they are interested in *utterances*, real time, irreproducible instances of language use in particular situations for particular purposes.

The third meaning of discourse, though, is probably what most clearly separates discourse analysts from other people interested in the study of spoken communication. In this definition, discourse means the way in which people create their social worlds through the way they use language, or, as the critical discourse analyst Norman Fairclough (1992: 3) puts it, the different ways people have of 'structuring areas of knowledge and social practice'. This definition is particularly influenced by the work of French philosopher Michel Foucault (1969, 1971), who argued that our practices of using language and creating and regulating texts (including 'spoken texts') end up not just constraining the way we talk and write, but also the way we think, the kinds of identities we can have, and the kinds of relationships of power that are produced and reproduced in society. A good example that Foucault (1976) gave which is directly relevant to the conversation I analysed above is the discursive construction of the 'homosexual person'. The idea of somebody 'being' gay, and of 'confessing' that to one's parent, according to Foucault, is actually a very recent thing, the result of particular discursive practices and forms of knowledge that developed in late-nineteenth-century Europe. What discourse means in this definition has to do with how different ways of *thinking* about things are tied up with different socially and historically situated ways of talking about things, which are inevitably tied up with different power relations in a society.

Sometimes people who adhere to one or another of these definitions criticize those who adhere to others. People who focus on the structure of texts and stretches of talk, for example, criticize those who are more concerned with broader issues of power and ideology for not paying sufficient attention to the small details of situated interaction, and people who are interested in these broader issues criticize those who focus on the small details of structure and sequence for emphasizing the trivial and not addressing the issues that really matter like justice and equality and discrimination. One of the main purposes of this book is to take us beyond such arguments, to present a model of spoken discourse that not only accommodates all three of these definitions, but also shows how they work together. People sometimes refer to the first definition of discourse (the ways texts and conversations are put together) as 'small d discourse', and the third definition (the ways we use language to construct social realities) as 'big D Discourse'. A central argument I wish to make in this book is that the main point of the study of spoken discourse is to understand the relationship between 'big D' and 'small d' d/Discourses. And the secret to understanding this relationship, I will argue, lies in the second definition, the ways spoken language is used to perform concrete actions in the world. It is in these moments of action that we can observe how the structures of conversations help to form the structures of our societies, and how the structures of our societies help to create the structures of our conversations. To paraphrase Bakhtin (1986), language enters life through concrete actions, and life also enters language through concrete actions.

What this means is that through studying language in use, discourse analysts are also studying things like justice, equality and discrimination. A focus on action as the locus of analysis gives us the potential to help social actors themselves understand more about how their actions are enabled and constrained by the discursive tools available to them in different situations and what they might be able to do about it. So to say that discourse analysis is the study of social action is the same as saying that discourse analysis is the study of *agency*, the capacity people have to take concrete social actions in the world, and the capacity they have to change that world.

How this book is organized

In the remainder of this book, I will develop some of the ideas about studying spoken discourse that I have introduced here. In the next chapter, I will provide a survey of the different disciplines that have contributed to the study of spoken discourse, including linguistics, anthropology, sociology and critical theory, and the main approaches to discourse to come out of these disciplines, such as conversation analysis, the ethnography of speaking, interactional sociolinguistics and critical discourse analysis. All of these approaches will figure prominently in the framework for analysing spoken discourse that I will introduce. At the end of this chapter, I will give an overview of this framework and describe some of its main concepts and analytical tools.

Chapter 3, entitled 'Technologies of Talk', will provide a survey of the various tools that people have available to them to engage in spoken discourse and how these tools are deployed and mixed in complex configurations with other tools. The 'toolbox' I will describe includes material tools like telephones, computers, architectural structures, furniture and other objects, as well as symbolic or 'semiotic' tools like languages, conversational routines and scripts, speech genres, social languages, social identities and social practices. I will illustrate how people 'design' interactions by creatively combining the different resources that are available to them and the consequences of these combinations on the kinds of social actions they can take. I will also consider how tools become tools in the first place – how for example, certain ways of talking come to be regarded as speech genres and social languages, how certain combinations of actions come to be regarded as social practices, and how certain ways of acting come to be regarded as social identities. I will use the word 'technologization' to describe the process by which objects, actions, behaviours and symbols are transformed into cultural tools or 'technologies of talk'.

In Chapter 4, I will focus on action, or, more specifically, mediated action as the unit of analysis in my framework. I will begin by exploring how different approaches to spoken discourse understand the relationship between discourse and action, with special attention to speech act theory and conversation analysis, which regard discourse itself as a kind of action. I will then explore another perspective, one in which discourse is seen not so much as a form of action, but as a mediational means used to take actions, and how different discursive resources function to make some social actions easier or more difficult.

In Chapter 5, I will explore the issue of *interaction*, how people manage to do things together. First I will explore the ways people manage the 'mechanics' of conversation, such as beginning and ending conversations, taking turns, and negotiating what to talk about, through the use of different 'technologies of talk'. Then I will discuss the different ways in which people can participate in interactions as 'ratified participants', and as 'bystanders' or 'eavesdroppers' of various sorts. Finally I will explore the effect of media on the ways people can participate in interactions, especially how new forms of media make available new ways of 'speaking', 'listening', 'by-standing' and 'eavesdropping'.

In Chapter 6, I will explore the issue of social identities and how they are constructed and negotiated in spoken discourse. I will discuss how identities are, on the one hand, *brought along* to interactions by participants as cultural tools – conventionalized combinations of ways of speaking, ways of acting, ways of interacting and ways of reproducing social structures associated with certain types of people – and, on the other hand, *brought about*, as people deploy these conventionalized identities in specific circumstances and negotiate their relationships to each other and to the activities they are engaged in. Finally I will discuss how identities and relationships are developed over time by individuals and groups through the 'identity projects' they engage in.

Chapter 7 focuses on how social groups, communities and institutions become resources for spoken discourse. I will discuss both how people 'imagine' different kinds of communities (speech communities, discourse communities and communities of practice) around different kinds of discursive tools, and how they use these communities as 'technologies of talk'.

In the final chapter, entitled 'Answerability and The Future of Talk' I will consider the ethical implications of the mediated action approach to spoken discourse developed in this book. I will argue that our main goal in the study of spoken discourse should be to understand how we can be more 'answerable' to one another in our daily interactions, and how, through being answerable, we can build better societies. I will also discuss the impact of new technologies of talk, such as digital video and the internet, and how they are changing our capacity to be answerable to one another in both positive and negative ways.

2

Studying spoken discourse

The study of spoken discourse is an interdisciplinary project that draws on fields such as linguistics, philosophy, anthropology, sociology and critical theory. While, different academic disciplines and the different approaches to discourse that have grown out of them are often based on different assumptions about things like language, society and communication, one thing that unites all of the approaches to spoken discourse that I will review in this chapter is a concern with *action*. Whereas linguists in the traditions of Saussure and Chomsky are primarily interested in language structures and how they are manifested in the way people speak, discourse analysts start directly with the way people speak and investigate how that affects how they *do* things in the world.

Below I will provide a brief survey of the different academic disciplines that have contributed to the study of spoken discourse and the approaches that have grown out of them. I should mention straight off that there is a great deal of interesting work on spoken discourse that I will fail to mention, and a lot of important ideas that will not find their way into this account. It is not, then, meant to be an exhaustive history of the study of spoken discourse. Rather, what I hope to do is to put the ideas that I will develop in this book in both a disciplinary and a historical context and begin to explore the different epistemologies these ideas promote and the different analytical tools they make available to us.

Linguistics

Although I begin with the discipline of linguistics, it may come as a surprise to readers that, of all of the disciplines I will be discussing, this is not the one that has contributed the most to the study of spoken discourse, and some linguists have even been downright hostile to many of the methods of studying spoken discourse that I will describe below. The main reason for this is that the primary project of linguistics in the twentieth century was, as Saussure (1916/59: 14) put it, 'separating language from speaking'. The goal of Saussure, and after him, Chomsky (1965), was to understand language as a *system* independent of the contingencies of its use. When we separate language from speech, Saussure wrote, 'we are at the same time separating: (1) what is social from what is individual; and (2) what is essential from what is accessory and more or less accidental' (13–14). For Chomsky, this dividing act consisted of separating what he called linguistic 'competence' from linguistic 'performance'. Rather than studying the way real language users employ the tool of language to deal with the unpredictablity of the real world, Chomsky took as his object of study the 'ideal native speaker', an imaginary creature who belongs to a completely homologous speech community, and is unburdened by lapses in memory, distractions, errors, limitations of the human body, constraints of the physical setting, and the contingencies of context.

In one sense, it is everything that Saussure and Chomsky leave behind, the messy and contingent nature of actual linguistic performance, that is of most interest to discourse analysts. That is not to say that we are interested in what Saussure calls the 'accidental' character of speech. In fact, much of what this book is about is understanding how everyday language use is far from accidental, how people deliberately design interactions to create order out of everyday experience. We are also not interested in speaking as an 'individual' rather than a social act. On the contrary, for discourse analysts, speaking is always social, not just because it always takes place in *dialogue* with other speakers, but also because it always both reflects and constitutes the social world.

Despite these differences, however, it is important to acknowledge the contributions that structuralist and generative linguists have made to the study of language more generally and specifically to the study of spoken discourse, and to acknowledge how revolutionary their ideas were at the time that they were developed. Saussure, for instance, was writing at a time when the study of language was dominated by philologists, who were obsessed with how languages 'progress' and 'decay', and phonologists and neogrammarians, who focused on compiling inventories of sounds and morphological variations for different languages. Saussure's big idea was that it is possible to study language itself (rather than just individual languages), and that language is more than just an inventory of units; it is a *system*. His other big idea, which severely rocked the boat of those studying spoken language at the time, was that the sounds of words have no direct relationship to their meaning. Meaning, he insisted, is neither phonological nor morphological, but psychological. Finally, despite his focus on the underlying structure of language rather than on the way it is actually used in everyday speech, Saussure at least affirmed the primacy of speech over writing, insisting that the subject of linguistics is the study of the spoken language, and that writing exists only to represent speech.

Chomsky, for his part, was reacting to behaviourist notions of language popular in the mid-twentieth century that saw it as little more than a conditioned response to a given stimulus (see Skinner 1957/91). Chomsky's big idea was creativity. How, he asked, is it possible for people to make so many different kinds of meanings and to produce utterances that they had never before heard (and may never before have been uttered) if language is merely 'verbal behaviour' that we learn through exposure to the speech of others? There must be something else going on. For Chomsky, that something else was the 'deep structure' that exists inside the heads of all speakers, which allows us to perform these creative feats of transformation. The 'ideal native speaker' is nothing less than a personification of this structure. As it turns out, though, creative as this ideal speaker is, he or she is not nearly as creative as a real speaker, who has to do a lot more than simply generate new meanings to get by in the world, including managing delicate social practices like 'coming out'. As Harris (1981/2002: 33) puts it, 'Armed only with deep structure the "ideal speaker–hearer," it might appear, is in fact a communicational cripple.'

There are certainly many scholars of discourse that have been heavily influenced by structuralist and generative approaches to language. In fact, the roots of discourse analysis are often traced to the work of Zelig Harris (1952), whose primary goal was to figure out how to apply the same kind of systematic syntactic analysis that linguists apply to sentences to longer texts, and one of the first widely accepted approaches to spoken discourse, that developed by John Sinclair and Malcolm Coulthard in the 1970s (Sinclair and Coulthard 1975), conceptualizes talk as a hierarchical system made up of units of different rank, (transactions, exchanges, moves, and acts) arranged according to structural rules. Even Labov's more sociolinguistic approach to spoken discourse, exemplified in his studies of oral narratives (Labov and Waletzky 1967) and psychotherapy sessions (Labov and Fanshel 1977) focuses primarily on finding structural regularities below the seemingly chaotic surface of talk. 'The fundamental problem of discourse analysis,' Labov (1972b: 299) asserts, 'is to show how one utterance follows another in a rational, rule-governed manner.'

In the later part of the twentieth century, partly as a result of influence from the sociologists, anthropologists and philosophers whom I will discuss below, some linguists became dissatisfied with formalist and mentalist approaches to language and began to suggest models for studying it that take into account the way in which it is actually used in the real world. The most influential of these was Michael Halliday (1973, 1978), whose systemic functional linguistics has left a strong mark on many approaches to discourse analysis, particularly critical discourse analysis. Halliday, drawing on the work of Firth (1937), who himself was influenced by the anthropologist Bronisław Malinowski (see below) proposed a model of grammar that focuses on language not as a matter of deep structure, but as a matter of *meaning potential*, potential that is only realized in the interaction between language and the social world.

Another famous dissenter from the Saussurean and Chomskyian paradigms was Roy Harris (1981/2002, 1996), whose 'integrationist linguistics' directly attacks the notion that languages and grammars have any existence at all apart from their emergence in actual communication. An integrationalist redefinition of linguistics, he declared, should dispense with ideas about linguistic signs being arbitrary, words having meanings, and grammar having rules, in favour of an approach which seeks meaning in the way language is *used* in actual contexts.

Yet another approach to language that veered away from Chomsky's mentalist paradigm is sociolinguistics, a sub-field of linguistics that concerns itself with the influence of things like age, gender, social class, topic and context on the way people talk. Sociolinguistics has itself come to encompass a rich variety of approaches such as variationist sociolinguistics, which seeks to connect different varieties of language to different kinds of speakers, and interactional sociolinguistics, which focuses more on variations in the ways people manage social interaction. More recently, scholars like Jan Blommaert (2005, 2010) and Ben Rampton (2008) have proposed a radically new way of doing sociolinguistics, one which questions the idea of languages themselves as bounded, autonomous entities, and instead focuses on the different *semiotic resources* that are available to different people in different circumstances. For such scholars, what is important about linguistic signs is not just their 'meaning' within a linguistic system, but also their *social value*, how their use helps people to present themselves as certain kinds of people and gives them access to certain kinds of rights and privileges.

Philosophy

To really get to the roots of contemporary approaches to spoken discourse one must go back a lot further than Saussure, and even the nineteenth-century philologists and phonologists to the philosophers of ancient Greece, in particular, the Sophists, who developed a field known as *rhetoric* – the study of the way people use words to achieve particular rational or emotional effects on listeners. Although the study of rhetoric reached its height around the fifth century BC in the teachings of Corax of Syracuse and other Sophists, the most famous textbook on the art of spoken discourse to come down to us from that time is Aristotle's *Rhetoric* (written around 350 BC). Although usually when we think of rhetoric today, we think of written compositions in Freshman English classes, Jacob Mey (2013) has argued that rhetoric as it was developed by the ancient Greeks should be seen as the true progenitor of modern pragmatics (see below). In fact, many of the aspects of spoken discourse which are central to the approach I will develop in this book were also of central concern to the Sophists and to Aristotle, including the relationship between speech style and the goals of the speaker, and the way people's speech influences how they are regarded by others (see also Hughes 2011).

The most important contributions that philosophy has made to the study of spoken discourse, however, came over 2,000 years later in the late twentieth century, starting with the period Hacking (1975) calls the 'heyday of sentences', when philosophers started to make questions of meaning and the nature of language central to their intellectual projects. Many, such as Bertrand Russell, Gottlob Ferge, Rudolph Carnap, and W. V. Quine focused more on the relationship between language and logic, often finding 'flaws' in everyday uses of language when it came to being able to accurately deal with ontological and epistemological questions. At the same time, another group of philosophers became interested in the way context affects meaning. This group, known as the 'ordinary language philosophers', consisted of John Austin, H. Paul Grice, and, at least in his later years, Ludwig Wittgenstein.

Austin's biggest contribution to the study of spoken discourse was to transform the typical questions that people were asking about language, at that time – questions regarding the 'meaning' or the 'truth' of utterances – into questions of a different sort: questions about 'action' and the effect of utterances on their hearers. Language, he suggested, is not simply a representational medium, but a tool to take action in the world. We do not just 'mean things' with words, we 'do things' with them (Austin 1962). His approach came to be known as *speech act theory*, and was later developed further by the American philosopher John Searle (1969).

Grice had a slightly different take on the question of meaning. His focus was on explaining why, despite the fact that people often do not say what they mean or mean what they say, we still manage to understand one another. The kind of 'logic' that Grice proposed to solve this problem was not the abstract 'mathematical' logic of his predecessors, but an *interactional* logic whereby people engage in conversations based on a few fundamental assumptions about how conversations are supposed to work and use these assumptions to try to work out the intentions of speakers.

Although Wittgenstein, in his earlier work, promoted a view of language as a logical and coherent system of meaning along the lines of earlier philosophers of language, by the end of his career he became one of ordinary language philosophy's most radical proponents. Language, he argued, in his

Philosophical Investigations, is not a form of meaning, but a form of action or, as he put it, a 'form of life' (1958/69: 8). To understand how language functions, one cannot look just at words or 'sentences', but rather one must look at the wider 'language game' of which particular words or sentences are a part. Wittgenstein's notion of 'language games' has had a profound impact on most of the approaches to spoken discourse that I will be describing in this book. In fact, one might argue, along with Hornish (8 May 2006: n.p.) that the goal of discourse analysis is 'to describe the game, to illuminate its often obscure rules, to clearly mark out its boundaries, and to identify its players, coaches and referees'.

The approach to spoken discourse that grew out of the work of the ordinary language philosophers is known as pragmatics. I will have much more to say about the tools that pragmatics provides for analysing *discourse as action* in Chapter 4. For now, the most important thing to note about pragmatics is the radical shift that it helped to bring about in the study of spoken language from focusing on meaning to focusing on action, from focusing on texts to focusing on contexts, from focusing on linguistic systems to focusing on social conventions, and from seeing interpretive processes as occurring inside the heads of speakers and listeners (as in the diagram of 'talking heads' I discussed in the last chapter) to seeing them as a matter of the interaction between the individual mind and the social world. At the same time, as the field of pragmatics developed, some practitioners, influenced by the 'cognitive turn' in linguistics ushered in by Chomsky, found themselves moving away from examining the role of context and convention in linguistic action, and more towards making conjectures about the inner psychological states of speakers. Sperber and Wilson's (1996) relevancy theory and what has become known as cognitive pragmatics (see e.g., Bara 2010) are examples of this move back towards mentalist models.

Anthropology

The person we probably have to thank the most for alerting scholars of spoken language to the importance of *context* and the centrality of *action* was anthropologist Bronisław Malinowski. As far back as 1923 (more than three decades before the 'ordinary language philosophers' whom I discussed above began promoting a similar view), in his paper, 'The Problem of Meaning in Primitive Languages', Malinowski argued that we can't understand what people in societies very different from our own are saying by simply translating their words; we must also have some kind of understanding of the situation in which they are speaking, of their customs, their cultural institutions, and, most important, what they are *doing* with their language. At first, Malinowski presented this as just a 'problem' with 'primitive languages', but he later argued that this is a feature of all language use, whether by a native of the Tobriand Islands where he did his fieldwork, or by a British earl (Malinowski 1935). 'Each utterance is essentially bound up with the context of situation and with the aim of the pursuit,' he wrote. 'The structure of all … linguistic material is inextricably mixed up with, and dependent upon, the course of the activity in which the utterances are embedded' (1923: 310–11). Based on this argument, he proposed that language should be studied 'not as an instrument of reflection, but as a mode of action' (1923: 315).

Another early anthropologist who had a profound influence on the study of spoken discourse was Franz Boas, sometimes referred to as the father of American anthropology, Boas's work on the native languages of the indigenous populations of the Pacific Northwest laid the foundation for an anthropological approach to spoken language based on ethnographic accounts of real people using real language in real situations. In contrast to Saussure, who at around the same time, on the other side of the Atlantic, was developing a structuralist theory of language that attempted to separate it from the contingencies of its use (and whose theories were to have their own profound effect on European anthropology), Boas and his followers considered language to be inseparable from social practices and social relationships. Boas's student, Sapir, in particular, developed the notion that language and culture mutually influence each other, and *his* student, Benjamin Whorf took this even further, developing the theory of *linguistic relativism*, widely known as the 'Sapir-Whorf hypothesis', at the heart of which is the claim that the structure of a language affects the way people think. Here is not the place to debate the merits of this controversial hypothesis, other than to note its general influence on the study of spoken discourse in notions of how discourse amplifies and constrains different ways of meaning, doing and being, and its specific influence on another important figure in the model of spoken discourse I will develop in this book, the Soviet psychologist Lev Vygotsky, whom I will discuss further below.

Among the most influential American anthropological linguist to come out of the Boasian tradition was Dell Hymes, whose model for the *ethnography of communication* has become one of the most popular methods for the study of spoken discourse. Like Malinowski and Boas, Hymes insisted that the study of language should not be limited to linguistic forms, but must also take things like community, culture and context into consideration. Unlike Malinowski and Boas, however, Hymes had a particularly formidable opponent in this debate in the person of Chomsky, whose theory of generative linguistics had, by the time Hymes was developing his ideas, become the dominant approach to language in American universities. Much of Hymes's model, then, was developed in direct response to Chomsky. His notion of 'communicative competence', for example, is offered as an alternative to Chomsky's focus on 'grammatical competence', and his vision for the scope of the study of language, incorporating as it does a wide range of social, cultural, contextual, and even aesthetic factors contrasted sharply with Chomsky's narrower mentalistic view. 'The place of language in the life of the community,' Hymes (1996: 70) insisted, should be 'understood as more than a matter of sounds, spellings, grammatical categories and constructions. It would be properly understood as involving varieties and modalities, styles and genres, ways of using a language as a *resource*.' (emphasis mine).

Finally, there is the work of other North American anthropological linguists such as Eleanor Ochs and Michael Silverstein, Richard Bauman and Charles Briggs. What Silverstein (2003) and Ochs (1993) contribute to the study of spoken discourse is their development of the notion of *indexicality*, an idea that originally came from the work of the semiotician Charles S. Peirce, who used it to talk about a relationship between a sign and what it signifies, in which the sign is related physically or causally to the signified, as smoke is to fire. In a sense, indexicality is another way of understanding the 'pervasive context-dependency of natural language utterances' (Hanks 2001: 119). In traditional linguistics, indexical signs include words such as 'I', 'you', 'this' and 'that' which 'point' to some aspect of the physical context (signs usually referred to as *deixis*), but Sliverstein, Ochs and other anthropological linguists are more interested in what they call 'non-referential' indexes, those that 'point' to aspects of the larger social context and, in so doing, 'presuppose' or 'entail' some kind of social meaning (such as a social value, a social relationship, or a social identity). Ochs (1993), for example, discusses how gender (masculinity and femininity) are *indexed* by certain styles of speech or bodily movements. Indexicality is an extremely valuable tool for considering ways people use linguistic resources to make meanings and perform actions that are *not* tied to the linguistic systems. It allows us, as Blommaert (2010: 181) puts it, to think of language 'semiotically' rather than 'linguistically', to see that the 'range of possible functions for linguistic signs is far larger than just their conventional linguistic functions'.

Anthropological linguists interested in performance (see e.g., Bauman and Briggs 1990; Duranti 1983; Hanks 1996) have contributed to the study of spoken discourse an account of how spoken discourse can sometimes be rendered 'portable', so that it is able to be lifted out of the context in which it originally occurs and introduced into new contexts, processes which they call 'entextualization' and 'recontextualization'. These processes were dramatically illustrated in the example of the YouTube video that I discussed in the last chapter in which a son's private performance of 'coming out' to his father is transformed into an episode on the son's YouTube channel about coming out in the military. Although these ideas were originally developed in the analysis of bounded performances such as oral storytelling and rituals, they have important applications to all spoken discourse. As I mentioned in the last chapter, all spoken discourse involves, to some degree, recontextualizing the past words of others and making one's own words available for future recontextualization. This observation reminds us that the boundaries that we sometimes place around the episodes of spoken discourse we analyse are ultimately artificial, and that a real understanding of what's going on in a specific encounter depends on accounting for how meanings and texts, and speakers and listeners, move across different contexts and different encounters (see also Blommaert 2005, 2010; Silverstein and Urban 1996; Wortham and Reyes 2015).

To summarize, the most important contribution that anthropology has made to the study of spoken discourse is to alert us to the complex ways in which social interactions are embedded in wider sociocultural contexts, contexts that extend out from the immediate situations of the encounters we are analysing to include other encounters, the histories of those involved, and the wider culture. This concern is reflected not just in the analytical tools that linguistic anthropology has left us with, but also in the tools they have developed for collecting data, among which is the method of *ethnography*, a method that compels analysts to look beyond the words that he or she has recorded or transcribed to find out about the social situations that gave rise to these words.

The Palo Alto Group

The Palo Alto Group refers to a loose association of anthropologists, psychiatrists, information scientists and cyberneticians who took their name from their collaboration on various projects at the Mental Research Institute and The Centre for the Advanced Study in the Behavioural Sciences in Palo Alto, California in the 1950s and 1960s. Among their members were anthropologists Gregory Bateson, Margaret Mead, and Ray Birdwhistle, communication theorist Paul Watzlawick, psychiatrists Frieda Fromm-Reichmann, and Norman McQuown, linguist Charles Hockett, and cybernetician Warren McCulloch. I am devoting a separate section to this group of scholars first because the interdisciplinarity of their work makes it difficult to fit them into more traditional disciplinary categories, and second because their contribution to current approaches to the study of spoken discourse is both profound and sadly under-acknowledged.

What was special about the Palo Alto Group was not just the variety of perspectives they brought to the study of spoken discourse, but their commitment to the careful micro-analysis of actual interactions, and their use of technology – in this case film – to aid in that analysis. The most famous example was their collaboration on the close analysis of a series of filmed interactions with a psychiatric patient and her family known as the 'Doris Film' from 1956 to 1968, what was likely the first example of the use of film for the micro-analysis of spoken interaction. The introduction of such new technologies for gathering and analysing data, as I will discuss further below, alters not just what analysts can see (and hear), but the way they can analyse it. In other words, technology does not just play a role in determining the kind of data we can gather, but also in facilitating the creation of new analytical and theoretical frameworks. Among the frameworks that grew out of this project was what Bateson (1971) called the *natural history method*, an approach which as Kendon (1990: 20) describes it, 'proposed the detailed description of whatever could be observed in an interaction … in terms of what there is to be observed, not in terms of pre-established category systems' (see also Erickson and Schultz 1982; Kendon 1990; Streeck1983).

Of all the members of the Palo Alto Group, Gregory Bateson is the one who has left the strongest mark on the study of spoken discourse. Among his most important ideas was that of *metacommunication* (Ruesch and Bateson 1951), the idea that along with a 'message', usually communicated through the words that we say, we also always communicate a 'message about the message', often expressed in very subtle ways through things like gaze, facial expression and tone of voice. Metamessages communicate a range of information about the speakers and the context, including how participants feel about what has been said and how they mean it to be interpreted, and about their relationship with the people with whom they are talking. But one of the most important things that metamessages communicate is what people think they are *doing* in the interaction, that is, what they take as the 'activity' within which the message is to be understood. Bateson called this information about 'what we are doing' the *frame* of the interaction. In his seminal paper, 'A Theory of Play and Fantasy' (originally published in 1954, reprinted in Bateson 1972/2000), he described observing monkeys playing in the zoo, noting how sometimes actions like biting and barring of teeth, which on the surface might seem hostile, can actually be interpreted as friendly if situated within a 'frame' of 'play'. This idea of 'frames' and 'framing' was later taken up and elaborated on by the sociologist Erving Goffman (1974, see below), and has since become a central concept in the analytical toolkit of interactional sociolinguists (see e.g., Tannen, ed. 1993).

Concepts like metacommunication and framing are part of a larger *ecological* view of communication promoted by Bateson and his colleagues, a view which not only sees spoken discourse as context dependent, but which sees context itself as a *dynamic* set of practices rather than a static set of circumstances, as something that social actors create as they go along (partly though exploiting the indexical nature of language that I discussed above). In this respect, rather than speaking of context (as a noun), it is really more accurate to speak of processes of *contextualization* (Auer and Di Luzio 1992; Gumperz 1982).

Sociology

Arguably the field that has had the most obvious influence on the study of spoken discourse is sociology, in particular, the micro-sociology of Erving Goffman and the ethnomethodology of Harold Garfinkel. Just as anthropologists like Boas challenged the 'top-down' perspective of anthropologists who preceded them with a more 'bottom-up' approach to the study of culture, Goffman and Garfinkel challenged the macro-sociological tradition of earlier sociologists like Émile Durkheim and Talcott Parsons – for whom the goal of sociology was to understand people's behaviour at the level of, and in relation to, large-scale social structures and abstract principles of social organization – with a more 'bottom-up' approach to the study of social life.

This more 'bottom-up' approach should not, however, be mistaken for one in which social behaviour is reduced to the motives, dispositions and actions of individuals (as in some psychological approaches). Like other sociologists, Goffman and Garfinkel are primarily interested in the constitution of the 'social order'. Only for them, the primary locus of social organization is not the family or the group or the institution, or even the society, but the *interaction*, or what Goffman (1983a) dubbed 'the interaction order'. In fact, it is Goffman in particular that we have to thank most for advancing the view that the concrete, situated social interaction is the best place to look to understand how both the individual self and broader social structures are produced and reproduced (Raymond and Sidnell 2014). It is 'situations and their men' (and, of course, their women) rather than 'men and their situations' that Goffman (quoted in Streeck and Mehus 2005: 384) encourages us to study. For it is only through the study of situations, Goffman, insisted, that we can begin to understand what he called 'the greasy parts of speech' (1964: 133), those aspects of spoken discourse that are less amenable to traditional linguistic analysis. All interactions, from Goffman's point of view, are fundamentally attempts by participants to come to terms with the situation, to work out 'what's going on here?' (Goffman 1974: 8). This question, says Goffman, is the basis of all social life, 'whether asked explicitly, as in times of confusion and doubt, or tacitly, during occasions of usual certitude,' and 'the answer to it is presumed by the way the individuals proceed and get on with the affairs at hand'.

Goffman's work is replete with useful concepts to describe the various ways in which people come to terms with 'what's going on' and to 'get on with the affairs at hand', many of which I will elaborate on in the remainder of this book. These include his view of social life as a 'performance' (1959), his concept of 'face' and description of how people acknowledge, grant, ratify, protect and loose face in social encounters (1959, 1967), his development of Bateson's concept of 'framing' to explain how people dynamically negotiate and strategically deploy different definitions of the situation in social interaction (1974), his account of the various ways in which people participate in social gatherings (1966), the different sorts of 'rituals' that they engage in (1967), and the stances that they adopt in relation to the words they say and the people with whom they are talking (1981).

The other sociologist who has had a profound effect on the study of spoken discourse is Harold Garfinkel. Like Goffman, Garfinkel was also interested in 'what's going on', but with a much stronger emphasis on the way people work together to make what's going on 'make sense' to themselves and others. Underneath the processes of defining (and negotiating) 'what's going on' that preoccupied Goffman is the more basic task that social actors have of appearing 'normal' to each other, what Sacks (1984) called 'doing being ordinary'. Being 'normal' may not seem a particularly difficult thing to do, but, as Garfinkel argued, it is actually not as easy as it appears: It's not just a matter of following externally imposed rules or 'going with the flow'. People have to actively work to create order in their everyday lives, and the field Garfinkel (1967) developed – ethnomethodology – is designed to help us discover the *methods* they have for doing this. Thus, the 'methodology' in ethnomethodology refers not so much to the methodology employed by the analyst, but rather to that employed by social actors in constructing their actions as 'sensible' and making sense of the actions of others.

Garfinkel's main strategy for uncovering the everyday sense-making methods of people was to try to disrupt them through what he referred to as 'breaching experiments' or 'tutorial problems' (Garfinkel 2002) in which he (or more often his students) engaged in unusual behaviour and observed how people reacted, and, more importantly, what they did to re-establish order. Perhaps the most important insight we can take from Garfinkel's experiments is the realization not just that people try to work together to maintain a certain orderliness in their interactions with others, but that they are *accountable* to each other for that orderliness. Throughout this book I will argue that all spoken discourse, no matter how trivial it might seem, has a *moral* or *ethical* dimension. Partly what I mean by this is that the way we treat one another in the course of our everyday actions, the way we are present to others and answerable to them in discourse (Bakhtin 2010), is linked to larger social orders and to issues such as equality and the way goods get distributed in societies.

But the basis of the moral orders in our societies lies in the everyday ways that we make ourselves accountable to one another in conversation (Samra-Fredericks 2010).

The two approaches to spoken discourse most influenced by Goffman and Garfinkel are conversation analysis and interactional sociolinguistics. Conversation analysis grew directly out of ethnomethodology through the work of sociologist Harvey Sacks, beginning with his analysis of telephone calls to a suicide prevention centre. Interestingly, Sacks was initially not especially interested in conversation *per se*, but more interested in how people describe and manage suicide threats. As he analysed his data, however, he became fascinated by the ways callers engage in everyday activities such as opening the conversation, identifying one another, making requests, and disagreeing with the other party (Wilkinson and Kitzinger 2011). From these observations, he began to develop a theory of how people use the apparatus of conversation to create the kind of 'orderliness' in their everyday interactions that Garfinkel spoke of.

Just as important as the theoretical contribution conversation analysis has made to the analysis of spoken discourse is its methodological contribution, particularly the way it appropriated the (at that time relatively new) technology of the portable audio tape recorder into its project. In fact, as with the use of film by Bateson and his colleagues, one might argue that it was not so much a matter of the technology being applied to the method as of the technology being the thing that made the method possible in the first place. It would not have been possible for Sacks to notice what he did in phone calls to the suicide prevention hotline if those calls had not been recorded and made available for him to listen to over and over again, and the kinds of features of talk that became the central focus of conversation analysis were to a large degree features that were only rendered analysable through the intervention of tape recordings.

Another important thing about the relationship between conversation analysis and technology which is sometimes forgotten is that it was the first serious attempt to analyse what we traditionally think of as technologically mediated communication, in this case, telephone calls. In fact, it was technologically mediated communication – not face-to-face talk – that served for Sacks and Schegloff as the baseline for the development of their theories. In this book, as I mentioned in the last chapter, I will be arguing that all conversations, including face-to-face conversations, are mediated through technologies of some kind. What the pioneering work of Sacks on telephone communication contributes to this argument is an early example of the analysis of the effects of mediation on the way people manage various aspects of spoken interaction, including identification, turn allocation topic development, and closing (see Chapter 5).

The other major approach to spoken discourse to grow out of sociology is interactional sociolinguistics, but whereas conversation analysts were more influenced by the work of Garfinkel, interactional sociolinguists have been more influenced by the work of Goffman, especially his concern with how people negotiate 'what they are doing' and 'who they are being' in conversation (Jones 2013). As Scollon (2001: 163) defines it, interactional sociolinguistics is an approach to spoken discourse which seeks to understand how social actors 'are able to strategize their own actions within a negotiative process with other social actors to achieve their desired social meanings, including their identities, footings, alignments with others and their positionings of themselves and others'.

Along with its debt to the micro-sociology of Goffman, interactional sociolinguistics has also been heavily influenced by the work of linguistic anthropologists, and so, unlike conversation analysis, whose main concern is describing the universal orderliness of everyday interaction, interactional sociolinguists, like variationist sociolinguists, are interested in the ways membership in different social groups (defined by things like age, gender and ethnicity) affects the way people communicate. The term was first used by the anthropologist John Gumperz, whose initial concern with interaction centred on questions of social justice, such as why members of less powerful groups had difficulty communicating with members of more powerful groups, especially in high stakes interactions like interviews (see Gumperz 1982). The answer he came up with was that people in different social groups develop different ways of managing interaction, including different ways of *contextualizing* utterances and of signalling aspects of their relationship with others.

Before leaving the discipline of sociology, it is important to mention one other approach to language that grew up within its borders in the late twentieth century, that of Pierre Bourdieu (1977, 1991, 1992). Like Garfinkel and Goffman, Bourdieu was also convinced that the best place to explore the workings of larger social structures was in the situated, embodied practices of social actors, and he was also, like Garfinkel and Goffman, fascinated by the minutiae of everyday life. But, whereas Goffman and Garfinkel were concerned primarily with how people accomplish social actions, Bourdieu was more interested in how they participate in social *practices*, that is, how the various norms of interaction and methods of sense-making that Goffman and Garfinkel so meticulously observed become embedded in the fabric of societies and in the embodied consciousness of social actors. The way we habitually perform social actions – how we speak, stand, walk and interact with others, is not just a matter of 'orderliness', he contended, but a reflection of the larger *social order* that has been subsumed into the individual. Bourdieu called this aspect of the individual the *habitus*. It constitutes the 'structured dispositions' that people acquire in their interactions with others and with society which leads them to reproduce the rules and structures of society in their subsequent interactions (1977: 72).

Another important notion that Bourdieu introduced to the study of spoken discourse is the idea that not all ways of speaking (or acting or moving) are regarded equally within the particular language game in which they are deployed. Bourdieu (1991) considered the resources we use for talk to be forms of 'symbolic capital', which, like forms of economic capital, are distributed unequally throughout society. Whenever we speak, we are claiming for ourselves and for our activities a certain value in the society in which we live, and our ability to claim that value comes from our access to and mastery of different semiotic resources (see also Blommaert 2005, 2010). At the same time, the ways we are able to claim value for ourselves and our practices helps to determine the kinds of semiotic resources that are available to us.

Critical theory

Bourdieu's critical sociology is just one of a raft of more 'critical' perspectives that have influenced the study of spoken discourse in the past several decades. What I mean by 'critical' is approaches that acknowledge that the kinds of resources that are available to people for social interaction, the kinds of 'language games' in which they deploy these resources, and the ways that they are accountable to one another for how they do so, are not ideologically neutral. Some players inevitably have certain advantages over others, and in many ways the rules of these games and the distribution of resources in them are designed to maintain the advantages of some and the disadvantages of others.

What is sometimes referred to as 'critical theory' includes scholarship from a range of disciplines including philosophy, sociology and literary theory. The critical theorist who has arguably had the most impact on the study of spoken discourse is the French historian Michel Foucault. It was Foucault, who introduced to discourse studies the third definition of discourse which I discussed in the previous chapter, the definition of discourse as historically constituted ways of talking, acting and thinking designed to enforce particular regimes of knowledge and systems of social organization. Foucault (1969, 1971) referred to these sets of discursive practices as 'orders of discourse'. I will, following Gee (2011), call them 'Discourses' (with a capital 'D').

What Foucault meant by 'orders of discourse' is that the way we use discourse is ordered through systems of exclusion, classification and access which determine what sorts of semiotic resources are available to what sorts of people and how they can be used. These systems ultimately determine not just *what* we can say, but also *who* we can be and what counts as 'knowledge' and 'truth'. Orders of discourse (or 'Discourses') are supported by institutions like schools, hospitals, governments, corporations and the military, and advance particular ideological agendas (such as 'globalization' or 'neoliberalism'). Every time we speak, every language or linguistic register, every genre, every social practice and every identity we deploy in social interaction connects us to some Discourse, and our ability to participate in the Discourse (to show ourselves to be, for example, certain kinds of soldiers or certain kinds of gay men or certain kinds of fathers) has a considerable impact on our status in society and our life chances.

Central to Foucault's thinking about orders of discourse, and to the thinking of many other critical theorists who came after him, was the idea that all texts and all utterances are in some way *connected* to other texts and other utterances, and that much of what a text or utterance means depends on these connections. Foucault (1969: 99) wrote:

> There is no free, neutral, independent statement. A statement always belongs to a series or a whole, plays a role among other statements, is part of a network of statements. ... There is no statement that does not presuppose others, that is not surrounded by a field of coexistences, effects of series and succession, a distribution of functions and roles. If one can speak of a statement as such, it is because a sentence or proposition figures at a definite point, with a specific position, in an enunciative network that extends beyond it.

Kristeva (1986: 37) referred to this phenomenon as 'intertexuality'. No text (and, presumably, no conversation) she argued is entirely original. Any text is essentially 'a mosaic of quotations ... the absorption and transformation of [other texts], which depends for its meaning on the web of intertextuality in which it exists'. In formulating her thoughts on intertextuality, Kristeva was influenced by the ideas of Bakhtin (1981, 1986) which I mentioned in the last chapter and will discuss further below, specifically his view that all texts are 'dialogic' and 'heteroglossic', 'uttered in multiple voices in response to multiple voices and in anticipation of polyvocal responses' (Scollon et al. 1998: 228).

Closely related to the notion of intertextuality is the idea of *iterability* advanced by the literary critic Jacques Derrida (1984). Iterability basically means repeatability. Derrida came up with the term as a critique of Austin's speech act theory. Whereas Austin argued that our ability to do things with words is chiefly a matter of how our words interact with the circumstances in which they are uttered, Derrida countered that the main thing that gives speech acts their 'force' is the fact that they are *recognized* by others as acts that have been performed before. In other words, communicating (and acting) are chiefly a matter of 'citing' or reusing the words of others, re-performing speech acts that countless others have performed before us. As a result, 'language constantly evokes other meanings that exceed, contradict, and disrupt the language user's intentions' (Kulick 2003a: 123). Austin's notion of performativity was taken up in a similar fashion by the feminist critic Judith Butler (1993a), who applied it to understanding social identities, particularly gender identities. Gender, she said, is not something we are, but something we perform (along with other people) though discourse. Like Derrida, Butler viewed performativity as essentially iterative: our performances are constrained by the performances that have come before us, and by the discourse about gender which our societies make available for us to 'cite'.

What concepts such as intertextuality and iterability introduce into the study of spoken discourse is yet another way of understanding context, not just as a matter of the physical, social or cultural circumstances in which texts are produced, but as a matter of the other texts that they are connected to. This understanding of context gives us a way not just to connect language to the material, social and cultural world, but also to the web of previously produced language within which it is entangled.

Many of these ideas have found their way into analytical toolkits of anthropological linguists (see, for example, Briggs and Bauman 1992; Hanks 1996), critical sociolinguists (see, for example, Blommaert 2005, 2010) and critical discourse analysts (Fairclough 1992; Wodak 1996). Whereas the micro-sociological and ethnomethodological approaches described above begin by analysing the moment by moment ways people make sense of the world in interactions as a way of understanding how they 'talk into being' (Heritage and Clayman 2010) the institutions and societies in which they live, critical discourse analysts and others influenced by critical theory tend to begin with broader assumptions about institutional or societal power and ideology and seek to discover how they are expressed (or concealed) in texts and conversations. As Wodak (2001: 53) puts it, such approaches are 'fundamentally interested in analysing opaque as well as transparent structural relationships of dominance discrimination, power and control when these are manifested in language'.

Overlaps and tensions

The main approaches to the analysis of spoken discourse to come out of the traditions discussed above are (a) pragmatics (coming out of the philosophical tradition, especially the work of the 'ordinary language philosophers'); (b) the ethnography of speaking (coming out of anthropology); (c) interactional sociolinguistics (influenced by the work of Bateson and others in the Palo

Alto Group as well as by the micro-sociology of Goffman); (d) conversation analysis (coming out of Garfinkel's ethnomethodology); and (e) critical discourse analysis (influenced by critical theory). These approaches share many common concerns, most of which I have already mentioned: they are concerned with language *in use*, the relationship between language and *action*, and between utterances and the *contexts* in which they occur. They are interested in speech as linguistic *performance* (rather than as a reflection of a linguistic system), and they are all, at least on some level, interested in the *ethical* and *political* dimensions of discourse, how conversations reflect and reinforce the ideologies and power relationships of the societies in which they occur.

There are, at the same time, many areas in which adherents of these approaches do not agree. I call these areas of tension among approaches the 'text/context problem', the 'structure/agency problem', and the 'macro/ micro problem'. None of these three problems are new, and none of them are exclusive to discourse analysis. In fact, an argument could be made that these three problems represent the key loci of debate in nearly all of the social sciences.

The 'text/context' problem has to do with understanding exactly what things we are analysing when we analyse spoken discourse and how these things are related to each other. As I said above, one of the key advances that was made in the study of language in the twentieth century was the recognition of the importance of *context* in the understanding of language in use. It should also be clear from the discussion above, however, that not all approaches to the study of spoken discourse see context as the same thing. Some view context rather broadly, seeing it in terms of the sets of customs, beliefs and social relationships that make up the cultures in which communication takes place. Others see it more in terms of the immediate physical settings in which conversations occur and the actions people are engaged in when conducting these conversations. Some, like conversation analysts, take an even narrower view of context, insisting that the only aspects of context that an analyst can legitimately attend to are those aspects that participants themselves explicitly orient to in their actual talk, and others like critical theorists, see it as the web of other texts that are evoked whenever people speak. Some analysts are more inclined to see context as a relatively stable set of circumstances, whereas others focus more on the contingent, dynamic, negotiated nature of context (or *contextualization*), insisting that contexts are not given, but rather that they are constituted by people as they interact.

The biggest problem with talking about context, however, is not with how big or small we want to make it but with the way the idea of context itself forces us into a bifurcated view of discourse in which its textual aspects are considered focal and the non-textual aspects are considered peripheral. In this view, the achievement of meaning is basically a matter, as Widdowson (1996: 126) puts it 'of matching up the linguistic elements of the code with the schematic elements of the context'. The problem with this approach is that, in any situation what Widdowson calls the 'schematic elements of context' are constantly changing as participants negotiate 'what's going on': context, it turns out is less 'schematic' and more dynamic. Another problem with this idea of context is that it reinforces a logo-centric view of discourse in which what we are supposed to be focused on is 'language', and whatever is not 'language' (gestures, objects, settings, relationships, identities and practices) is seen as secondary. Cook (2011: 434) argues that this tendency for analysts to 'artificially separate' text from context is 'at odds with the aim of [discourse analysis] which is to deal with the realities of language in use rather than with linguistic abstractions'. What is needed instead, he suggests, is 'a more holistic approach which regards discourse as irreducible rather than as a simple addition of context and text'.

The second problem, what I call the 'structure/agency problem' is also one that has preoccupied social scientists from a range of disciplines (see e.g., Bourdieu 1977; de Certeau 1984; Foucault 1969; Giddens 1986). For us, this problem chiefly has to do with the relationship between discourse and action. As I mentioned above, nearly all of the approaches to discourse analysis that I have discussed are interested in one way or another with how we 'do things with words'. If words and other semiotic tools allow us to do certain things, however, there must also be things that they prevent us from doing. To what extent are our actions determined by the resources that our societies make available to us to act? In other words, to what extent do words (and other semiotic tools) 'do things' with us? This is really the problem that Butler was confronting in her examination of Austin's concept of performativity: since all discourse 'emerges in the context of a chain of binding conventions,' she reasoned (Butler 1993a: 225), it is really more accurate to think of discourse producing the speaker rather than of the speaker producing discourse.

The final problem, the 'macro/micro problem' has to do with where we as analysts should focus our attention: on the broader social orders (ideologies, institutions) that conspire to enable and constrain what we can say, or on the smaller 'interaction orders' in which people attempt to manage their actions and relationships on a moment by moment basis? In other words, should discourse analysts focus more on 'big D Discourses' or on 'small d discourse'? The development of many contemporary approaches to spoken discourse, especially in anthropology, and sociology has followed a movement from more top-down or macro-level perspectives to more bottom-up or micro-level perspectives. At the same time, the critical turn in discourse studies, influenced by poststructuralist and Foucauldian models of discourse has pulled attention back to the way 'forces from above' act to shape or determine what people can say and do in social interactions. Those advocating a narrower perspective sometimes accuse those who take a wider perspective of reifying abstract Discourses without sufficient empirical evidence about how they actually affect everyday talk, while those advocating a wider perspective sometimes accuse those who take a narrower perspective of getting lost in the minutiae of everyday talk and failing to see the 'big picture'.

Mediated discourse analysis

The primary framework I will be using to organize my discussion of spoken discourse in this book is called *mediated discourse analysis*, a perspective on discourse developed by Ron Scollon and his colleagues beginning in the late 1990s (Norris and Jones 2005; Scollon 1998, 2001; Scollon and Scollon 2004) which draws heavily on the work of sociocultural practice theorists such as James Wertsch (1991, 1994) and Michael Cole (1998), and of 'new literacy' scholars like James Gee (2011, 2012), as well as on the insights of many of the scholars discussed above such as Bateson, Garfinkel, Goffman, Gumperz and Hymes. Saying that I will adopt this framework does not mean that I will be using it *instead of* the other approaches to spoken discourse I have mentioned: pragmatics, the ethnography of speaking, conversation analysis, interactional sociolinguistics, and critical discourse analysis. In fact, what is useful about mediated discourse analysis is that it gives us a way to make use of tools from all of these approaches and to integrate them in a way that helps us address the three problems I discussed above: the text/context problem, the structure/agency problem, and the micro/macro problem.

The two scholars that have been most influential in the development of mediated discourse analysis belong to none of the disciplines I have discussed so far, though they have influenced all of them. They are a developmental psychologist – Lev Vygotsky – and a literary critic – Mikhail Bakhtin. Vygotsky (1962) was a Soviet psychologist of the early twentieth century who pioneered an approach known as cultural-historical psychology. Vygotsky's psychology challenged individualistic notions of the mind and of learning that were prevalent during the time he was writing (and persist today); learning, he insisted, is not an individual mental phenomenon, but rather essentially a *social* activity mediated through the various *tools* which our cultures make available to us. Some of these tools are physical (what Vygotsky called 'technical tools'), such as axes and ploughs, and others are psychological (or, as I will be calling them, 'semiotic'), such as languages, counting systems, forms of expression, and conventions invoking particular social practices and social identities. The tool he was most concerned with was language: influenced by Sapir's ideas about the affect of language on thought and culture (see above), he conducted a range of experiments on how children's development of concepts is influenced by the structures of language, work which he reported in his classic *Thought and Language* (1962). The important thing about language and other cultural tools, for Vygotsky, is that they link our individual minds to the societies in which we live: they are given to us by our societies and carry with them the histories of their previous uses. In this way, all action, all work, all communication, and even all thought can be considered cultural phenomena.

Bakhtin was a Soviet literary scholar who lived around the same time as Vygotsky. Although much of his work focused on the aesthetics of written texts – specifically the novel – he regarded authors and their characters as 'speaking subjects' and tried to understand how their 'voices' manifested and interacted with one another in literary works. He began by asking the seemingly simple question 'who's speaking here,' but soon realized that for any utterance the answer to this question is far from simple. When a novelist puts words in the mouth of one of his or her characters, for example, who is speaking: the novelist or the character? And when a character parodies the speech of other characters or of the authorities of his day, or of certain types of people, who then is speaking?

Bakhtin explained this complex relationship between 'voice' and speaker using two concepts: the concept of *heteroglossia*, and the concept of *dialogism*. First of all, all utterances are heteroglossic or 'many tongued'; that is, they are formed by borrowing the words, languages, genres and 'accents' of others. It is, in fact, impossible to speak without borrowing the words of others. We must not only appropriate some code or 'language' with certain lexical or grammatical conventions in order to be understood, but we must also appropriate certain conventional genres such as ways of telling stories or ways of 'coming out', as well as certain registers or styles of speaking in order to be recognized as doing certain kinds of things and as being certain kinds of people. Quite often, we even repeat the actual words that we have heard from others, sometimes attributing them to their sources, but usually not. So when we speak, we never speak as just ourselves: we 'ventriloquize' the voices of those who have used these languages, genres, and styles of speaking and who have uttered these words before us.

The second way that utterances are connected to other utterances (and speakers to other speakers) is in the inherent *dialogism* of all utterances. It is impossible, for any utterance to stand alone and make sense. All utterances are basically *responses* to previous utterances, and invite responses in future utterances. As Bakhtin (1986) put it, 'any utterance is a link in the chain of speech communication' (84); 'utterances are not indifferent to one another, and are not self-sufficient; they are aware of and mutually reflect one another' (91). Just as for Vygotsky, every individual action we do and every thought we think (mediated as they are through cultural tools) are essentially social, linked to the history of those tools and the societies from which they come, for Bakhtin, every word we utter is also social, embedded in a complex web of relationships with other words and other speakers.

These ideas have important implications for the study of spoken discourse. They suggest that to really understand what's going on in a conversation, we have got to look not just at what you say to me and what I say to you, and not just at what you and I are 'doing with our words' or how these actions are influenced by the contexts in which these words are uttered. We've got to look at how what you and I say and do is made possible and shaped by the tools that our social environments make available to us, and how these sayings and doings are connected up with the words and actions of many other people who may not be obvious participants in the conversation you and I are having. In other words, we have got to consider how our day-to-day conversations are actually part of what Gee (2011) calls 'Big C Conversations' that take place within our communities, societies and cultures, and among different communities, societies and cultures. In the remainder of this book, I will be introducing five key concepts that will help us to understand how our everyday engagement with spoken discourse both situates us in the societies in which we live and creates opportunities for us to change those societies for the better. Those concepts are *mediation, action, interaction, identity,* and *community.*

Mediation

The most important concept in a sociocultural approach to spoken discourse is *mediation.* As I said in the last chapter, most people, when they think of mediated communication, think of things like television, radio, telephone calls and computer-mediated communication, and work on the effects of such media on communication and social interaction over the past half a century has yielded many important insights, not least of which is the understanding that media are not simply neutral channels through which our messages flow, but that they also play an important role in shaping these messages and in shaping the relationships and social identities of the people who are sending and receiving them; as McLuhan (1964/2001) succinctly put it, 'the medium is the message' (see also Innis 1951).

The conceptualization of mediation I am using in this book, however, based on the ideas of Vygotsky, is much broader than that employed by most media scholars. From a Vygotskyian perspective, *all* communication is mediated, and mediational means (or, as I will be calling them, 'technologies of talk') include not just computers and telephones, but also languages, gestures, styles of speaking and acting, forms of talk like stories or arguments, social practices like 'coming out', social identities like 'gay', and even social groups and institutions like the US military. Taking this broader approach to mediation helps us to see that, just as telephones and computers affect the kinds of messages that we can exchange and the kinds of relationships we can create with other people, so do all of these other tools (languages, speech styles, genres, social practices, etc.). It also reminds us that studying spoken discourse is always about more than just studying language: conversation always involves an array of mediational means, both physical and semiotic.

The most important characteristic of these 'technologies of talk' is that they make some kinds of talk (and, therefore, some kinds of social actions, social identities and social relationships) more possible and others less possible. As I mentioned in the last chapter, I will refer to the characteristics of mediational means to amplify or limit the potential for action as *affordances* and *constraints* (Gibson 1986). Because all technologies involve affordances and constraints, they are inevitably *biased* (Innis 1951) towards certain kinds of actions and certain kinds of interactions, and these biases reflect the interests and ideologies of the societies in which these technologies have developed and the histories of their past use. The affordances and constraints of technologies of talk, then, constitute an important way in which social structure functions to constrain human agency. At the same time, the affordances and constraints of technologies are not entirely deterministic of what users can do with them. Technologies are, by their very nature, multifunctional, open to being appropriated and mixed with other technologies in all sorts of innovative ways which can create new kinds of affordances for and constraints on social action. The relationship between individual speakers and the technologies of talk that they appropriate is always dialectical, technologies acting to afford or limit certain actions, and individuals constantly adapting them to fit the contingencies of particular circumstances and goals. As Wertsch (1994: 204) puts it, there is always a 'tension between the mediational means as provided in the sociocultural setting and the unique contextualized use of these means in carrying out particular concrete actions'.

Finally, it is important to realize that these various technologies do not exist independent of one another. Rather, they operate together in configurations or 'toolkits' which tend to be associated with certain groups of people. These configurations of technologies are really what Gee is talking about when he refers Discourses with a capital D, which he defines as 'ways of combining and integrating language, actions, interactions, ways of thinking, believing, valuing, and using various symbols, tools, and objects to enact a particular sort of socially recognizable identity' (Gee 2011: 29). We can never just appropriate a particular technology of talk without in some way aligning ourselves with the Discourse from which that technology comes.

Action

Mediated discourse analysis shares with many of the approaches I described above a concern with *action*. Where it differs is the way it conceptualizes the relationship between discourse and action. While most other approaches to discourse such as pragmatics and conversation analysis start with discourse and ask what people are 'doing' with it, mediated discourse analysis starts with action and asks what role discourse plays in its accomplishment. This may seem like a subtle difference, but it's actually very important, because it has the effect of reminding us that there may be many other mediational means involved in performing an action which are as important or more important than what we traditionally regard as discourse (i.e., language), and that often the relationship between discourse and action is more complex than either speech act theory or ethnomethodology conceives of it.

As Scollon (2001: 4) puts it:

> Many theories of language and of discourse start out with a focus on 'social action' such as speech act theory, pragmatics, interactional sociolinguistics, and CDA but then somehow in practice tend to become focused only on text. Other aspects of social action and other mediational means than language and discourse are backgrounded as 'context'. Unfortunately, this can lead to a distorted understanding of the relationship between discourse and social action.

As this quote implies, one of the main advantages to taking action (or, to be more exact, mediated action) as the unit of analysis is that it helps us to resolve the text/context problem: we no longer need to argue about which aspects of context need to be considered since our analytical focus is no longer on 'text'; it is on action. Things that are regarded in other approaches as 'context', including cultural norms, physical settings, interpretative frames, interpersonal relationships, social practices and social identities, as well at things normally regarded as 'texts', such as utterances, exchanges, genres and registers, are all regarded equally as 'technologies of talk', and whether or not any one or combination of these technologies should be the focus of our analysis has only to do with if and how it is deployed by social actors to take particular social actions.

Rather than thinking in terms of conversations (texts) that take place in particular contexts, then, mediated discourse analysts think in terms of unique, irreproducible actions taking place at particular points in time/space at which particular people, particular technologies, and particular social orders meet in such a way that particular actions become possible. We call these points: 'sites of engagement'. Scollon (2001: 3–4) defines a site of engagement as the 'real-time window that is opened through an intersection of social practices and mediational means that make that action the focal point of attention of the relevant participants'. Rather than existing independent of the social actors and their actions, sites of engagement are essentially 'focal points' (Jones 2005) at which social actors orient to particular technologies of talk, particular social relationships, particular social identities, and particular communities in order to perform particular social actions. What is created through these orientations is not a static 'context' in which utterances can be inserted, but rather a range of possibilities for *entextualization* and *contextualization*, depending on how social actors engage strategically with the technologies of talk that are available to them. In other words, action is not just about 'doing things with words' (and other cultural tools), but also involves actors dynamically constructing the *social situations* in which those actions become possible.

Interaction

The focus of most studies of spoken discourse has been not just on action, but on *interaction*, the ways people 'do things with words' *together*. Interaction is not something that we have to figure out how to do from scratch whenever we find ourselves in a new situation: it is governed by sets of rules and expectations which Goffman (1983a) referred to as the *interaction order*. These rules and expectations enable and constrain who is allowed to participate in different kinds of social encounters, what sorts of roles they are allowed to play, and how they are expected to conduct themselves. Interaction orders, are, of course, socially and culturally conditioned, but, as Goffman insisted, they also play a role in creating our societies and cultures 'from the ground up'. Thus the ways we work out with others 'what we are doing' and 'who we are being' in interaction, the ways we negotiate our interactional rights and responsibilities, and the ways we are *accountable* to one another for our words and our actions all function to produce and reproduce the broader moral orders that guide our societies. That's why the way people conduct themselves when they participate in practices such as 'coming out' is so important: because it affects not just the relationship between the people involved but also affects and reflects broader societal expectations about how people are meant to treat one another in situations where things like identity and group membership are at stake.

It should be clear by now that, from the sociocultural perspective I am adopting, the whole idea of social interaction is much more complicated that one person having a conversation with another. All conversations involve multiple forms of interaction: interactions between speakers and listeners, interactions between the different technologies of talk that they are deploying in their conversation, interactions among the different social groups to which they belong, and interactions among the multiple intersecting and overlapping sites of engagement at which conversations take place.

This broader perspective of interaction has at its foundation Bakhtin's concepts of dialogism and heteroglossia. As I explained above, dialogism is the idea that utterances never stand alone: they are responses to previous utterances by previous 'speakers'. When somebody responds in conversation, they are responding not just to the person to whom they are speaking, but also to a whole host of 'invisible participants': people, groups, and institutions whose previous utterances have somehow set the terms for the present conversation.

Heteroglossia is the idea that all utterances necessarily contain the 'voices' of other people. Whenever we appropriate a technology of talk, we are inviting into our conversation the 'voices' of the Discourse from which that technology has come, and of the people who have used that technology in the past. When a speaker says, 'I'm gay', for example, he or she is 'giving voice' to a Discourse of identity and sexuality that is the result of many different voices and many different conversations over the past hundred years or so, and when somebody replies to this with the words, 'God made Adam and Eve, not Adam and Steve', he or she is not just repeating something they have heard before, but also 'giving voice' to another Discourse which, although this phrase seeks to connect it to Biblical times, is also only about a hundred years old. And so when people have conversations like this, they are not just engaging in private chats. They are participating in the ongoing 'Big C Conversation' between these two Discourses.

Identity

As I have noted before, spoken discourse is not just a matter of what we are 'doing with our words', but also a matter of *who we are being*. Whenever we engage in conversation, we both bring to and create through those conversations certain social identities – identities like father, son, airman, and YouTube celebrity, and our ability to enact these identities is intimately tied up with the histories of our past experiences and the ways we have been socialized into using different technologies of talk.

Identity is a complex and contentious concept with many different definitions in the social sciences. Some regard it as something tied to the individual, the unique, core 'self' (or collection of 'selves') that we develop over the course of our lives, whereas others see it as more a matter of the social roles that we play in different situations. An approach to identity informed by discourse analysis avoids both of these extremes, seeing identity instead as essentially an interactional phenomenon: something that, on the one hand, we 'bring along' to interactions as a result of our personal histories and the histories of the societies in which we live, and something that we 'bring about' in interaction

Everybody enters into interaction with a certain collection of 'prefabricated identities' or 'identity kits' (Gee 2012, 2014) that they can use to perform social actions. Claiming identity is not just a matter of, for example, asserting 'I'm gay'. It also requires getting that identity *recognized* by others by showing that one is a competent user of whatever identity kit one is deploying. At the same time, even when these prefabricated identities are recognized and legitimately granted, we must still negotiate the contours of these identities in moment to moment interaction with other people. We cannot be 'just gay' or 'just a soldier' or 'just a Lady Gaga fan': we must negotiate how these 'brought along' identities affect our relationships with those with whom we are interacting, what interactional rights we are able to claim based on them, and how these identities fit into the ongoing 'storylines' that we are composing in our interactions with others (Davies and Harré 1990). These ongoing negotiations of identity, in turn, have an effect on the way these identity kits can be deployed in the future by ourselves and others. Whenever an individual claims to be 'gay' or a 'soldier' or a 'Lady Gaga fan', he or she is contributing to the ongoing evolution of this identity as a cultural tool within a particular community.

Communities

The final concept that I will be focusing on in this book is the idea of community. Whenever we interact, we interact as members of groups, and much of what we are doing in our interactions involves claiming or denying membership in particular communities. This insight, in fact, has been the focal point of much of the work in variationist sociolinguistics, whose aim has been to show, as le Page and Tabouret-Keller (1985), observed, how people produce certain linguistic patterns in order to affiliate themselves with groups that they would like to be identified with and to distance themselves from groups they do not wish to be identified with.

My focus, however, will be less on how people use particular technologies of talk to align themselves with certain groups and more on how groups themselves are 'imagined' (Anderson 1991) around different technologies of talk, and how, through such processes of imagining, communities themselves become tools that people can use to take social actions. Some communities, as le Page and Tabouret-Keller (and other sociolinguists in the same tradition) have shown, are imagined around certain ways of talking (dialects, registers, or social languages). Others, however, are imagined around other technologies of talk such as speech genres and social practices. As communities form around these different cultural tools, they play a role in socializing new members into the way these tools are used, and so in preserving and transmitting technologies of talk across time and space. At the same time, communities also play a role in changing technologies of talk as members work together to adapt the tools they share to new circumstances.

The study of technologies of talk as they are used to take mediated actions at concrete sites of engagement, then, is ultimately the study of how people are able to use these tools to build communities and societies. The study of spoken discourse is not just the study of language or communication or interaction. It is the study of how we manage to live together.

3

Technologies of talk

'Coming out' revisited

Five months before he came out to his father online, Randy Phillips, the YouTube celebrity who goes by the name AreYouSuprised, made his first coming out video entitled 'Coming out to everyone as a military man'.[1] This video is in many ways very different from the one I analysed in the first chapter. First of all, it is a monologue rather than a conversation. Second, it is framed so that viewers cannot see the speaker's face. All we see is his torso clad in a white tee-shirt, and all we hear is his voice speaking directly to his online audience. This framing is not just a clever filming technique: it's what makes this video – filmed before the military's 'Don't Ask, Don't Tell' policy was officially lifted – possible in the first place. Without the ability to conceal his identity, Randy would not be able to say the things that he does:

```
1    hey (0.2) u:h^ (0.3) what's goin on (0.8) this is going to be my
2    (0.3) first^ YouTube video^ (0.6) e::h maybe a series (1.1) if (.) if
3    this is what y'all like^ (0.9) but let me introduce my self^ (1.1) I'm
4    not gonna say my name↓↑ (0.4) but I'm a:: (1.3) active duty United
5    States military member^ (1.7) I am from^ (1.1) here↓↑ (cut to: map
6    of US with words 'Bible Belt' written underneath. 3.0 secs) (1.5)
7    I'm currently stationed^ (1.3) here↓↑ (0.3) (cut to map of Europe
8    labelled Europe. 2.9 secs) (1.4) a::n I a::m currently deployed to^
9    (0.8) here. (0.2) (cut to: map of Middle East labelled SAND BOX.
10   3.0 secs) (1.3) uh the whole point of this video^ (0.2) uh (0.3) is
11   (0.6) to:: t'come out↓↑ (1.0) that's that's even hard to say^ (0.6) uh
12   (1.7) to a lot of people^ (0.9) my parents of course^ (1.3) my entire
```

---

[1]Original url: https://www.youtube.com/watch?v=R6U-Ocm3Nq0. Available at: https://youtu.be/BwNPq1p7QTk.

13　family^ (1.5) my best friend↓↑ (1.7) my other best friend. (1.3) my:
14　↓↑ (1.4) girlfriend^ (1.6) everyone I work with (1.0) of course not
15　yet. (.) this is (0.6) it's gonna be a while because^ (1.0) u:h (0.4) the
16　whole don't ask don't tell thing is not^ (0.2) completely
17　implemented (0.7) but (0.5) I'm not gonna show my face and I'm
18　not gonna really (0.5) give a whole lotta detail (0.8) but if you
19　wanna follow me on my journey^ (1.2) it may ta:ke (1.6) a year↓↑
20　(1.0) or so for this to finally get over with^ (0.6) uh (0.4) but I just
21　wanna (1.2) t'document this (0.7) let other people^ (0.6) follow me
22　(0.2) I'm a hundred percent closeted (1.0) absolutely nobody knows
23　(1.8) but I'm sure (1.3) of this and I (0.3) definitely wanna come out.
24　(0.9) so↓↑ (0.8) if y'like this please subscribe mm there're gonna be
25　more videos to come (0.7) maybe one every few wee:ks:^ (0.3) I'm
26　not gonna make another video if nobody's watchin' these (0.5) but if
27　I can get maybe^ (0.4) a hundred subscribers^ (0.9) and a thousand
28　views on this (.) as soon as I get that (0.6) I'll definitely post another
29　video and (.) and keep everybody updated (0.4) uh (0.8) please uh
30　send me yer questions what you'd like to know^ (0.7) what you'd
31　like to know about me nothing personal I'm not gonna tell you who
32　I am^ (1.2) but (0.4) I just wanna sh (0.4) show the journey and I'll
33　(0.4) share all my struggles with you.

Almost three months later, Randy posted another video, this one documenting his coming out to a friend and comrade.[2] In this video, he is still not visible, since he is the one holding the camera pointed towards his friend, who is in the driver's seat of a military vehicle. As the friend talks to Randy, he mostly keeps his eyes on the road, though occasionally he glances over at the passenger seat, holding the steering wheel with one hand and gesturing with the other.

1　Friend　(inaudible) are you watching my speed?
2　Randy　I'm not watchin your spee::d
3　Friend　Sir I was not speeding (0.4)
4　Randy　no (1.1) I just always wanna get something (0.6)
5　　　　　like on video^ (0.2) like I've never seen
6　　　　　(1.0)
7　　　　　hey Sherwood^
8　　　　　(2.1)
9　Friend　°yup°

---

[2]Original url: https://www.youtube.com/watch?v=OsP3DeTJ1I0. Available at: https://youtu.be/3gYHQOUeZag.

10	Randy	(0.5) ↓I'm ↓gay
11		(1.0)
12	Friend	it's all good ↓↑ (0.2)
13	Randy	<u>is</u> it? (0.1)
14	Friend	ye[ah.
15	Randy	[are you cool with it? like^=
16	Friend	=well
17		I <u>honestly</u>::=
18	Randy	=don't say my <u>name</u>
19		(1.2)
20	Friend	Sir^ (0.4) [I couldn't] give a <u>rat's</u> <u>ass</u> (.)
21	Randy	[o k a y]
22	Friend	hey love is love (0.7)
23	Randy	$don't sayit like <u>that</u>$ [it sounds so <u>rude</u>
24	Friend	[it's <u>true</u>::
25	Randy	(0.2) okay^
26	Friend	(1.2)
27		fuckin don't ask don't tell^ (.) go ahead and tell.
28	Randy	(0.3) yeah?
29	Friend	(0.6)
30		goin t'hang yahs (0.2)
31	Randy	shhh <u>what</u>? =
32	Friend	= he he he he he (.) he heh
33		(0.7)
34		oh <u>ma</u>::n (0.6) I don't give a shit about that stuff (0.1)
35	Randy	really? yeah I know you don't that's why I wanna
36		tell ya
37	Friend	ma::n [(inaudible)] just the same
38	Randy	[so]
39		aright
40	Friend	(1.8)
41		you wanna swing that way^=
42	Randy	=heh
43	Friend	(0.9)
44		it's all good↓↑ (1.2) want watcha can't touch↓↑
45	Randy	[ha]
46	Friend	[I don't know]
47	Randy	(0.7) ha you're a ginger [right?
48	Friend	[ha ha ha ha ha
49	Randy	(0.2) I'm good.
50	Friend	(0.8) I'm more like the Pillsbury Dough Boy^=
51	Randy	=heh

These two videos illustrate some of the different tools that people have available to them when they engage in spoken discourse in different situations. In the first, the range of resources for communication is fairly constrained: we cannot see the speaker's face, and, for the length of the video, his arms remain motionless at his sides. Nevertheless, the speaker still draws on an abundant range of resources, including the formidable meaning making potential of the English language, the ability of the human voice to communicate through stress and intonation, and a rich collection of formulaic phrases, stylistic devices, generic conventions and cultural references. He also uses written texts like maps with humorous labels like 'The SAND BOX'.

In the second video, Randy and his friend have a wider range of tools available: they move their bodies and arms, glance at each other, and display an array of facial expressions (though mostly not visible to the audience of the video). But even in this case, the way in which they can use these tools is constrained by the physical environment in which this conversation is taking place and other demands on their attention (such as driving). Since they are conducting a real-time conversation, rather than just a monologue as in the first video, they also must do more with these tools: they must use them not just to express their thoughts and feelings, but also to coordinate the *joint action* of 'having a conversation' with each other, and to coordinate that action with the other actions (driving and shooting a video) in which they are engaged.

Tools and toolkits

The main premise of this book is that all spoken discourse is mediated through 'technologies' or 'cultural tools', and the way people appropriate and mix these tools affects the kinds of actions they are able to take, the kinds of meanings they are able to make, the kinds of relationships they are able to form, the kinds of people they are able to be, and, ultimately, the kinds of societies they are able to create. One consequence of this approach is that we should not regard the 'new' kinds of conversations that people are engaging in nowadays, mediated through technologies like mobile telephones and social networking sites, as fundamentally different from face-to-face interactions, nor should we regard face-to-face interaction as some kind of 'pure', 'unmediated' form of communication. Certainly there are important differences between the way people conduct conversations using different technologies: 'coming out' over the phone, for example, or over YouTube, or to a friend sitting next to you in a truck are all very different, but what makes these different conversations different is not the fact that some are mediated and others are not. Coming out 'in person' depends just as much on 'technologies' as broadcasting a

YouTube video – technologies that are both physical (like human bodies and the interiors of motor vehicles) and semiotic (like languages, speech genres and social identities). It's just that the technologies involved have different affordances and constraints on the things that people can do with them and the kinds of interactions they can have. All social interactions are sites where people must work together to 'orchestrate' the use of whatever sociocultural and material resources they happen to have available for expressing meanings, for showing who they are, and for accomplishing whatever actions they are trying to accomplish.

In this chapter, I will attempt to give an account of the different kinds of tools that are available to people to engage in spoken discourse and to discuss the kinds of social actions that these tools make possible. One risk of such an endeavour is that it may appear at first that I am reifying these tools, or assuming that particular tools have the same configurations of affordances and constraints regardless of the situation into which they are appropriated. I hope it will soon become clear that what I am more interested in doing is describing the dynamic and contingent nature of mediational means as they are used to take action in social life. Cultural tools are never the same across different uses and circumstances, first because every time they are used, they accumulate the history of that use which they carry into future uses, and second because the affordances and constraints of any tool depend not just on the tool itself but on how the social actor adapts it to particular goals and mixes it with other tools. A tool's utility does not reside in the tool itself, but originates at the point of contact between the tool and the conditions of its use.

The notion that spoken discourse is a matter of how people deploy different tools or technologies of talk is not unique to the approach I am taking in this book. Many of the approaches that I discussed in the last chapter use similar language to talk about the resources people draw upon when they engage in conversation. Conversation analysts, for example, often describe things like turn types, adjacency pairs and membership categories as 'devices', 'apparatuses' or 'technologies' (Hutchby and Wooffitt 2008; ten Have 1990; Sacks 1992b: 332). In his very first lecture on conversation analysis, Sacks (1992a: 10–11) argued that conversations are mediated through what he referred to as 'social objects'. 'Of the enormous range of activities that people do,' he said, 'all of them are done with something. ... What we want then to find out is, can we first of all construct the objects that get used to make up ranges of activities, and then see how it is those objects do get used.'

The two most influential metaphors for spoken discourse, Goffman's dramaturgical metaphor and Wittgenstein's notion of 'language games' also implicitly see social interaction as mediated through tools. For Goffman (1959: 22), performers depend on various kinds of 'expressive equipment' – things like props, costumes, scripts and physical settings – in order to play their parts successfully. Wittgenstein similarly envisions players in 'language games' having available to them different kinds of tools. One aspect of these tools that he highlights is the fact that what one can actually do with a particular tool depends crucially on the game into which it has been appropriated. He writes (1958/69: 6e):

> Think of the tools in a tool-box, there is a hammer, pliers, a saw, a screwdriver, a rule, a glue-pot, nails and screws – The function of words is as diverse as the functions of these objects. (And in both cases there are similarities.) Of course, what confuses us is the uniform appearance of words when we hear them spoken or meet them in script and print. For their application is not presented to us so clearly.

Although Wittgenstein never gets much beyond words in his conception of the toolbox we use to communicate, one of the chief advantages of a toolbox approach to spoken discourse is that it opens up space for us to consider things other than language as important resources for talk. As Gee (2014a: 142) reminds us:

> People build identities and activities not just through language but by using language together with other 'stuff' that isn't language. If you want to get recognized as a street-gang member of a certain sort you have to speak in the 'right' way, but you have to act and dress in the 'right' way, as well. ... You also have to use or be able to use various sorts of symbols (e.g., graffiti), tools (e.g., a weapon), and objects (e.g., street corners) in the 'right' places and at the 'right' times. You can't just 'talk the talk,' you have to 'walk the walk' as well.

Finally, this approach resonates with a range of work in sociology and anthropology, such as that of Swidler (1986: 273), who sees 'culture' as basically a '"toolkit" of symbols, stories, rituals, and world-views, which people ... use in varying configurations to solve different kinds of problems'. A key feature of this perspective is that it emphasizes both the enabling and constraining nature of cultural artefacts, values and beliefs. 'Culture's causal significance,' writes Swindler (273), lies 'not in defining ends of action, but in providing cultural components that are used to construct *strategies of action*' (emphasis mine, see also Alexander 2003; Bruner 1987).

There is a big difference between seeing language and other semiotic resources as cultural tools (Everett 2012) and seeing them as sets of 'rules' or 'deep structures' as many theoretical linguists do. It means that the meanings that people are able to make and the actions that they are able to take with these tools are not determined by the tools themselves, but also by the way people are able to deploy them in specific situations. The 'technology' of conversation that Sacks (1992b) spoke about, for example, should not be seen as a 'casual framework within which humans mechanically operate in uttering their turns at talk', but rather as 'an organizational substratum' which people deploy in strategic ways depending on what they are trying to achieve (Hutchby 2001: 156; see also Button 1990). As Voloshinov (1973: 68), a contemporary of Bakhtin's, put it, 'what is important for the speaker about the linguistic form is not that it is a stable and always self-equivalent signal, but that it is an always changeable and adaptable sign'.

This 'tension' between what tools do, and what we do with tools is, in fact, one of the main reasons focusing on tools and how people use them is such a powerful way to approach spoken discourse, because it can help shed light not just on how social structures influence individual actions, but also on how individual actions influence social structures. 'A toolkit approach', says Wertsch (1991: 94), 'allows group and contextual differences in mediated action to be understood in terms of the array of mediational means to which people have access and the patterns of choice they manifest in selecting a particular means for a particular occasion.'

The way in which we understand the relationship between what tools can do and what we can do with them is in terms of what I referred to in the last chapter as *affordances* and *constraints*. The idea of affordances comes from the work of perceptual psychologist James J. Gibson (1986), who used it to describe the potential that things in the environment have for serving as tools to perform certain actions. Affordance are, as Gee (2014b: 16) puts it, 'what things are good for, based on what a user can do with them'. The important thing about this definition of affordances is the idea that affordances do not reside in tools, but in the *interaction* between tools and users. As Gibson (1986: 127) wrote, 'I mean by ... [affordance] something that refers to both the environment and the animal in a way that no existing term does. It implies the *complementarity* of the animal and the environment.' 'Affordances are only affordances,' Gee (2014: 16) explains, 'given that a potential user of the object has the ability to use the object to carry out the action it affords. The user must have what we can call an *effective ability*, the ability to effect (carry out) the affordance.' Effective ability, however, is not the same as what Chomsky refers to as competence, by which he chiefly means an individual's knowledge of the grammatical system of a language. Effective ability is more than just knowledge: it is the ability to adapt a tool to changing circumstances and a sensitivity to the ever-changing conventions of use that grow up around particular technologies. It is the ability to cope with not just the 'patterned, abstractable, universal, [and] repeatable' nature of tools, but also the aspects of tools that are 'variable, locally adapted, saturated by context, never quite the same, and constantly adjusting to the world beyond their own limits' (Hanks 1996: 7).

Technologies of talk

As I mentioned in the last chapter, technologies of talk can include material technologies like telephones, computers and the human voice, and semiotic technologies like languages, genres, identities and practices. In some ways, however, this is an artificial distinction, since all technologies of talk have both material and semiotic dimensions (Wertsch 1998a). As McLuhan pointed out four decades ago, material technologies do more than just transmit messages; they also have an effect on the *meaning* those messages have. Apart from what you say when you are breaking up with your girlfriend, the material technology you employ to do it – whether you call her, write her a letter, change your relationship status on Facebook or invite her to an Italian restaurant – itself carries meaning (Gershon 2012). By the same token, all semiotic tools have material dimensions. Spoken language must take material form as sound waves in order for it to be transmitted from one person to another, and genres like business letters, television programmes and text messages are instantiated as physical texts in ways that make them inseparable from the material means (paper, television sets, mobile phones) that are used to transmit them. In other words, when considering the affordances and constraints of different technologies, we must understand how these affordances and constraints are always a matter of how these technologies are deployed together with other technologies, and especially how material and semiotic dimensions of technologies interact.

Material technologies

I will be referring to material technologies of talk as *media*, including in this category those tools which we normally think of when we think of media (such as telephones and televisions) as well as physical objects, built environments, and, perhaps the most important material means for engaging in spoken discourse: the human body and voice. Media provide the basis for the deployment of all semiotic tools – you cannot (under normal circumstances) speak without the medium of the voice, gesture without the medium of the body, or engage in social gatherings of various types without the media of different kinds of built environments. Hutchby (2001: 1) defines media as 'channels by means of which individuals or groups can be situated in co-presence'. Of course, different media make different kinds and degrees of co-presence possible, but it is only through the accomplishment of some sort of connection, some capacity to perceive others and to be perceived by them, that we can engage in conversations.

The most basic media that we use to interact with others are our voices and bodies. The human articulatory organs allow us to produce a wide range of sounds that can be combined in ways that express meaning, to project our presence over a certain distance, and to modulate the volume of our voice to make it audible to people at different distances from us. In some kinds of interactions, such as telephone conversations, our voices also serve as the primary means through which we accomplish co-presence. In face-to-face communication, on the other hand, the body functions as the primary means through which we become present to one another.

We use our bodies to display our availability for interaction, to gain and hold other people's attention, to keep them informed of our involvement with them (Goffman 1963, 1971), and to mark off interactional 'territories' from the surrounding world (Kendon 1990). Our bodies also allow us to use space as a canvas for social interaction. We can lean in close to people, move away from them, arrange our bodies with other bodies in various formations that facilitate certain kinds of conversations and certain kinds of social relationships (see Kendon 1990; Hall 1966/90). Finally, our bodies are also equipped with all sorts of moving parts, our hands, head and eyes, for example, with which we can point and gesture, not to mention our faces, the parts of which we can move together in coordinated fashion to make expressions of incredible variety.

Disembodied media such as megaphones, telephones and computers, as well as things that we may not normally think of as media such as tables, chairs, rooms and the interiors of motor vehicles, are normally seen as *extensions* of our bodies and voices. Telephones and microphones extend our voices. Vehicles like cars and bicycles extend our legs. And chairs and tables extend the ability of our bodies to assume certain postures (McLuhan 1964/2001). Another way of seeing such media, however, is as *environments* within which we can deploy our bodies and voices in different ways (Meyrowitz 1985). Like our bodies and our voices, the main way these environments function is by allowing us to enact different forms of interactional co-presence. In some ways media enable co-presence, but in other ways they constrain it, by, for example, restricting the range of semiotic modes that can be deployed (as a telephone restricts the use of gaze, gesture and facial expression) or the extent to which people can monitor each other. Because of this, media provide ways for users to strategically manage how they want to be perceived by others, to control what kinds of information they want to make available and what kind of information they want to withhold. An excellent illustration of this is the first example above, in which Randy uses the affordances of digital video to reveal things inside of its frame and conceal things outside of it in order to hide his face from the audience (see also Jones 2008b). This effect of media to simultaneously amplify and restrict presence can also be seen in the second example in which Randy and his friend are interacting within the confined space of a motor vehicle. On the one hand, this environment forces participants into close physical proximity, allowing rich opportunities for mutual monitoring, but, on the other hand, it also constrains their access to each other by the way it forces them to sit side by side (instead of face-to-face), and by the constraints on the driver's ability to gesture and gaze towards his or her interlocutor imposed by the need to attend to the mechanics of driving and the traffic conditions outside the vehicle (for more on the effect of driving on interaction, see Mondada 2012; Nevile 2012).

Media also consist of various material objects like the clothes we wear and the ornaments we use to decorate our bodies, objects that we carry like handbags and briefcases, tools such as eating utensils, eyeglasses, and writing implements, and the stationary or movable objects that surround us such as lamps, street signs and traffic signals. Some of these objects are specifically designed for communication, functioning as carriers of particular semiotic modes: newspapers carry the printed word, paintings carry colour and form, and mobile telephones carry the human voice (as well as graphical information). What is often neglected when it comes to such objects, however, is their materiality, the way they function to regulate co-presence. A mobile telephone placed on the table in a restaurant, for example, may signal something about the owner's commitment to participation in various sorts of interactions. A newspaper opened in front of a subway passenger's face may function not just to transmit information about current events to the reader, but also to shield the reader from involvement with other passengers, or, as in old detective movies, to allow him or her to surreptitiously monitor them.

A final important point about media has to do with their role in what Bauman and Briggs (1990) call *entextualization*, the 'the process of rendering discourse extractable, of making a stretch of linguistic production into a unit – a text – that can be lifted out of its interactional setting' (73). As I mentioned in Chapter 1, this ability for discourse to be taken out of one context and transported into another plays an important role in allowing people to make connections between the present interaction and interactions in the past, and between one particular interaction and the broader norms of interaction in the wider society. All interactions are *heteroglossic*, made possible by acts of appropriating and recontextualizing past moments of discourse, and this is only possible through *entextualization*. Of course, different media are able to preserve discourse and actions with different degrees of durability. Words uttered through the human voice are notoriously impermanent, but they can still be stored in the memories of the people who have heard them, repeated and passed on by 'word of mouth'. Writing makes words much more durable, though it is less effective at preserving other aspects of discourse (such as gestures and prosody). Newer media like tape recorders and video cameras are more effective at storing rich, multimodal texts, and their ubiquity in modern life has changed people's understanding of the permanence of spoken discourse and their ability to recontextualize and 'remix' segments of past discourse into present interactions (Knobel and Lankshear 2015). Traces of past discourse and action can also be stored in objects and environments as 'frozen actions' (Norris 2004: 13–15) – which is why detectives can often 'read off' of crime scenes the past actions that occurred in them. In fact, all objects and environments, as Iedema (2001) points out, are essentially *resemiotizations* of past discourse: a building, for example, is the physical embodiment of countless texts and meetings, blueprints and conversations that occurred in the course of its being built. The way media allow us to entextualize and recontextualize discourse plays an important role not just in helping us to link one interaction to another, but also in creating a sense of continuity to social identities, social relationships and social practices, and transmitting sociocultural knowledge across expanses of time and space.

Semiotic technologies

Coming up with labels for semiotic technologies is much more challenging. When you consider Vygotsky's (1981: 137) list of what he called 'psychological tools', what you find is a dizzying array of different kinds of things: 'language; various systems for counting; mnemonic techniques; algebraic symbol systems; works of art; writing; schemes, diagrams, maps, and mechanical drawings; all sorts of conventional signs; and so on'. Some of these tools are what linguists would call 'codes', systems of meaning making not very different from those abstract systems that Saussure and Chomsky concerned themselves with (e.g., 'languages', 'algebraic symbol systems'). Others are closer to what more contemporary scholars of discourse like Kress (2009) refer to as 'modes' (e.g., 'writing'). And still others constitute texts or text types (e.g., 'works of art', 'schemes, diagrams, maps, and mechanical drawings').

My way of classifying semiotic technologies will attempt to take into account all of these different kinds of tools and to provide a way of understanding the relationship between them. The first type of semiotic technology I will be concerned with, and the type that establishes the basis for all the other technologies I will discuss, is the *mode*. Modes are socially conditioned resources for making meaning (Kress 2009; Kress and van Leeuwen 1996). They include things like speech, writing, gaze, gesture and object handling. While modes are not the same as 'codes' (what we usually think of as 'languages'), they do present to users certain sets of 'meaning potential' that come to be conventionalized over time by particular groups of users. The advantage of thinking in terms of modes rather than codes is that it helps us to avoid seeing speech or other semiotic modes as abstract systems that can be applied in the same way across different communicative contexts. It also helps to alert us to affordances – or, as Hockett (1960) calls them, 'design features' – that go beyond their capacity to generate 'meaning' in the Chomskyinan sense of the word. When it comes to speech, for example, among the design features that Hockett observed are its capacity to be monitored as it is produced by the person who is producing it (something we normally cannot do in the same way with facial expressions and gestures), its capacity to be repeated (allowing messages to be easily entextualized and carried into different contexts), the fact that it allows us to talk about things and to create contexts that are independent of the physical settings that we inhabit, and, perhaps the most important design feature of them all, the ability to *talk about talk*, making speech an ideal tool, as I will describe below, for the *technologization* of other tools.

Other modes such as gaze, gesture, proxemics and object handling have different design features. Gaze, for example, allows people to communicate their attention to or engagement with different aspects of the physical environment, other people, or different activities taking place without having to refer to them explicitly in speech (Goodwin 1981; Norris 2004; Stivers and Heritage 2001). It also gives people ways of showing how they feel about or understand what other people say or do (Haddington 2006), and of regulating the flow of talk and managing the conversational floor (see e.g., Goodwin 1981; Kendon 1967, 1990). The mode of gesture allows people to use physical space as a canvas for communication, giving them ways to express meanings that can be used either independent of words or in concert with them (Birdwhistell 1952, Kendon 1975). One of the things people can do with gestures (as well as with paralinguistic modes like stress and intonation) that they can't do with language is express meaning *topologically*. Language expresses meaning typologically, separating the world into different categories like big and small, red and green, happy and sad. Gesture and paralanguage allow for the expression in finer gradations or 'shades' of meaning: rather than saying something is big or small, for example, we can hold our hands at a certain distance to communicate a more exact estimate of size, and when a word like happy doesn't express how we feel with enough specificity, we can accompany the word with a certain gesture or say it in a certain tone of voice to slightly alter its meaning (Lemke 1999).

Finally, 'disembodied modes' (Norris 2004) like images, music and writing, have their own particular affordances. We can change the way people understand our speech, for instance, by accompanying it with visual aids like pictures or diagrams, and we can change the way people interpret texts and images by adding to them a verbal commentary. Goodwin (1994), for example, shows how expert testimony in a courtroom often depends on the skilful mixing of speech with images (see Chapter 8).

Spoken discourse is, by its very nature, *multimodal*, that is, we almost always deploy multiple modes at the same time when we speak, and the kinds of meanings that we are able to make with one mode are dependent on the other modes that are deployed along with it. There is also an intimate relationship between modes and media: media are the material carriers of modes. Paper, computer screens and other surfaces are the carriers of writing; the voice is the carrier of spoken language; and the body is the carrier of modes like gaze, gesture and posture. Certain media only allow for the transmission of certain modes (the conventional telephone, for example, only allowing for the transmission of speech), and while other media allow for the transmission of multiple modes, they may amplify some modes and mute others, or allow users to strategically foreground certain modes and background others (Norris 2004). Depending on the way the message is composed, for instance, the medium of digital video allows users to foreground or background different modes including the speech of actors, their gestures and facial expressions, different physical settings, and different objects in those settings (Harley and Fitzpatrick 2009). It also allows users to introduce other modes as well such as images, written texts, background music and sound effects, which they can laminate onto or edit into the spoken message, as Randy does with his maps in the first example above.

A closer look at the second example above illustrates how the affordances and constraints of different modes, as they are deployed through different media, affect one another. In the following version of the transcript, the descriptions of the non-verbal behaviour of Randy's friend appear in bold type underneath the spoken utterances with which this behaviour co-occurs.

```
 7   Randy    hey Sherwood^
 8            (2.1)
 9   Friend   °yup^°
              (gaze towards passenger)
10   Randy    (0.5) I'm gay
11            (1.0)
12   Friend   it's all good ↓↑ (0.2)
13   Randy    is it? (0.1)
              (gaze towards passenger)
14   Friend   ye[ah.
15   Randy      [are you cool with it? like^=
16   Friend                        =well
17            I honestly::=
              (one beat gesture with hand out the window,
              palm open-hold)
18   Randy             =don't say my name
19            (1.2)
```

20 Friend **Sir^ (0.4) [I couldn't] give a <u>rat's</u> <u>ass</u>** (.)
            (beat gestures on each word with hand out window palm
            open to the side)
21 Randy   [o k a y]
22 Friend **hey love is love (0.7)**
            (hand raised out window, fingers parted slightly – hand
            drops at end of utterance)
23 Randy $don't sayit like <u>that</u>$ [it sounds so <u>rude</u>
24 Friend   [it's **<u>true</u>::**
            (beat gesture hand raises slightly)
25 Randy   (0.2) okay^
26 Friend (1.2)
27   fuckin don't ask don't tell^ (.) **go ahead and tell.**
            (quick glance to passenger on pause, beat gesture out of
            window palm down)
28 Randy   (0.3) yeah?
29 Friend (0.6)
30   goin **t'hang yahs (0.2)**
            (gaze towards passenger)
31 Randy   shhh <u>what</u>? =
32 Friend   = *he he he he he* (.) **he heh**
            (*raises head slightly,* **gaze toward passenger)**
33   (0.7)
34   oh <u>ma::n</u> (0.6) I don't **give a shit** about that stuff (0.1)
            (gaze left out of window)
35 Randy   really? Yeah I know you don't that's why I wanna
36   tell ya
37 Friend and I **don't care**
            (beat gesture with hand out window and quick glance to
            left)
38 Randy   =so
39   aright
40 Friend (1.8)
41   you **wanna swing that way^=**
            (gesture with hand out window, palm up, two beats at end)
42 Randy   =heh
43 Friend (0.9)
44   it's all good↓↑ (1.2) **want watcha can't touch↓↑**
            (gesture with hand out window, palm pointing forward,
            places palm on chest)
45 Randy   [ha]
46 Friend [I don't know]
47 Randy   (0.7) ha you're a ginger [right?

As I said above, a driver's use of the mode of gaze when he is driving is severely constrained by his or her need to attend to traffic conditions. Nevertheless, drivers still manage to gaze at passengers when they are talking to them, and to use the mode of gaze in strategic ways (Nevile 2012). In the example above, Randy's friend gazes at him five times in this excerpt: The first time is after Randy's 'pre-announcement' in line 9 ('hey Sherwood'), this gaze functioning as a way of ratifying Randy's right to the floor and attending to the news that is about to be delivered. The second time is when Randy elicits a confirmation of his friend's initial positive assessment of the news in line 13 ('is it?'), this gaze functioning again as a way of orienting to Randy's question and also possibly of communicating the sincerity of the assessment. The third gaze, in line 27, punctuates the brief pause between the phrases, 'fuckin don't ask don't tell^' and 'go ahead and tell'. The final two gazes towards Randy in lines 30 and 32 serve as 'contextualization cues' (Gumperz 1982, see Chapter 4), which 'frame' the friend's words ('goin t'hang yahs') as a joke. There are also times at which the driver directs his gaze in the *opposite* direction, looking briefly to his left out of the side window; both of these instances accompanied by utterances communicating his lack of concern about Randy's sexuality, in line 34 when he says, 'I don't give a shit,' and line 37, when he says, 'I don't care.' What is interesting about this account is that it demonstrates, even in this short excerpt, and even with all of the constraints on the mode of gaze associated with driving, the range of functions that gaze can serve, helping the driver to communicate his attention, to regulate the rhythm of the conversation, to signal contextual shifts, to manage the conversational floor, and to communicate metaphorically about his thoughts and attitude. What is perhaps even more interesting is that the driver does all of these things with his gaze while continuing to attend to the demands of driving.

Along with gaze, Randy's friend also makes ample use of gestures, even though one of his hands is occupied with steering. All of the gestures he makes are with his left hand out of the side window, and all of them serve in some way to supplement his speech. In some cases, the gestures serve as metaphorical representations of what he is saying, as in line 22, when he raises his hand with his fingers parted when he says, 'hey love is love', and then drops it abruptly, as if to say 'and that's that', and in line 41, when he opens his palm upward when uttering the words 'you wanna swing that way^' and then follows the utterance with two short beats with his open palm: open palmed gestures typically communicate uncertainty or openness (Müller 2003), and are often accompanied by rising intonation, as in the conditional clause uttered here (Bolinger 1983); the short pulses at the end serve to complete the utterance, a way of saying, 'if you wanna swing that way, *that's fine.*' A contrast to this palm up gesture is the palm down gesture that he makes when he says 'go ahead and tell', palm down gestures typically signalling closure or dismissiveness. In other cases, gestures serve more of a timekeeping function, as when he emphasizes the words 'I couldn't give a rat's ass' with five beats of his hand. Such gestures, commonly referred to as 'beat gestures' (McNeill 2005; Norris 2004) help people to manage the rhythm and information structure of their speech, to give prominence to certain words or phrases, and to coordinate their speech and actions with those of people with whom they are talking and with the cognitive demands of other tasks they might be engaged in.

The point of this brief analysis is not just to show how great a role non-verbal modes like gaze and gesture play in spoken discourse, even in situations where speakers also have to use their hands and eyes for other things, but also how speakers use different modes together in coordinated ways that help them to overcome constraints placed on communication. The obvious limitation of this analysis is, of course, that we do not have access to Randy's non-verbal behaviour (since he is taking the video). If we did, we would likely find that Randy's gestures, gaze and other body movements are, in various ways, synchronized with those of his friend (Erickson 1990; Goodwin 1981; Kendon 1970). We might also gain insight into ways in which, nowadays, pointing a video camera or smart phone at someone has become an important new form of non-verbal behaviour which has an inevitable effect on the way in which modes like speech, gesture and gaze are deployed.

Speech genres and social languages

Apart from these basic modal resources like speech, gaze, and gesture, social actors also typically have access to more complex semiotic technologies, technologies made up of patterned combinations of verbal and non-verbal signs that have, over time, come to be conventionalized. Among these are what Bakhtin (1986) calls 'speech genres' – conventionalized methods of structuring discourse associated with different kinds of 'social practices' (such as 'coming out') – and 'social languages' – styles of speaking (involving particular word choices, grammatical patterns, and phonological features) that are associated with different kinds of people such as 'soldiers', 'gay men', 'southerners' and 'psychiatrists'.

Speech genres are particular forms of spoken discourse that are, as Bakhtin (1986: 87) puts it, characteristic of 'particular situations of speech communication'. Among the examples that he gives are 'genres of greetings, farewells, congratulations, all kinds of wishes, information about health, business, and so forth ... genres of salon conversations about everyday, social, aesthetic, and other subjects, genres of table conversations among friends, intimate conversations within the family, and so on' (79–80). It's obvious from this list that what he meant by speech genres ranges from the simplest of conversational routines to rather lengthy and elaborate forms of interaction. The kinds of discourse features that set one speech genre apart from another are also wide ranging, including features like the conventional sequential ordering of particular utterances, particular patterns of turn taking and topic management, the use of particular rhetorical forms or stylistic devices, and particular formulaic utterances or exchanges.

One way of thinking of speech genres is as 'scripts' that people follow when they interact in different kinds of circumstances (Schank and Abelson 1977; Scollon, Scollon and Jones 2012). These scripts govern, sometimes loosely and sometimes rather strictly, who should say what to whom and in what order. But a better way of seeing a speech genre is as a series of *actions* which people take to accomplish social practices (Bhatia 1993). From this perspective, we might consider the basic building blocks of speech genres to be 'speech acts' (Austin 1962; Searle 1969), utterances which, by being uttered, accomplish some social action (see Chapter 4). The utterance 'I'm gay', for example, can be seen to constitute the speech act of 'coming out', which changes the status of the person who utters it (Chirrey 2003). But this speech act is normally uttered in the context of a larger 'speech genre' in which this utterance is one action in a conventionalized series of actions. This genre, as I explained in the first chapter, usually involves at least three actions, a move that prepares the listener for the announcement of new information ('hey Sherwood'), a move in which the new information is revealed ('I'm gay'), and some kind of response or reaction to the information ('it's all good'). The most important thing about speech genres, however, is that they link these actions to larger *social practices* – cultural activities or 'definitions of the situation' (Goffman 1959) which have become recognizable to members of a particular community. According to Wertsch (1998a), practices are chains of actions that have a *history* within a particular group of social actors and within the cognitive development of an individual. Along with these histories, practices also carry with them a certain amount of ideological 'baggage', including ideas as to why that practice is the way it is, for what purposes, and whether it is good or bad (van Leeuwen and Wodak 1999). Thus, when people appropriate the speech genre of 'coming out', they normally do so within the context of the larger *practice* of 'coming out', which comes with a whole set of political and ideological assumptions that go beyond just telling someone that they're gay. This is why the genre of 'coming out' does not easily transfer to societies where people have different political and ideological assumptions (about, for example, things like sexuality, selfhood and kinship) (Chow 2000; Scollon, Scollon and Jones 2012). While it is possible to perform the action of 'coming out' without using the speech genre of 'coming out' or invoking this larger practice (see e.g., Kitzinger 2000; Liu and Ding 2005), and it is also possible to participate in the *practice* of coming out without appropriating this speech genre (see e.g., Liang 1999; Chapter 4), such occurrences represent particular strategic uses of language in which speakers are, for one reason or another, either downplaying their performance of particular speech acts or disassociating themselves from particular social practices.

At the same time, the speech genre of 'coming out' is not the only genre associated with the practice of 'coming out': other genres include the 'coming out narrative' (Bacon 1998; Liang 1997), in which people relate their experiences of coming out in the past, and, the 'coming out video' (an example of which I began this chapter with), in which people reveal their sexuality to a mass audience over social media sites like YouTube (Alexander and Losh 2010).

Thus, when we use the label 'coming out', we might be referencing one of three things: (1) the *speech act* of 'coming out', in which a speaker utters words such as 'I'm gay', thereby accomplishing the action of 'becoming gay' in the eyes of the person to whom they are uttered; (2) the *speech genre* of 'coming out', consisting of a series of conversational moves of which the speech act of 'coming out' forms a part; (3) and the social practice of 'coming out', consisting of a broader set of ideas about things like what it means to reveal that one is gay to other people, and what it means to be gay in the first place.

While speech genres are forms of talk which show others 'what we are doing', social languages are forms that show others 'who we are being'. They consist of certain *styles* of speaking which index particular social identities. People who approach speech from a purely linguistic perspective normally analyse it in terms of the 'languages' people speak (such as English, German, Russian or Chinese). For Bakhtin, the notion of standardized 'national languages' is actually an 'academic fiction' which serves to obscure the fact that within any national language there are myriad dialects, varieties and registers spoken by certain groups of people and serving particular 'socio-political purposes' (Wertsch 1991: 58). Blommaert (2010: 37) calls these varieties 'clustered and patterned language forms that index specific social personae and roles'. They may be characterized by particular lexis, jargon or formulaic phrases (such as 'I don't give a rat's ass ...'), particular grammatical patterns, or particular phonological features, and the social identities they can index can be very specific identities (such as a 'radical feminist lesbian of colour') or rather general relational identities such as 'son', 'father' and 'friend' (see Chapter 6).

Most people have access to many different social languages, which they can draw upon in different situations and sometimes mix in strategic ways, either 'switching' from one language to another to manage their roles and relationships in interaction, or blend together to form hybrid social languages (which might later come to be technologized as new social languages in their own right) (Gee and Green 1998).

Just as speech genes are dependent on the broader social practices that they index, social languages only work as social languages if people share a set of recognizable social identities with which these ways of speaking can be associated, identities like 'soldier', 'gay man', 'father' and 'Christian'. Different societies (and different communities within societies) have different sets of socially sanctioned identities that people can appropriate to take action in the world. Like social practices, social identities come with all sorts of baggage related to the *value* that societies and communities give to them, and how they are seen to fit with other identities, and the kinds of social practices that are associated with them. Certain social identities make certain kinds of social actions possible: you can't, for example, operate on my brain unless you have access to the identity of a brain surgeon (which requires not just that you have certificates from the right schools, but also that you have mastered a certain social language – that you know how to *talk* like a brain surgeon). At the same time, some social identities can preclude people from participating in certain social practices, as the identities of gays and lesbians precluded them from joining the US military until the 1990s. Of course, the set of socially sanctioned identities in a particular community can change over time, as can the values and social statuses afforded to these identities.

The idea of social languages does not mean that all brain surgeons or gay men or Christians talk in the same way, just that there are certain ways of talking which, in certain sociocultural contexts, have come to *index* these identities. As with speech genres and social practices, people sometimes appropriate social languages and social identities in inventive ways in order to take strategic action. An adolescent boy might, for example, imitate a social language associated with gay men in order to show that he is *not* gay (see Chapter 6), and a gay man might avoid using a social language that society associates with gay men in order to resist the stereotypes that that association serves to reinforce. This last point highlights the fact that social practices and social identities are technologies that are directly implicated in issues of social justice, equality, and access to social resources. The affordance of these technologies is that they allow us to conduct interactions using a kind of social shorthand: To be able to bring to interactions 'prefabricated' identities like 'soldier' or 'doctor', and to be able to engage in certain prefabricated activities like 'coming out' or 'conducting a medical examination' makes life a whole lot easier. At the same time, as soon as we find ourselves 'labelled' as particular kinds of people, or find ourselves implicated in particular kinds of social practices, our abilities to deploy tools not associated with these identities and practices can be limited.

Technologies and technologization

So far in this book I have been using the words mediational means, cultural tools and technologies fairly interchangeably. The time has come to clarify these terms. A mediational means is simply anything that serves to mediate a social action. A rock picked up off the ground and hurled towards an enemy or prey is a mediational means. It might also be considered a cultural tool, if throwing rocks has become a recognized cultural practice among a particular group of people. It becomes a 'technology' when people start paying more attention to how rocks are thrown, making rules about who should throw them and who shouldn't, and even taking the rocks and fashioning them into more efficient weapons like arrowheads. In other words, technologies are tools that become associated with bodies of knowledge and collections of *techniques* as to how to use them (including when to use them, where to use them, and the kinds of people who are allowed to use them, and the other tools that they should be used in conjunction with), and which have accumulated a certain amount of 'ideological baggage' as a result of this. I have been calling the communicative resources I discussed in this chapter (media, modes, speech genres, social languages, social practices and social identities) 'technologies of talk' because they are more than just physical objects or linguistic forms: they also have certain collections of techniques and certain social values associated with their use, and they are situated in complex webs of relationships with other tools in larger 'toolkits' which I have been calling Discourses.

Technologies are not static. People develop new technologies as their material and social conditions change, and old technologies are constantly altered as people adapt them to new circumstances. I will refer to the process by which tools come to be associated with techniques for using them and to be integrated with other tools within Discourses as *technologization* (Jones 2002a, 2013; Scollon 2001). Technologization is at the very root of social change; it allows us to develop new technologies to deal with our ever-changing material and social circumstances. But it can also function to inhibit social change. Computer scientist Jaron Lanier (2011) talks about the problem of 'lock in' when it comes to technologies, a phenomenon in which we become so used to the ways a particular tool allows us to do certain things that we become less able to imagine doing things in any other way. Lanier's discussion focuses mainly on material technologies like computers, but this can just as easily happen with semiotic tools – speech genres can lock us into certain kinds of interactional routines and perpetuate certain kinds of social relationships, and social identities can harden into stereotypes which can be used to limit the range of action afforded to certain people. Technologization can also have the effect of 'locking out' certain kinds of people, restricting access to a particular technology of talk to those who belong to certain social groups or who have not been socialized into certain bodies of knowledge.

What sorts of conditions are needed for a tool to become technologized? The most important condition is tied to the notion of iterativity that I discussed in the last chapter. Tools accumulate conventions regarding how they should be used, by whom, and under what circumstances through the repetition of concrete social actions. In this regard, every time someone uses a particular object or word or gesture in a certain way, speaks in a particular accent, tells a particular kind of story, or identifies him or herself using a particular identity label, he or she is contributing to the ongoing technologization of that object, word, gesture, social language, speech genre or social identity.

But repetition is not enough. These iterative instances of tool use normally need to be supported by a community of users who validate certain conventions for using tools and pass them on to novice members of the community through processes of socialization. Practices like stamp collecting are technologized through the interaction of people who share with one another certain ways of acquiring, archiving, trading and 'reading' stamps (Swales 1990). Similarly, identities like 'soldier' or 'gay man' are technologized through the interaction among people who share affiliation to these identity labels. The relationship between technologies of talk and communities is dialectical. Not only do communities serve as sites where tools are technologized, but technologies of talk also serve as a means through which communities themselves are technologized and individuals claim membership in them (see Chapter 7).

One of the main ways in which communities contribute to the technologization of tools is through the way they help to create and reinforce the connections between different kinds of tools in the larger 'toolkits' of which they are part. So, for example, not only does being a certain kind of soldier require dressing in certain ways, talking in certain ways, producing certain kinds of speech genres, using certain kinds of physical tools at certain times and in certain places, and differentiating people based on various identity markers (such as rank), but the ways each of these technologies is deployed depends on the other technologies that are deployed along with it. Particular ways of speaking are associated with particular speech genres or particular kinds of people, or accompanied by particular ways using other tools. In other words, one of the main ways that tools become technologized is through becoming integrated with other tools in more or less systematic ways within Discourses. In this respect, whenever a technology is used, it invokes (or 'indexes') the whole toolkit of which it has become a part. A military uniform invokes certain ways of talking, acting and thinking, even when its wearer doesn't say a word.

Finally, technologization usually involves the emergence of external representations of the tool and the conventions of use associated with it. For physical tools, such representations may take the form of texts like user's manuals or instructions. For semiotic tools, they typically take the form of what is known as *metadiscourse*, people talking about the way they talk. Parents, for example, typically produce for their children explicit instructions about what to say to whom, when, where and how ('Say thank you to the nice lady,' 'Don't talk that way at the dinner table,' 'Nice girls don't say things like that'), or expose them to comments about the way other people talk which link them to certain social identities or invoke value judgements such as 'rude' or 'polite'. Sometimes, the 'rules' for using semiotic tools are compiled in written texts like dictionaries, grammar books and etiquette manuals. Representations of 'certain kinds of people' talking in particular ways in particular circumstances are also circulated through media and public discourse.

One good example of technologization is what Agha (2005, 2007) calls *enregisterment*, the process through which linguistic registers (what I have been calling social languages) come to be regarded as a socially recognized way of speaking that are linked to certain kinds of people. Central to Agha's understanding of how different ways of talking become enregistered is the notion of 'metalanguage'. He writes (2007: 17):

> The study of language as a social phenomenon must include the study of metalinguistic activity for a simple reason: language users employ language to categorize or classify aspects of language use, including forms of utterance, the situations in which they are used, and the persons who use them. Such reflexive classifications shape the construal of speech (and accompanying signs) for persons acquainted with them.

Although this idea of 'talking about how we are talking' may seem rather strange, it is actually something that we do all the time. In fact, much of what Randy does in his coming out videos on YouTube is metadiscourse – talking about the discursive technologies associated with the practice of coming out, and commenting on what to say to whom, when, where and how. The first example above contains a number of instances of metadiscourse such as:

a) uh the whole point of this video^ (0.2) uh (0.3) is (0.6) to:: t'come out↓↑ (1.0) that's that's even hard to say^ (lines 10–11)

b) I'm not gonna show my face and I'm not gonna really (0.5) give a whole lotta detail (lines 17–18)

c) I just wanna (1.2) t'document this (0.7) let other people^ (0.6) follow me (line 20–21)

d) I'm sure (1.3) of this and I (0.3) definitely wanna come out (line 23)

e) I just wanna sh (0.4) show the journey and I'll (0.4) share all my struggles with you. (line 32–33)

These examples show the range of different ways in which metadiscourse can function to create reflective representations of spoken discourse and, in so doing, contribute to the technologization of certain ways of talking, certain social practices and certain social identities. Metadiscourse might, for instance, serve to explain the purpose of a particular genre or way of speaking (examples a, c and e), thus linking it to certain social functions like 'documenting' or 'sharing'. It might serve to link a particular genre or way of talking to a person's identity, or feelings, or degree of investment in a particular technology of talk (as in examples a, b and d). Or it may set the 'ground rules' for the way a particular technology of talk will be deployed (as in example b). All of these functions contribute not just to the speaker's ongoing construction of his own identity and management of his own 'coming out', but they also contribute to the ongoing technologization of 'coming out' as a social practice and of the identity of a 'military man' at this particular historical moment in the United States.

This sort of metadiscourse is not just characteristic of reflective monologues such as the first example, but is also an important part of conversations, such as that in the second example above, where metadiscourse plays a role in helping participants negotiate their shared deployment of different technologies. In this conversation, after Randy has made his revelation and his friend has responded, there ensues a conversation in which Randy and his friend *reflectively evaluate* that exchange. In fact, what takes up most of this conversation is not the 'coming out', but the conversation about the 'coming out' which follows it.

```
15   Randy    [are you cool with it? like^=
16   Friend                              =well
17            I honestly::=
18   Randy                  =don't say my name
19            (1.2)
20   Friend   Sir^ (0.4) [I couldn't] give a rat's ass (.)
21   Randy               [ o k a y ]
22   Friend   hey love is love (0.7)
23   Randy    $don't sayit like that$ [it sounds so rude
24   Friend                           [it's true::
25   Randy    (0.2) okay
26   Friend   (1.2)
27            fuckin don't ask don't tell^ (.) go ahead and tell.
```

Here we can see metadiscourse functioning in many of the same ways it functioned in Randy's monologue, to interpret and evaluate various aspects of the conversation ('$don't sayit like that$ it sounds so rude'), to link different aspects of the conversation to particular kinds of social identities and particular ideological stances ('fuckin don't ask don't tell^ (.) go ahead and tell'), and to set and enforce 'ground rules' for the conversation ('don't say my <u>name</u>').

Metadiscourse, however, does not always consist of such straightforward commentary on what is being said. Sometimes people comment less directly on the discursive practices they are involved in through joking, irony or parody, as, for example in the following exchange:

```
30  Friend   goin t'hang yahs (0.2)
31  Randy    shhh what? =
32  Friend                = he he he he he (.) he heh
```

Here Randy's friend metadiscursively comments on what he believes the proper response to coming out should be by parodying what he believes is the improper response. Parody and other forms of intertextuality (such as 'fuckin don't ask don't tell^ (.) go ahead and tell.') metadiscursively comment on utterances or speech genres by comparing them to some prior utterances or genres (in this case, the past practice of hanging soldiers for offences, and the 'Don't Ask, Don't Tell' policy).

The sort of metadiscourse evident in these two examples is typical of most spoken discourse. Sometimes, however, these more dynamic activities of commenting on, evaluating and setting ground rules for discourse solidify into sets of standard rules or regulations about speech which come to exert pressure on participants in a community so that not only does the use of certain technologies of talk signal 'membership', but the failure to talk in the 'correct' way can result in exile from the community. This is, in fact, what occurred with the 'Don't Ask, Don't Tell' policy, which was essentially a *metadiscursive policy*, the purpose of which was to regulate social practices and social identities by regulating spoken discourse.

*

In this chapter, I have elaborated on the concept of mediation that forms the basis for an approach to spoken discourse informed by mediated discourse analysis. I have offered a brief and admittedly sketchy taxonomy of the kinds of technologies of talk people use to engage in spoken discourse, a taxonomy which I will further fill out in the coming chapters. I have also discussed how these tools function to make some kinds of social actions possible in certain situations while constraining other kinds of social actions. In the next chapter, I will focus more on exactly *how* people use technologies of talk to engage in social actions.

4

Talk in action

In October and November of 2014, university students in Hong Kong occupied three large areas in the city's shopping and financial districts for seventy-nine days to protest against a plan for constitutional reform that called for candidates for chief executive to be approved by a committee of 'representatives' mostly loyal to the Beijing government. Among the most pervasive symbols of the movement was the yellow umbrella, 'technologized' as an emblem of the movement after students had used umbrellas to protect themselves from tear gas and pepper spray from police.

The protests put university presidents in the city in an awkward position. On the one hand, they felt responsible for upholding their students' right to free speech and for expressing concern for their safety. On the other hand, as presidents of publicly funded universities they could not afford to be seen as challenging the authority of the government too directly. One test of university presidents' ability to walk this fine line came in November when Hong Kong universities normally hold their graduation ceremonies. On these occasions, some students took the opportunity to express their political views through such actions as wearing yellow ribbons on their gowns and unfurling yellow umbrellas during the ceremony. Some of the presidents reacted positively to these actions. Professor Chan Fan-Cheong, president of Hong Kong University of Science and Technology, for example, praised his students as both outspoken and creative. The president of Hong Kong Baptist University, Professor Chin Sun-Chi, however, criticized students' actions, saying that they were disrespectful.

What is of interest to us here for the study of spoken discourse is not so much the different stances that these presidents took, but rather how these stances were instantiated in concrete social actions. Graduation ceremonies in Hong Kong, as elsewhere, are highly technologized social practices involving a number of conventional and strictly choreographed speech genres. If we were to apply Goffman's central question 'What's going on here?' to a graduation ceremony, we would have to conclude that the main action being accomplished is that of the president, or other representatives of the university, *conferring degrees* on the graduating students. This action is normally supported by the concrete action of *handing* – the president handing a certificate to a student, often accompanied by other actions such as the student's name being read, the student shaking hands with the president, and the students' parents talking photos. In other words, the focal action of such an event is an act of one person physically handing a certificate to another person, which has the effect of changing that person's status.

The problem with the graduation ceremony at Hong Kong Baptist University in November of 2014 was that this action of handing ended up being disrupted when one student knelt before the president professor Chan and offered him a folded yellow umbrella, saying, '校長呢個係我哋嘅小小心意，希望你接受我哋嘅訴求.' ('This is a little gift from us students. We hope the president can listen to the students' demands.'). In response to this gesture, the president motioned for the student to leave without handing him his diploma.

In the context of the practice of a university graduation, a university president's refusal to hand a student his diploma is what in linguistic jargon we would call 'marked'; it is inconsistent with what is normally expected, and so, by virtue of being unexpected, it creates some kind of special meaning or accomplishes some kind of special action. But the meaning expressed and the action accomplished by occurrences of marked behaviour are not always so clear cut. Indeed, different social actors on this occasion interpreted the gesture differently. For President Chan, it was meant as a rebuke of the student's break with protocol. It was not the symbolic meaning of the umbrella that he objected to, he said later, but the fact that the action violated the 'solemnity of the occasion'. The student, of course, had a different idea about what he was doing by handing the president the umbrella, and what the president was doing by refusing to hand him his diploma. In his mind, his act of handing was an exercise of his right to express his political views, and by refusing to hand him his diploma, the president was, in some way, attempting to constrain that right or punish him for his views.

So one of the most important factors in interpreting these actions has to do with the activity (or 'social practice') that they are seen as part of – the practice of exercising political speech or the practice of participating in a 'solemn ceremony' – each of these practices being associated with both particular ideological assumptions and particular practical expectations about the rights, roles and responsibilities of social actors. What is also interesting is that the one thing that this gesture of not giving the student his diploma did *not* accomplish was to deny the student his diploma. As on many such occasions, what was being handed was not actually a diploma but an empty binder. The actual diploma was obtained by the student in another, less ceremonial act of handing involving a low-level clerical worker in the office of the university registrar.

The reason I've given so much attention to this incident is that it illustrates quite dramatically something very important about the relationship between discourse and action, the fact that we make meanings through actions, and also take actions through discourse. It also illustrates how even a simple action like handing can have multiple possible meanings and perform multiple possible actions.

In the first chapter of this book, I emphasized that one of the main things that distinguishes the study of spoken discourse from the study of 'speech' or the study of 'language' is that the study of discourse always involves a focus on action, what people are *doing* when they are using language. In this chapter, I will further explore the relationship between discourse and action, arguing that there are basically two different ways analysts of spoken discourse can understand this relationship. One way is to see discourse as itself a form of social action. The other way is to see discourse as a tool with which we perform actions and negotiate with others what actions we are performing. The first approach is more associated with pragmatics and conversation analysis, and the second is more associated with interactional sociolinguistics and mediated discourse analysis.

Discourse as action

One of the most important things about the acts of handing and not handing that I talked about above is that even though they don't involve 'speech', they can be regarded as forms of spoken discourse, or 'speech acts'. In other words, both the student, by handing the umbrella to the president, and the president, by *not* handing the diploma to the student, were not just doing things. They were also 'saying' things. By the same token, most of the spoken language in the event was not just a matter of 'saying things' but also of 'doing things'. When the master of ceremonies asked participants to stand for the National Anthem of China, he was not just saying something. He was issuing a *directive*, and as a result of this directive, everybody stood. Similarly, when a particular student's name was called out, this was not just a matter of identifying the student by name; it also functioned to *summon* the student onto the stage to receive his or her diploma. In other words, one of the key ways in which we can understand the relationship between discourse and action is to realize that discourse is a kind of action (that we *do* things with words) and that action can be a kind of discourse (that we *say* things with actions).

This understanding of communication is, of course, very different from Saussure's 'circuit of speech' in which communication is seen as a matter of 'messages' being passed from one person to another through the medium of spoken language. In that model, the 'meaning' – what is being communicated – resides in the message – what is being transmitted. In a view of communication that sees discourse as a form of social action, there is often a more indirect relationship between the 'meaning' that is being communicated and the message in the words that are being transmitted. Sometimes, the meaning resides more in the *act of transmission* than it does in the words. And so, the tricky part about this seemingly simple formulation – discourse is action and action is discourse – is that there is not always a simple and direct relationship between the language we are deploying to do a certain action and what we are doing, or between what we are doing and the words we are speaking. In fact, one of the biggest challenges we face as analysts is to figure out what people are doing with their words and saying with their actions, and sometimes, as the analysis above illustrates, we often have no way of settling on a clear answer. Was the student being respectful by kneeling to the president, or was he being disrespectful? Was the president attempting to stifle the student's right to speak, or was he attempting to protect the solemnity of the occasion? This, of course, is also a challenge that participants themselves face. In essence, all social interaction involves people making *guesses* – what we call *inferences* – about what different actions 'mean' and about what different meanings 'do'. This might seem to be a recipe for disaster, but as it turns out, we are extremely good at working out what people are doing with their words and meaning with their actions. That's not to say that our guesses always exactly match their intentions. Sometimes, dealing with the ambiguity of this discourse/action relationship is a matter of coming up with a range of hypotheses that we can test as the interaction progresses. Furthermore, when people are not clear about what they are trying to say or trying to do, this does not necessarily mean that they are being uncooperative. Sometimes it means that they are being 'polite' or 'strategic' by creating space for a range of interpretations of their words or actions, which can then be negotiated with the other person. There are times, of course, as in the example above, that people come to social occasions with such different ideas about what they should or should not say or do that they end up communicating at cross purposes.

The main school of discourse analysis concerned with understanding how people figure out what other people are doing with their words and saying with their actions is called pragmatics (Levinson 1983; Leech 1983). As I mentioned in Chapter 2, pragmatics comes out of the work of what were known as the 'ordinary language philosophers', most importantly John Austin, John Searle and H. Paul Grice. Expressed within the framework of mediation I introduced in Chapter 2, the focus of pragmatics is on the processes by which people combine material and semiotic tools in strategic ways in order to 'do things' with their utterances or to figure out what others are doing with theirs.

Austin explained this process by means of a theory of 'speech acts', a theory that he developed at a time when philosophers of language were mostly interested in the 'constative', or *descriptive*, function of words. The foundation of 'speech act theory' is Austin's important insight that there are some utterances that 'do not describe or "report" or constate anything at all, [and] are not "true or false."' Rather, 'The uttering of the sentence is, or is a part of, the doing of an action, which again would not normally be described as, or as "just" saying something' (1962: 5). Among the examples that Austin gives are a bride or groom saying 'I do' at a wedding ceremony; a dignitary saying, 'I name this ship queen Elizabeth' while smashing a bottle of campaign against the bow; and the sentence, 'I give and bequeath my watch to my brother' occurring in a will. Such utterances, Austin pointed out, do not just contain 'meanings', but they also 'perform' actions. It is by their very utterance that people become married, that ships come to have particular names, and that brothers become the rightful owners of their dead brother's watches. Austin called such utterances *performatives*.

The important thing about performatives is not their 'meaning', but their 'force', their ability to get things done. As Austin saw it, utterances have three kinds of force – the force of having been said, which he called *locutionary force*; the force of the action they perform, which he called *illocutionary force*; and the force of the result of that action, which he called the *perlocutionary force*.

Illocutionary force, the ability of utterances to perform actions, is not just a matter of the words in an utterance. It's a matter of how those words interact with the conditions under which they are uttered. 'I do', said by a person sitting in the pews at a wedding does not result in a marriage. A drunk passing a ship moored at the docks and smashing his bottle of cheap whisky against it, saying, 'I hereby christen this ship Lady Gaga,' has no effect on the name of the ship. And a man writing 'I give and bequeath my watch to my brother' in his will does not result in the transfer of property if he does not own a watch, or if he does not have a brother. Understanding the *conditions* under which performatives 'work' is really the main task of speech act theory.

From this starting point, Austin moved very quickly to the conclusion that these 'special' kinds of utterances that he was calling 'performatives' are not actually so special, that *all* utterances can actually be seen to perform actions – actions like inviting, warning, apologizing or even just 'asserting'. In fact, he ended up asserting that it is actually impossible *not* to perform an action with an utterance. Every time we say something, we inevitably do something with our words. He used the example of 'It's raining.' Certainly, on one level, this could be understood simply as a statement of fact. But in an actual situation, there must be some accounting for why a statement of fact is made. It may be an act of 'informing' someone who is not aware of the fact that it's raining. Or it could be a way of 'reminding' someone to bring their umbrella before they leave the house. Or it could be a way of 'refusing' an invitation to take a hike in the woods.

What *is* special about the kinds of performatives that Austin initially noticed (such as 'I do [take this man …]' and 'I hereby christen this ship …') is that they make explicit the action that they are performing. We can also do this with promises by saying 'I promise I will come,' and with warnings by saying 'I'm warning you!'. In such cases, there is a direct relationship between the semantic content of the utterance and the action that it is performing. But often when we warn someone we don't use word 'warning' (we might say, for example, 'Mind the gap'). And when we threaten someone, it would be unusual to say, 'I threaten you' (see Thomas 1995). In fact, threats often come in the form of assertions or even 'promises', such as 'I will light you up!' (see Chapter 8) or 'if I ever see you here again, I promise I'll punch you in the nose'. At one point during the pro-democracy protests in Hong Kong in the autumn of 2014, a police officer said to a group of protesters, '對住禁多人打人，我都唔想禁樣做' ('I don't want to have to use force in front of so many people') (see Chapter 7). This was really not so much a statement of the officer's desire so much as it was a threat to use force unless the protesters followed his orders to step back.

Speech acts in which the action performed is not explicitly stated are called *indirect speech acts.* Just because these acts are indirect, however, does not necessarily mean that they are less effective. Sometimes part of their effectiveness comes from their indirectness. A threat in the form of a promise, for example, might seem even more threatening. In any case, the vast majority of the speech acts that we perform are of the indirect variety. And so the question when it comes to speech acts is how people are able to work out what act is being performed if this is not made explicit in the words that people say, and when sometimes people even 'mislabel' their speech acts, calling threats promises, and so forth.

This problem takes us back to Austin's idea that performatives only 'work' under certain conditions involving things like who says them and where they are being said. He called these conditions 'felicity conditions'. As I discussed in Chapter 1, for example, for something to 'count' as 'coming out', certain conditions must be met. 'Dad, I'm gay,' counts as coming out only if the person who utters it is really gay, and if the person to whom it is uttered is not aware of that fact. But there are other conditions as well. A five-year-old boy saying this to his father would probably not be considered as performing an act of 'coming out'. Not that he may not actually be gay, but because in most societies in which 'coming out' is a recognized action, it is usually reserved for people of a certain age.

Similarly, there are certain conditions that need to be met for an utterance to 'work' as a threat. The question of whether something should be interpreted as a threat or not, in fact, is not just a linguistic question, but also a legal one, since some civil and criminal cases depend on determining whether or not what one person said to another constitutes a threat (Shuy 1996). If we apply Austin's idea of felicity conditions to deciding whether or not an utterance constitutes a threat, we can come up with a number of conditions that usually (but don't always) adhere to threats. One set of conditions has to do with the people involved: a threat from someone who is incapable of carrying it out does not 'work' as a threat. Another set of conditions has to do with the future action that is stated or inferred in the threat: it must be an action that the speaker believes will be harmful to the hearer. We don't normally threaten to buy people ice cream cones or take them to the circus. The most important set of conditions, however, and the most difficult to pin down, are conditions having to do with the intentions of the speaker. For an utterance to count as a threat, the speaker must have the intention to threaten someone. That is to say, by uttering the threat they mean to communicate their intention to in some way do harm to the hearer (Martínez-Cabeza 2009).

If we apply these conditions to the utterance by the police officer to the line of protesters which I referred to above: 'I don't want to have to use force in front of so many people,' it's easy to see why a reasonable person might interpret this as a threat. First of all, the officer explicitly refers to a future course of action that would be potentially harmful to the recipients (the use of 'force'). He is also capable of carrying out this action, equipped as he is with a truncheon and pepper spray, and accompanied by a large number of colleagues similarly equipped. Where this statement starts to get complicated is when it comes to the intention of the officer. Although it seems that he is willing to use force, the semantic content of his utterance explicitly denies this intention ('I don't want to …') and also disavows agency (if he does use force, it is because he 'has to'). In fact, the interesting thing about this utterance is that the officer manages to issue a threat by saying that he is *not* doing so, and by shifting the blame for any harm that might come to the protesters onto the protesters themselves.

These problems of communicating intentions and of what constitutes the interpretation of a 'reasonable recipient' are problems that were taken up by another 'ordinary language philosopher', H. Paul Grice. For Grice, in fact, the main factor determining whether or not communication is successful is the degree to which the hearer is able to figure out what the communicative intention of the speaker is. If a customer in a bar spills beer on another customer and says 'oops!' in a certain tone of voice, the utterance will likely be taken as an apology (Bach 2006: 153). Of course, one could easily analyse this as the speech act of 'apologizing' and list the various conditions that obtain to make it successful. It's real success, however, depends on the speaker saying 'oops!' in such a way that the hearer is able to recognize the speaker's intention to apologize, and on the hearer giving the speaker the 'benefit of the doubt', that is, assuming that, by saying 'oops!' he or she is trying to communicate something relevant to the action of spilling beer and that what is being communicated complies with accepted norms of behaviour in bars (where customers don't normally pour beer on each other). As Grice (1957/89: 220) put it, in communicating, a speaker intends his or her utterance 'to produce some effect in an audience by means of the recognition of [his or her] intention'. Had the hearer in this situation been unable or unwilling to recognize the speakers' intention to apologize and had he responded by retaliating in some way, we would no doubt regard the hearer as either drunk or unreasonable or both.

So how do 'reasonable recipients' go about recognizing people's intentions, especially when people don't always say what they mean or mean what they say? For Grice, the main way they do this is by testing what people say against a set of assumptions about what it means to be a 'reasonable' communicator, which he called 'maxims'. These maxims are based on the idea that people, when they are communicating, generally try to cooperate with each other. When they perceive that these maxims are being violated in some way, they don't automatically assume that people are being uncooperative, but rather give them the benefit of the doubt and assume that there must be some 'reasonable' explanation for what they have said or done. And that reason is usually that they are trying to say/do something in an indirect way. Grice called this form of indirect communication 'conversational implicature'.

The first expectation that people bring to conversations, according to Grice, is that others will tell the truth (the Maxim of Quality). When Randy's friend in the conversation that I considered in the last chapter says 'gonna hang ya' after Randy comes out to him, Randy laughs. He does this because the falsity of this statement is so obvious that he immediately assumes it to be a joke. Of course, for conversational implicature to work it requires effort from both the speaker and the hearer: the speaker must violate the maxim in a way that he assumes that the hearer will detect as a violation, and the hearer must do the inferential work of trying to figure out why the maxim was violated.

The second expectation that people bring to conversations is that speakers will not say any more or any less than they need to (Maxim of Quantity). When people say less than we think they are supposed to, as when Randy's mother replies to his revelation that he's gay by simply saying 'okay', we are likely to assume that they are implying something (in this case, that it is *not* 'okay') (see Chapter 6).

The third assumption people bring to conversations is that what people say will be relevant to the topic that they are talking about. If, for example, a son called his mother from Germany to announce that he is gay, and the mother responded with questions about the weather or about Oktoberfest, it would be reasonable for him to infer that his mother does not wish to talk about his sexuality.

The last assumption that we bring to conversations, in Grice's list of maxims, is the assumption that people will be clear and orderly in their communication, that they will avoid ambiguity. This is probably the most violated of all maxims since, as I noted above, so many speech acts are expressed indirectly, and much of what we do when we make inferences is a matter of coming to terms with ambiguity. When the police officer I mentioned above says, 'I don't want to have to use force in front of so many people,' he is, in some respects, obfuscating what otherwise might have been a clear and direct threat ('Stand back or I will use force').

It should be clear from this example that Grice's maxims are not like rules that we are meant to follow if we want to have successful communication. In fact, sometimes we can achieve what we want to achieve much more effectively in conversation by *not* being truthful, concise, relevant or clear, in the same way that we can make a threat much more potent by framing it as a 'promise' or 'advice' or an 'assertion' about what we 'do not want to do'. The reason for this is that effectively getting things done with discourse is not the same thing as effectively expressing meanings. In fact, it is often the *indirect* relationship between words and the actions that they produce that makes 'doing things with words' effective. For one thing, it allows us to do things 'without doing them'. Some gays and lesbians, for example, are unsure of how the people around them will react if they 'come out' directly, and so they engage in various acts of implicature (such as avoiding using gendered pronouns to describe their partners) in order to 'test the waters' (Liang 1999). Often we do things indirectly in order to produce 'plausible deniability', allowing us to deny our intentions or disavow agency for our actions ('I don't want to have to use force in front of all of these people.'). And sometimes we are indirect in order to be polite (Leech 1983); by asking 'do you have a pen?' rather than saying 'give me a pen', for example, we give the hearer an opportunity to refuse in a way that doesn't make him or her seem ungenerous. Listeners can also make creative use of ambiguity by treating an utterance as ambiguous even when it might not have been intended that way by the speaker, or by interpreting an utterance in ways that fit their own purposes ('But you *said* I could drop by anytime!').

Another affordance of this indirect relationship between discourse and action is that it allows us to perform different actions with different people based on our understanding of the different assumptions that they are bringing to the conversation. A gay man uttering the words 'she's not really my type' on having a beautiful woman pointed out to him may be conveying one thing to the people present who don't know he's gay and another thing to those who do. Finally, the indirect relationship between discourse and action allows us to do more than one thing at a time, 'laminating' different communicative goals onto a single utterance. Searle (1969: 70–1) gives the example of a wife saying to her husband at a party: 'It's really quite late.' The utterance, Searle writes, 'may be a statement of fact, an objection, a suggestion, a request or a warning.' The fact is, it doesn't have to be just one of these things. The indirectness of the speech act allows her to observe how her husband takes it before deciding on her next move. This is one weakness of Grice's focus on the intention of the speaker. In actual communication, sometimes what speakers actually intend is to be ambiguous, for ambiguity on the level of a speech act allows them to more effectively accomplish some higher-level action.

What all of this suggests is that things like speech acts and conversational implicature are not just a matter of abstract procedures of logical reasoning that go on in the minds of speakers and hearers, but also a matter of what goes on *between* them, a kind of real-time negotiation in which my intentions and your interpretations can change dramatically as the interaction progresses. An approach to the relationship between discourse and action that attempts to take this negotiative dimension of speech acts into account is conversation analysis. Like pragmatics, conversation analysis is chiefly concerned with how people do things with words. As Schegloff (1992: xxix) puts it, the two main questions that conversation analysts ask are: 'What is someone doing by saying this thing, and how do they come to be doing it?' Where conversation analysts differ from pragmaticists is in their emphasis on how people do things with words *together*: conversational actions are always seen as 'joint actions' (Clark 1992), contingent upon what the other person has done before, and partly determinative of what he or she can do next. In other words, the solution that conversation analysts offer to the problem of figuring out what people are doing with their words is not applying the rules of logic or assumptions about context that are external to the interaction, nor making conjectures about speakers' intentions, but trying to understand action in terms of how it is situated in relation to other actions.

This focus on *sequence* is perhaps conversation analysts' greatest contribution to understanding the relationship between discourse and action. Speech acts, they remind us, do not occur in isolation from other speech acts, nor do they exist as abstract cognitive exercises. They are always part of a *flow* of interaction between two or more people. As Goodwin and Duranti (1992: 29) put it, 'Whatever is said is always said in some sequential context and its illocutionary force will be determined by reference to what it accomplishes in relation to some sequentially prior utterance or set of utterances.'

Conversation analysts, therefore, do not see speech acts in terms of individual utterances, but rather in terms of, at the very least, *pairs* of utterances. The utterance pair, or what Schegloff and Sacks (1973) call the 'adjacency pair' is seen as the minimum basic unit of action. They define adjacency pairs as pairs of adjacent utterances, each produced by a different speaker, which exist in a relationship of 'conditional relevance'. In other words, the meaning or 'relevance' of one half of the pair is conditional on its being produced together with the other. Examples they give of such pairs are 'question-answer', 'greeting-greeting' and 'offer-acceptance/refusal'. What this means is that the production of 'speech acts' like questions, greetings and offers is not just dependent on a single speaker, but is a matter of cooperation between speakers. But it's not just a cooperation based on giving the speaker 'the benefit of the doubt' or trying to figure out what they 'really meant', as in Grician pragmatics. For conversation analysts, hearers cooperate with speakers not by what they think, but by what they *do*. Hearers help to make questions questions by answering them; they help make greetings greetings by producing their own greetings in response; and they share in the production of offers by following them with acceptances or refusals. As Schegloff and Sacks (1973: 296) put it:

> What two utterances produced by different speakers can do that one utterance cannot is: by an adjacently positioned second, a speaker can show that he understood what a prior aimed at, and that he is willing to go along with that. Also, by virtue of the occurrence of an adjacently produced second, the doer of a first can see that what he intended was indeed understood, and that it was or was not accepted.

Adjacency pairs don't just provide evidence of how hearers interpret speakers' actions. They also provide a way for hearers to create implicature by not answering a speaker's action with the expected complementary action, and so to achieve (or avoid) actions in ways that make them less accountable. In fact, many of Sack's lectures on conversation focused on the various ways in which people exploit the pairwise organization of talk in order to do things indirectly. In his very first lecture, for instance, he analyses how callers to a suicide hotline avoid giving their names by filling in the 'slot' in which they would normally be expected to do so with other moves like requests for repetition or clarification, ensuring that 'the place where the return name fits is never opened' (Sacks 1992a: 6):

A: This is Mr Smith may I help you
B: I can't hear you.
A: This is Mr Smith.
B: Smith.

In this example, speaker B avoids filling in the slot created by speaker A by creating a diversion. In other cases, though, a speaker's unwillingness to provide the expected second part of an adjacency pair is more obvious, creating implicature by being 'heard' as 'officially absent' (Schegloff 1968: 1083). That is, the absence of the contribution itself is taken as 'doing something'. Consider the following exchange between a woman and her boyfriend:

    A: I love you.
    B: ...

The absence of the utterance 'I love you too', which is the normative way to fill in the slot created by a declaration of love in this context, is likely heard by the woman not just as silence, but as the *absence* of a declaration of love, and interpreted as signalling trouble in the relationship.

Many adjacency pairs allow for alternative second parts. For example, an offer can be answered with either an acceptance or a refusal. Coming out can be greeted with either acceptance or rejection. And an assessment can be followed by either an agreement or disagreement. In such cases, however, the two alternatives are not 'created equal'. There is always one response that is regarded as the preferred response, because it is the response that contributes to the most efficient accomplishment of the 'interactional project' (Schegloff 2007) initiated by the first part of the pair. An acceptance efficiently completes an invitation; and agreement efficiently completes an assessment. That is not to say that when an invitation is refused, the invitation is not regarded as having been accomplished. What it means is that the completion of the 'project' of inviting often requires some kind of extra work on the part of the person refusing the invitation; he or she normally must mitigate or account for or even apologize for their refusal. Pomerantz (1984) calls this tendency for one kind of response to be preferred over another the 'preference organization' of the pair. She came up with the notion when studying 'assessments' (statements in which a speaker evaluates something or someone). What she found was that when hearers agree with assessments, they often only produce rather short responses, for example:

    B: Isn't he cute
    A: O::h he::s a::Dorable
        (Pomerantz 1984: 60)

Disagreements, however, are often much longer and more complicated, involving hesitations, qualifications and/or explanations. In the following example, for instance, rather than simply disagreeing with B's assertion that a sense of humour is something that you are born with, A answers first with a qualified agreement, marked by all sorts of hesitations and disfluencies, before she issues her disagreement, which is hedged with the phrase 'I think' and qualified with a heavily stressed 'too.'

B: ... a sense of humor, I think is something yer <u>born</u>
      with Bea.
A: Yes. Or it's c- I have the- eh yes. I think a
      lotta people <u>are</u>. but then I think it can be
      developed, <u>too</u>.
      (Pomerantz 1984: 71)

The only exception to this Pomerantz found was when people produce self-deprecating assessments, in which case disagreements are the preferred response and so can be produced with no additional interactional work:

L: ... I'm so dumb I don't even know it hhh! –
W: y-no, y-you're not du:mb, ...
      (Pomerantz 1984: 85)

Just as the failure to answer the first half of an adjacency pair with the expected second creates implicature, so does providing a dispreferred response without the interactional work that usually accompanies it. We might, for example, communicate that we are angry with a friend by answering her invitation with a bald refusal, or we might joke with her by answering her self-deprecating remark with a frank and concise agreement. In other words, both the 'rules' of pragmatics and the 'rules' of conversation analysis are not exactly like the rules of grammar in that communication is often accomplished 'as much in their breech as in their observance.'

Because these methods of doing things with words outlined by the frameworks of pragmatics and conversation analysis often work through exploiting the ambiguity of language use in context, they depend a great deal both on a certain 'pragmatic competence' (Thomas 1983) on the part of users, as well as on some degree of good faith among speakers and hearers that they really will cooperate. This is why novice users of a particular variety of spoken language often have difficulty getting things done with words (even when they have a strong command of grammar and vocabulary), and also why legal disputes about what people were or were not doing with their words (in the case of things like threats and bribes) are often so difficult to litigate.

One example of the ways the tools I described above can actually make it *more* difficult for some people to do certain kinds of things with words can be seen in Kitzinger and Frith's (1999) study of sexual refusal by women. The problem Kitzinger and Frith address is the fact that many instances of date rape are attributed to women not adequately performing the action of 'refusal', which is portrayed in both rape trails and in materials used in 'refusals skills training' as a matter of 'just saying no.' The problem with this advice, as Kitzinger and Frith point out, is that it doesn't conform to the rules of preference organization usually associated with refusals, in which, as 'dispreferred responses', refusals are usually issued *indirectly* and accompanied by excuses, or justifications. In fact, issuing a direct refusal in such circumstances might create an implicature that the refuser does not wish to create. In other words, women's difficulty in giving a clear and direct 'no' in response to sexual advances may not be a matter of 'defective refusal skills', but simply a matter of 'doing refusals' in the way they are normally done in most other circumstances. Indeed, in most situations it is not necessary to 'say no' in order to accomplish the act of refusing. Simply pausing, hedging and producing accounts or excuses are enough to signal refusal. In such cases, it is really the men that are displaying defective communication skills by claiming not to have understood 'perfectly normal … ways of expressing refusal which they themselves routinely use in other areas of their lives' (Kitzinger and Frith 1999: 301).

Discourse in action

While the 'discourse as action' approach described above goes a long way in helping us to understand how people 'do things with words', there are many aspects of social interaction that it cannot account for. Although pragmatics helps to reveal how actions are performed through the strategic interaction between words and the contexts in which they are used, the view of context that it promotes is both too static (failing to take into account how identities, situations and intentions can change over the course of interactions), and oblivious to the possible effects of culture on assumptions about context and cooperation. Much of what is taken for context, in fact, is restricted to rather fixed ideas about the situation and the operation of (context-free) logical processes within the minds of speakers and listeners (Goodwin and Duranti 1992; Goffman 1983b). And although conversation analysis helps us to understand how speech acts are dependent on the flow of the conversation, it locks us into a linear understanding of action that focuses on sequentiality but ignores *simultaneity* (Blommaert 2005; Norris 2004; Norris and Jones 2005), and it focuses our attention on such a narrow window to that flow: the adjacency pair, that it runs the risk of distracting us from the ways conversational actions are embedded in broader social practices and histories that may affect interactions even when participants don't explicitly orient to them (Cicourel 1992).

Perhaps the biggest limitation of the 'discourse as action' approach, however, is that it focuses only on how people 'do things with words', and so takes attention away from how people 'do things' with other technologies of talk (such as gestures, objects, identities, and social practices). In fact, in many situations, the focal action that people are 'doing' is not a 'speech act' in the normal sense of the term, and in many social actions language plays more of a supporting than a starring role.

In contrast, a 'discourse *in* action' approach does not assume that 'words' are the only tools that people 'do things with' and seeks to understand the role of discourse in the complex combinations of people, practices and technologies that go into forming *sites of engagement*. In Chapter 2, I defined sites of engagement as points where certain people and certain technologies come together in certain situations to make certain social actions possible. In this approach, as Jones and Norris (2005: 9) put it, the relationship between discourse and action is seen as 'dynamic and contingent,' 'manifested in the *tension* between the kinds of actions that discourse and other cultural tools make possible and the ways people purposefully mix these tools in response to their immediate circumstances.' In other words, a 'discourse in action' approach is less interested in how 'texts' and 'contexts' interact to create actions (the main focus of pragmatics and conversation analysis), and more interested in the ways that different mediational means and different social actors come together to make various forms of *entextualization* and *contextualization* possible.

One example of the this can be seen in a kind of 'handing' very different from that I discussed at the beginning of this chapter – the handing of AIDS prevention pamphlets to gay men cruising for sex in public parks in China, a social action which I studied as part of my PhD research in the late 1990s (Jones 2002a, b). Today in China, gay men have a wide range of opportunities to receive information about how to prevent AIDS, but at that time, when the public discussion of homosexuality was severely constrained, it was much more difficult for health promotion workers to reach this vulnerable population. The solution decided upon by the AIDS prevention workers I was studying was to hand out AIDS prevention pamphlets which had been especially designed for gay men in public parks that sometimes served as venues for men to meet sexual partners, a practice referred to in the argot of the community as 'fishing'. Since men who visited such places to engage in 'fishing' risked arrest or harassment if detected by police, they had to be particularly circumspect in their behaviour, making use of subtle cues to signal to other members of the community their availability for interaction. The problem that AIDS prevention workers faced, then, was how to distinguish the appropriate people to hand these materials to from other members of the public who were simply out for a 'walk in the park'. Because of this, many of the interactions I observed began not with any explicit mention of AIDS or safe sex, but rather with exchanges like the one below;

A:　今天人不多。
　　(*Not many people here today.*)

B:　...
　　(...)

A:　你认为人多不多？
　　(*Do you think there are a lot of people or not?*)

B:　不知道。我不是本地人。
　　(*I don't know. I'm not from around here.*)
　　(Jones 2002b: 373)

The purpose of such exchanges was not to accomplish the action of handing people health promotion pamphlets, but rather to *create a context* in which that action might reasonably take place. What participants (both the AIDS prevention workers and the gay men who gathered in these parks) were doing with their words and with the various subtle signals that they were sending with their gazes and gestures, was negotiating what Goffman (1959) called the 'definition of the situation' (are we 'taking a walk in the park' or are we 'fishing'?) and thereby claiming and imputing social identities based on these definitions.

Interactional sociolinguists call these 'definitions of the situation' 'frames' (Goffman 1974; Tannen 1993), and the ways we signal to others with things like our words, voice, gaze and gestures how we are defining the situation that they call 'contextualization cues' (Gumperz 1982). 'Frames' are really technologized 'social practices', which include sets of expectations about the where, when, how, why and by whom these practices are normally conducted. They are based on shared understandings among participants about what it means to be 'playing' or 'fighting' (Bateson 1972), 'fishing' or 'talking a walk in the park'. As Tannen (1993: 6) puts it, 'frames' are essentially 'what people think they are doing when they talk to each other'. 'Contextualization cues' then work primarily by 'indexing' these social practices (Silverstein 1992). In situations like the one I described above, certain ways of walking, standing, looking at other people, as well as certain utterances like 'Not many people here today' said in a certain way serve to *index* the social practice of 'fishing' for members of this community (though to non-members these cues might be incomprehensible, or they might index *other* social practices like 'taking a walk in the park'). Like all indexicals, then, contextualization cues are inherently indeterminate and potentially polysemous (Briggs 1988; Hanks 1996; Johnstone and Kiesling 2008), entirely dependent on listeners being able to connect the sign to the aspect of context that it is meant to 'point to'.

It is because of this inherent indeterminancy, in fact, that gay men cruising in parks (and health promotion workers targeting them for 'intervention') are able to use the overlapping frames made available at this particular site of engagement to conceal one social practice inside another (concealing the practice of 'fishing' within the more socially acceptable practice of 'taking a walk in the park', and concealing the practice of 'health promotion' within the practice of 'fishing'). In this case, it is indexical signs, in the form of contextualization cues, rather than 'speech acts' that serve as 'the semiotic glue that binds communicative activity to … stances, social acts and social activities' (Puckett 2000: 8; see also Ochs 1993: 341).

At the same time, these 'frames' are often deployed contingently, and are sometimes revised or abandoned as the interaction proceeds. If an interlocutor in the above situation fails to respond in the expected way to one or more cues indexing the practice of 'fishing', the 'fisher' might shift frames, signalling that he is just out for a 'walk in the park'. Or participants might respond to particular framings in ambiguous ways, keeping open the possibility of more than one 'definition of the situation'. This is what happens in the excerpt above when B says, 'I don't know. I'm not from around here.' With this response, he neither commits himself to the 'fishing' frame, nor rejects it. Not surprisingly, such strategies are very common in situations like this in which, because of the risk of arrest should participants invite the wrong person into the 'fishing' frame, participants often go to great lengths to test and reconfirm their understandings of the contextualization cues issued by their interlocutors.

As this example illustrates, different sites of engagement make available different sorts of resources for people to engage in contextualization. Nearly all of the 'technologies of talk' I discussed in the last chapter can be used to create contextualization cues. People can signal the social practice they take themselves and others to be engaged in with semiotic tools like their choice of linguistic code, through various semiotic modes (including gesture, gaze or proxemics), the use of particular social languages or speech genres, or they can do it with material technologies like objects, physical settings or electronic media like mobile phones. Signalling that one was 'fishing' in public parks in China in the 1990s involved talking in certain ways and about certain topics, dressing in certain ways, standing, moving, gesturing and (most importantly) gazing in certain ways, handling objects like cigarettes in certain ways, and even being present in certain regions of the park or interacting in certain ways with aspects of the physical environment like benches and street lamps. Nowadays 'fishing' in China might take place in a venue like Starbucks, and participants might send contextualization cues by opening a GPS-enabled social networking app like *Grindr* on their mobile phones, an app that users can use to detect others in the immediate vicinity who also have the app installed and send them messages, in which case a message like 'Not many people here today' would have a very different meaning.

So doing things with words is not just about producing utterances within particular contexts; it is also about producing particular contexts around our utterances. Instead of searching for a stable set of rules or maxims that people use to produce and interpret speech acts, a 'discourse in action' approach is more interested in understanding how speakers at particular sites of engagement select among *different* sets of rules and maxims based on different possible definitions of the situation, and how they sometimes revise their selection as they go along to adapt to the ever-changing landscape of the interaction.

An inevitable consequence of contextualization is that participants end up not just producing definitions of the situations, but also definitions of themselves as certain kinds of people, specifically, as people who are 'qualified' to engage in the social practice being indexed. For Austin and Searle, the 'felicity' of a speech act is often a matter of the identity of the person who is performing it (i.e., only certain kinds of people can perform actions like marrying, arresting and 'coming out'). From a 'discourse in action' perspective, identity does not precede speech acts so much as it is performed *through* them (Butler 1990/2006), partly as a consequence of the act, and partly as a consequence of the contextualization that people engage in to make the act possible. Part of what people are doing when they negotiate 'what's going on here' is attempting to establish what Erickson and Schultz (1982: 35–7) call 'situational co-membership'. In the context of the situation I described above, this actually requires participants to, on some level, establish something about their sexual identities. In other words, the practice of 'fishing' is in some ways contingent on participants accomplishing the action of 'coming out' to each other.

At the same time, we would never characterize 'what's going on here' as 'coming out', and this is a very important point. There is a big difference between the *action* of 'coming out', which involves a simple act of disclosure, and the *social practice* of coming out, which entails all sorts of expectations about the context of this act: the participants involved, the conversational rights and responsibilities of those participants, and the purpose and consequences of the action. Randy's conversation with his father that I analysed in the first chapter constitutes the practice of 'coming out'. One gay man signalling to another in a public park that he might be 'up for it' does not.

Kitzinger (2000) provides another example of how someone can accomplish the action of 'coming out' without participating in the practice of 'coming out'. The conversation that she examines takes place in a university seminar in which students are discussing the issue of intersex people. While contributing to this discussion, a student named Linda inserts the action of 'coming out' into her contribution:

```
08  CK:    So y- (0.4) inst- (.) I mean, >I think a lot of lesbians
09         and gay people use that argument anyway which is that
10         it's not < (.)
11  Kate:  [mmm]
12  CK:    [ t h e ] sex, it's the person [I think]
13  Kate:                                 [Yeah, I]
14         think my brain w'ld, it'd do it that way.=
15  Linda: =It does, it does have an effect on you because (0.2)
16         If you've thought of yourself as heterosexual (1.0)
17         and you (.) >suddenly find yourself attracted to a woman
18         °it happened to me, < (0.2) a few years ago°
19         it's very (0.8) disturbing, [in a] way it's=
20  CK:                                [mm]
21  Linda: =it's (0.2) makes you very anxious (.)
22         because you then don't know how you're supposed to respond=
23  CK:    =mm[mm=
24  Linda: = [and (.) if you e- found out that your partner was an
25         intersex you would wonder (.) >how do I respond to this
26         person sexually < I don't know (.) how to approach, how
27         to be romantic how to (.) what this person expects
28         from me, whereas if you (.) think of- you know of
29         yourself as heterosexual, then you know (0.2) the
30         responses you know how to interact.
```

Kitzinger refers to what Linda does in this extract as 'coming out without anyone noticing'. While Linda accomplishes the action of 'coming out', in that she does manage to reveal to her classmates (at least those who are paying attention) that she is a lesbian, she does not engage in the *practice* of coming out. Coming out as a practice, as Kitzinger points out, is generally framed as a 'news announcement', often accompanied by what in Chapter 1 I referred to as a *preparation*, accomplished with utterances like 'Can I tell you something?' Basing her argument on principles from conversation analysis, Kitzinger also points out that another reason this does not 'count' as a 'coming out' is because the listeners do not supply the requisite second part (a *reaction*) to Linda's revelation (other than a non-committal 'mmmm'). It is not, Kitzinger insists, that they don't want to, but that Linda does not allow them to, because she fails to create a 'slot' for them by ending her turn at the logical 'transition relevance place' (Sacks, Schegloff and Jefferson 1974, see next chapter) for the practice of 'coming out', which is immediately after the revelation, but instead carries on with her turn.

Linda's ability to 'come out' without 'coming out', however, is not just a matter of what she is 'doing' with her turn, and what her classmates are doing with theirs. It is also a matter of the way Linda has *contextualized* her coming out using the various technologies of talk available to her at that moment, including the physical setting of the classroom, the speech genre of the classroom discussion, and the social language of academia, which tends to speak of things in terms of abstract generalizations ('If you've thought of yourself as heterosexual', and 'you then don't know how you're supposed to respond') rather than in terms of specific individual experiences. The only time Linda uses a first person pronoun is in the short, muted statement: '°it happened to me, < (0.2) a few years ago°' by which she performs the action of revealing herself as a lesbian, but which is immediately followed by a return to more distanced talk of 'you' and 'what you might do'.

What then is the purpose of 'coming out' by not 'coming out'? Kitzinger suggests a couple of possibilities. By not indexing the practice of coming out, she says, Linda manages to accomplish the action of coming out without having to deal with the possible embarrassment that her classmates' (not necessarily positive) reactions might have caused. Another possibility that Kitzinger suggests, however, is that by eschewing the social practice of coming out, Linda is making a kind of political statement, in effect saying that if homosexuality is as 'normal' as heterosexuality, then one should be able to speak of it as a mundane phenomenon rather than have to frame it as a 'news announcement'. The approach to contextualization that I've been developing in this chapter – an approach which sees sites of engagement as sets of multiple overlapping 'frames' – suggests that both might be true. That is to say, Linda's 'coming out' might be designed to be interpreted in different ways by different members of her audience. This, in fact, is another common affordance of contextualization, that the inherent indeterminancy of indexicals allows speakers to invoke different contexts for different audiences simultaneously.

Of course, whether or not someone is engaging in (or indexing) a social practice depends on how that social practice has been technologized within a community, and in some cases, the sets of expectations about different social practices might be different for different people in an interaction. It is safe to say that the practice of 'coming out' in the conversation that I analysed in the first chapter is something rather different for Randy than it is for his father. Randy's father most likely sees it as a kind of 'speech event' in which his son makes a revelation and he is expected to respond to it, but for Randy, this practice may involve years of struggle, involving the process of 'coming out to himself' and a long series of sometimes tentative or partial revelations to others and gradual integration into the 'gay community' (Bacon 1998; Coleman 1982).

What this means is that, from the point of view of many gay, lesbian, bisexual and transgendered people, it might be possible to engage in the *practice* of 'coming out' without actually performing the action of 'coming out'. This is one way we might interpret a story that Randy tells in a video entitled 'Coming out in the military – baby steps',[1] in which he relates an incident with a fellow airman, an incident which dramatically illustrates how people can make strategic use of contextualization to create implicature. He begins the video by bemoaning the difficulty he has had working up the courage to come out to a good friend of his, and then goes on to relate the following incident as evidence that he is making incremental progress (taking 'baby steps') in his 'process of coming out'.

```
14   I think he'll be okay with it^ but sjust (.) been really hard (0.5) ah for
15   me to sayit^ (0.9) so ↓↑ (0.2) ah I have a eh an even smaller step in my
16   journey (0.6) um (.) there's a newspaper that we get here^ (0.2) it's call
17   the stars in stripes^ (0.7) and anyway the other day (0.4) they wrote an
18   article (0.7) and it was just about you know um the repeal of don't ask
19   don't tell^ (0.5) and::↓↑ (0.5) I I was reading it (.) and (0.4) somebody
20   came up to me: (1.0) and said oh ↑↓ (0.2) °y'know° (0.2) did (0.3) did
21   you (0.4) $heh: did you::$ (0.4) it said don't ask don't tell (0.4) y'know
22   did you write that? (1.3) $an heh and I said$ not↓ (0.4) Jodie Smith
23   wrote it he's a much (0.3) better writer than I am (0.8) and they
24   just kinda like looked at me like what? I mean y'know they were
25   just trying to joke around and I (0.4) I kinda (0.3) y'know told
26   them um (0.5) yeah I'm I'm actually reading this (0.7) and so I know
27   it sounds like a really small step (0.4) but it was (0.2) pretty (0.2)
28   big to me (0.2) t'say:: (0.5) um:: (0.9) y'know I'm I'm I'm okay with
29   this and just it was just like one person and (0.4) Idunno (0.5)
30   somebody may have overheard it but it really wasn't that big of a
31   deal and they didn't even questions and probably didn't even
32   realise what I was tryin to say. (0.6) um^ (0.2) but (0.7) pretty big
33   (.) to me (0.7) so I'm sorry that these eh I'm takin like such baby
34   steps but (0.5) it's a rea:lly:: (0.3) it's been (.) really (0.2) ah a lot
35   harder'n I thought (0.2) but I have set a deadline hm (.) $for
36   myself$ when I'm gonna tell my parents I actually wrote a date^
37   (0.4) on my calendar it's a re it's a long way away but I said y'know
38   by (0.1) by this time I (.) I really wanna (0.5) um^ (0.9) I really
39   wanna tell.
```

[1]Available at https://youtu.be/-osYqoDJ4Tk.

In this incident, Randy makes use of a practice normally not at all associated with coming out, reading a newspaper, in order to try to communicate something about himself and his attitudes to his interlocutor. That may, of course, not have been his initial intention when he took up the newspaper to read, but the opportunity to appropriate it as a mediational means was created when his interlocutor endeavoured to create a particular kind of context around his action of reading (and, particularly of reading a specific article dealing with the 'Don't Ask, Don't Tell' policy) by asking, 'Did you write that?' This, of course, is not a serious question. What this person is doing by asking it is joking. An important part of this joke is the implicature he creates with this question that Randy is either gay or sympathetic to gay causes. For Randy to understand what he is 'getting at', however, and the fact that it is a joke, is more than just a matter of applying maxims and or searching for felicity conditions. It's also a matter of understanding something about the 'culture' in which this remark is made, one in which the speech genre of the anti-gay joke (especially when it involves imputing on others non-hetero-normative identities) is a common way of showing solidarity and reinforcing masculine identities (Bérubé 2010; Kimmel 2001; Lyman 1998). In other words, the context that he is creating with this genre is dependent on the larger context of values, beliefs, identities and practices in which it takes place. It is a remark that derives much of its 'force' through what I described in Chapter 2 as iterativity – the fact that it bears the stamp of countless similar jokes that Randy has no doubt heard before.

Randy's response to it is to refuse to acknowledge the 'joking frame' and to treat the remark as serious, responding with 'no↑↓ (0.4) Jodie Smith wrote it he's a much (0.3) better writer than I am.' With this answer, Randy is also creating implicature, but the source of the implicature is not that he is flouting any Gricean maxims, but rather, that he is *not* flouting them (delivering a response that is unassailably truthful, clear, concise and relevant to his interlocutor's question). In other words, he counters his interlocutor's way of being 'normal' by engaging in anti-gay joking not by explicitly challenging it, but by indexing another equally legitimate way of being 'normal'. The effect of this reframing to disrupt the questioner's default assumptions about gay identity and its appropriateness as a topic for joking can be seen in his reaction: 'they just kinda like looked at me like what?'

This is not just my interpretation. It is also the interpretation that Randy gives in his explanation that follows the narrative:

24   ... I mean y'know they were
25   just trying to joke around and I (0.4) I kinda (0.3) y'know told
26   them um (0.5) yeah I'm I'm actually reading this (0.7) and so I know
27   it sounds like a really small step (0.4) but it was (0.2) pretty (0.2)
28   big to me (0.2) t'say:: (0.5) um:: (0.9) y'know I'm I'm I'm okay with
29   this

The important thing to notice about this example is the fact that Randy's action of communicating that 'I'm okay with this' is accomplished not just through his words ('no↑↓ (0.4) Jodie Smith wrote it he's a much (0.3) better writer than I am'), nor just through the meaning he implies with these words ('I'm actually reading this'), but also through the social context that these words help him to create. By interpreting his interlocutor's joke about what he is reading as a 'serious question' and responding to it with a 'serious answer', he reframes the topic of LGB rights in the military from a 'joking' frame to a frame in which it becomes a legitimate topic of serious conversation. This is an example of the ideological power of frames, that they have the ability to render some topics and utterance that appear within them more legitimate, and others less legitimate.

Another thing this example illustrates is that people bring expectations about normative 'definitions of the situation' and normative practices of contextualization to particular situations, expectations and practices into which they have been socialized through previous experiences in similar situations. This is one reason, according to Gumperz (1982, see also Tannen 1984), that people from different 'cultures' encounter miscommunication: not just because they might speak different language varieties, or even because they hold different beliefs or values about the right way to behave, but because they have been socialized into different expectations of normative frames and normative practices of contextualization. In the conversation above, for example, Randy's interlocutor's expectations that issues related to gays and lesbians are natural resources with which to engage in joking are so strong that he is a bit taken aback when Randy doesn't take the bait. These normative practices of framing function to reproduce the values and ideologies of particular groups, and one way people can challenge these beliefs and ideologies is, instead of attacking them directly, operating interactionally to try to dismantle the 'frames' that support them, as Randy endeavours to do in this example.

Action and history: Opening up the circumference

The upshot of the argument I have been making in this chapter is that it is difficult to understand 'what's going on here', and to fully account for the complex relationship between discourse and action if we restrict our analysis to discrete speech acts or speech events or to the narrow conceptualizations of context that pragmatics and conversation analysis offer us. We need to see context as, first of all, *dynamic*, something that people actively negotiate over the course of interactions, and *historical*, the result of a coming together of multiple historical trajectories (what Scollon 2008 calls 'itineraries'): the histories of the individuals involved, of the relationships between these people, and of the various resources or 'technologies of talk' (such as anti-gay jokes) that they have available to them to take action. Our ability to 'do things with words' is crucially dependent on how these various historical trajectories intersect.

This is, in a way, the point that Derrida (1984) makes in his critique of Austin's speech act theory when he points out that what creates the illocutionary force of a speech act is not just the way a person's words interact with the context in which they are uttered, but rather, the way the utterance connects the present context to previous contexts: all 'speech acts', Derrida insists, are inevitably *entextualizations* or *iterations* of previous speech acts. A university president's action of handing a diploma to a student during a graduation ceremony makes sense to us only because countless university presidents have engaged in such acts of handing countless times in the past. Similarly, the student's action of handing a yellow umbrella to the president makes sense to us only if we understand the history of this object and the meanings that it accumulated in the weeks prior to this graduation ceremony. Even within the shorter historical timescale of the graduation ceremony itself, certain actions only make sense through the way in which they serve to *cite* actions that occurred before them: after the president of Baptist University refused to hand a diploma to the umbrella-wielding student, for example, several students who subsequently were called to the stage refused to accept their diplomas from the president, an action which took its meaning from the president's previous action. As Hanks (1996: 166) puts it, 'Context may be organised out of the vivid present of utterances, but it is equally performed by histories and social facts that linger in the blank spots and silences of speech.'

Another example of how these longer historical trajectories can affect the ways speech acts are accomplished and interpreted can be seen in the 'threat' from the police officer that I analysed above: 'I don't want to have to use force in front of so many people.' As I said above, this is a complicated utterance since the officer's intention to use force is enfolded within a denial of that intention and a disavowal of agency. It is also complicated because of the *history* of the use of force by police in the days prior to this utterance, and of the practice that had developed among protesters of using their mobile phones to video these displays of force and post them on social media sites as proof of 'police brutality'. It is not just that the threat to use force becomes more credible in the light of the fact that force has been used before. It is also that the officer, by adding the phrase 'in front of so many people' is *citing* the practice of protesters documenting the use of force by police officers like himself, and implying that he will not be deterred by that practice.

Finally, Randy's videos and his whole coming out process dramatically illustrate how specific social actions depend upon the histories of the people and the technologies that come together to make actions possible, and how those actions then become part of trajectories that make future actions possible. All of the tools that Randy and his interlocutor take up in the conversation that Randy narrates in the example above, for example, come with their own histories: The newspaper Randy is reading not only connects the conversation to a long history of practices of journalism and practices of newspaper reading, but also to the history of this particular newspaper, *Stars and Stripes*, which in many ways represents the 'official voice' of the US military. The headline in the paper links the conversation to a long history of policy debates and policies about gays and lesbians in the US military. The practice of 'joking' about gays and lesbians engaged in by Randy's interlocutor is also linked to a long history of 'homophobia' in the military, and in other traditionally masculine institutions. The video in which he recounts this story is linked to a trajectory of videos on his YouTube channel chronicling his 'journey' of coming out (each video with its own history of comments from viewers). And this story itself is linked to the actual conversation of which the story is a retelling. People themselves enter into moments of spoken discourse along their own trajectories, bringing to their actions 'an immense stock of sedimented social knowledge' (Hanks 1996: 238), and there are also the trajectories of people's relationships, the interaction orders that build up over time in particular settings and institutions and the personal histories that people have with one another.

While what makes particular actions possible at different sites of engagement is more a matter of contextualization, the way these actions get linked with other actions in historical trajectories is more a matter of entextualization (Bauman and Briggs 1990). It is the affordances that language and other technologies of talk make available for transforming actions into discourse so that they can be recontextualized into other sites of engagement that create historical trajectories. Thus, it is Randy's entextualization of his interaction with his colleague into a narrative that allows him to connect the context in which the interaction took place with the context of his speaking (Wortham and Reyes 2015), and it is the affordance of digital media to entexualize this narrative into an artefact that can be broadcast to millions of people over the internet that connects the context of his narrative to the many contexts which the viewers of the video inhabit, and, in a very concrete way, connects his struggle with coming out to their struggles. Finally, it is the affordance of discourse to project actions into the future (in the form or promises, resolutions, and dates circled on calendars) that connects Randy's seemingly insignificant conversation with someone about a newspaper article to a longer trajectory that will eventually involve him coming out to his parents:

    33   … so I'm sorry that these eh I'm takin like <u>such</u> baby
    34   steps but (0.5) it's a rea:lly:: (0.3) it's been (.) really (0.2) ah a lot
    35   harder'n I thought (0.2) but I have set a deadline hm (.) $for
    36   myself$ when I'm gonna tell my parents I actually wrote a <u>date</u>^
    37   (0.4) on my calendar it's a re it's a long way away but I said y'know
    38   by (0.1) by this time I (.) I really wanna (0.5) um^ (0.9) I really
    39   wanna tell.

What this insight suggests is that the important thing about the relationship between discourse and action is not just that discourse is a kind of action and that action is a kind of discourse, but that the affordances that technologies of talk provide for us to transform discourse into action and action into discourse along historical trajectories help us to create a sense of continuity as we move from one site of engagement to another, to make past actions meaningful, and to make future actions possible.

5

Talk in interaction

In this chapter, I will consider the way participants in spoken discourse manage the task of interacting. Typically, the term 'interaction' refers to the processes through which two or more entities affect each other through mutual reciprocal action. In the context of spoken discourse, we think of synchronous spoken conversation as the paradigmatic form of social interaction, but interaction does not have to involve speech. A line-backer tackling a quarterback is also a form of interaction. Interaction can also involve different degrees of presence and synchrony. We can interact face-to-face, by phone, by email and even a performer on television or a YouTube celebrity like Randy Phillips can be said to be interacting with his or her audience (Frobenius 2014; Haviland 2007: 150). Finally, we don't just interact with other humans. We also interact with animals, machines and objects of all kinds. Withdrawing money from an ATM machine, for example, is a form of social interaction. We might call it a kind of 'conversation': I insert my card, and the machine asks me for my 'PIN'; I respond with my PIN, and the machine 'asks' me what I want to do; I choose an option (withdrawal money), and the machine asks me how much; I input the amount, and the machine asks me to wait while it processes my instruction; I wait, and the machine asks me to take my card; I take my card, and the machine gives me my money.

At least that's how I am used to this conversation occurring, because that's the way it always occurs at ATM machines in Hong Kong where I live. But it doesn't always go this way. On more than one occasion, when visiting other countries, I have ended up leaving my ATM card in the machine, because the sequence of actions is different: the machine gives me my money *before* giving me my card back, and I am so accustomed to the part where I take the money being the 'end' of the conversation, that I take the money and run, leaving my card behind. There are a couple of things that we can learn from my mistake. The most important is that conversations are mediated through 'scripts', which influence the sequence of actions, and that these scripts operate through a principle of mutual reciprocity or what I referred to in Chapter 4, drawing on the work of Sacks and other conversation analysts, as *conditional relevance*. What this means is that each contribution to the conversation is a response to the previous contribution, and creates the conditions for the subsequent contribution. My entering an amount of money is a response to the machine asking me how much I want, and creates the conditions for the machine giving me that amount. In other words, the relationship between moves in this 'conversation is not merely serial, it is *sequential* (Suchman 2007). As I said in the last chapter, this sequential relationship between actions plays a crucial role in how social actions (like refusing a sexual advance) get accomplished. It also plays a crucial role in people being able to do actions together: being able to *interact* successfully. The study of interaction, then, is basically the study of how speakers and hearers jointly influence one another during the course of utterances (Goodwin 1981). This joint influence is both enabling and constraining. It enables parties in a conversation to make sense of what each other is doing and to work together towards a common goal. But it also locks us into certain trajectories of action. As conversation analysts John Heritage and Max Atkinson write (1984), there is 'no escape or timeout; from the sequential logic of conversation'. Or as Erickson (1986: 316) more colourfully expresses it, having a conversation is like 'climbing a tree that climbs back'.

But what my 'conversations' with 'foreign' ATM machines also teaches us is that the sequential relationship between utterances doesn't always end up producing the desired actions. Sometimes, the two parties in the conversation employ different sets of expectations about the relationship between moves, in which case, miscommunication can ensue. This is what sometimes happens in intercultural communication (see e.g., Scollon, Scollon and Jones 2012). It's also what happens to me when I use an ATM machine in a foreign country. Intercultural miscommunication, it seems, can occur just as easily with machines as it can with people.

At the same time, there's a deeper question that arises from this example, the question of who exactly I am interacting with. Obviously, I'm not only interacting with a machine: the machine is interacting with me on behalf of an institution: a bank, and this interaction is actually part of a complex chain of interactions which involves both humans (like the customer service representative I call to report my lost card) and other machines (such as the computer that records my transactions).

Even participation in that immediate interaction is something that is quite complex. Often, for example, there are people standing in a queue behind me while I am interacting with the ATM machine. None of them, however, can be considered to be participants in the interaction between me and the machine. In fact, they are normally at pains to separate themselves entirely from this interaction by, for example, glancing away to show that they are not watching me as I enter my PIN. They are still, however, interacting with me and the other people in the queue, that is to say, they are involved in a form of coordinated action governed by rules of mutual reciprocity and conditional relevance. Just like other interactions, queuing in front of an ATM machine is mediated by a script which dictates the sequential order of moves: one person leaving the machine is a signal for the person directly behind him or her to approach the machine. It is also governed by other rules of conduct concerning things like the way participants should stand, where they should look, and what sorts of things they should talk about if they talk.

The point I'm trying to make is that often what seems like a simple interaction between two parties can actually involve multiple participants, and that often more than one interaction might be occurring at one time: In the case of my withdrawing money from the ATM machine, I am interacting not just with the machine, but also with various employees of the bank, and with the other people queuing up behind me. There may in fact be other interactions as well, that I may not be fully aware of, such as that between the customers and the security guard watching us from the corner, or the security camera recording our every move. Like the example of the YouTube video with which I began this book, the number of participants and the roles they take in these multiple, overlapping interactions makes this seemingly simple situation much more complex than is immediately apparent. Furthermore, all of these various interactions are mediated through sets of expectations about what kinds of rights and responsibilities different people have.

And this brings me to the final point I want to make about interaction in this introductory section: the fact that all interactions have a certain 'moral' dimension. The queue is of course a perfect example of this. Goffman considered the queue as 'one of the ... most *moral* of all social encounters precisely because it has the least external organization and requires the purest commitment to the interactional order for its own sake' (Rawls 1987: 142 commenting on Goffman 1983a). The moral dimension of my interaction with the ATM machine is not just related to the fact that I should not peek to gain access to another user's PIN. It also has to do with to a more fundamental set of responsibilities to conduct myself within the terms of the *interaction order* that is normally in place in such situations. And so, when we speak of the 'moral' dimension of interactions, we may, of course, be interested in things like power, fairness and justice, but we really cannot attend to these broader issues of morality until we first come to terms with the more local moral demands of the interaction order.

The interaction order

In Chapter 2, I said that what differentiated Goffman and Garfinkel from other sociologists of their day was that they were less interested in studying the 'social order' in terms of broad structures like classes or institutions, and more interested in what Goffman (1983a) called the 'interaction order'. It is, they insisted, the rules, risks, rights and responsibilities that govern everyday mundane interactions like queuing at an ATM machine that end up determining what sorts of larger social orders we are able to have.

So what is an interaction order? We can think of an interaction order as a set of expectations about *participation* and *conduct* that becomes relevant to participants in certain sites of engagement. These sets of expectations are supported by many of the mediational means I discussed in Chapter 3, including physical tools like rope barriers and surveillance cameras, and semiotic tools like speech genres and social identities. The interaction order at any particular site of engagement is not fixed: it must, to a certain extent, be negotiated by participants as they appropriate and adapt these various mediational means in the service of their particular goals. At the same time, these mediational means link these locally negotiated interaction orders to larger social orders. The queue that I negotiate with my fellow customers at the ATM has its own unique characteristics based on the particular people who are there, but at the same time it is reflective of larger social and institutional structures (including the regulations of the bank and the cultural models of queuing in the society in which I live).

The most basic requirement of an interaction order is that it involves one or more social actors who are to some degree 'present' to each other. An interaction order is, as Goffman (1983a: 2) puts it 'an environment in which people are in one another's response presence', or, as he puts it elsewhere (1964: 135), 'an environment of mutual monitoring possibilities'. This notion of 'mutual monitoring' is really at the heart of all interaction, since without it we would not be able to sustain the kind of reciprocal relationship between the actions of different parties that interaction requires. This fact is obvious in face-to-face interactions, but perhaps less obvious in situations in which participants are not physically co-present such as telephone conversations, computer chats, email exchanges and YouTube videos, since the ability people have to monitor each other in these situations is more constrained. Nevertheless, interactions carried out using these technologies still involve mutual monitoring. Although people are not physically co-present, they are still 'present' to each other in some way. Even Goffman (1983a) recognized that media like the phone and mail afford a kind of distant presence. While there is a tendency to view the kinds of presence afforded by such technologies as 'reduced versions of the primordial real thing' (Goffman 1983a: 2), some digital technologies involve possibilities for mutual monitoring that go *beyond* those available in face-to-face communication. Online social networks, for example, sometimes allow users to monitor where their friends are geographically and other aspects of their day-to-day activities, and a mobile phone makes the person carrying it constantly available to people who are not physically co-present. In fact, one common complaint about digital technology is that it creates a situation in which we are *perpetually present* to one another, or, as Baron (2010) puts it, 'always on'.

Mere presence, however, is not sufficient for an interaction order. Parties who are present to each other must also have some means by which to enter into interaction, of regulating who is allowed into the interaction and of figuring out what rights and responsibilities they have once they are in it. They must also have the means to negotiate what the interaction is 'about' and to ensure that it proceeds in a smooth and orderly manner. Finally, they need to have ways of getting out of the interaction when they want to. These different requirements for an interaction order can be divided into two kinds of tools: *rules of conduct* and *frameworks for participation*.

Conducting interaction

The most common way for discourse analysts to approach interaction is to focus on rules of conduct – what Sacks and his colleagues (1974) called the 'formal apparatus' of conversation that enables people to coordinate their joint action. As Goffman (1983a: 5) put it, 'The workings of the interaction order can ... be viewed as the consequence of systems of enabling conventions, in the sense of the ground rules for a game, the provisions of a traffic code, or the rules of syntax of a language.'

What sort of 'ground rules', then, are needed for interaction to take place in an 'orderly' fashion? Essentially, three things are required. First, there must be some way for participants to move from a non-interactional state into a 'state of talk'. Second, there must be some mechanism to maintain mutual reciprocity, some way to make it possible for participants to manage their turns so they don't 'crash into' each other, to extend Goffman's metaphor of 'traffic rules'. Related to these rules are those that govern the relationship between turns and the way participants negotiate what the interaction is 'about'. Finally, there must be an orderly way for people to end interactions. Of course, most interactions (especially among people who know each other) are not so much ended as suspended, with the understanding that parties will take up where they left off in subsequent interactions, and similarly most interactions, begin, in a sense, *in medias res*, taking up topics, relationships and interactional projects from previous interactions. And so, just as it is necessary for people to have ways of putting boundaries around interactions, it is also important that they have ways of *linking* interactions to past interactions and anticipating future ones.

The first thing we need to have an interaction is a way to begin it, a way for participants to move from a state of 'non-interaction' to what Goffman (1966, 1967) called a state of 'mutually ratified participation'. Face-to-face interaction often involves a complex set of procedures by which people coordinate their entry into interaction involving mutual perception, recognition, negotiation of one's availability, and (often quite elaborate) greeting sequences (Kendon and Ferber 1973). Communication mediated through technologies such as telephones involves similar steps, but because of the different possibilities for mutual monitoring, they are achieved differently. For example, whereas in face-to-face interactions, 'recognition' is usually achieved visually, in telephone conversations this is either achieved verbally or through written text (in the case of the caller identification function on mobile phones that display the caller's name).

Common sense tells us that most interactions begin with greetings. But when we look at greetings more closely, we realize that they tend to involve a range of complex interactional work that goes beyond just 'greeting'. Scollon (1998), drawing on the work of Schegloff (1968), notes that opening an interaction always demands that participants complete three tasks: they must open the channel of communication, they must ratify the identities of the potential parties in the interaction, and they must negotiate the purpose (or topic) of the interaction. These tasks are often (though not always) achieved through three kinds of conversational exchanges: (1) a summons–answer sequence; (2) an identification sequence; and (3) a topic introduction sequence. Schegloff refers to these kinds of sequences as *preliminaries*, since they must be accomplished as a prerequisite to other things happening. Conversations, also involve other kinds of *preliminaries* that may occur later in the interaction, such as *pre*-offers, *pre*-request, *pre*-announcements (Terasaki 2000), and *pre*-closings (see below).

Of course, the most important preliminary for an interaction is the summons–answer sequence, the main purpose of which is to open the channel of communication. In face-to-face communication, this may be done verbally, as when one party 'hails' another with words like 'hey' or 'hi', or it may be done non-verbally with a wave, eye contact, the action of physically moving towards another person, or a combination of such non-verbal cues. Often in face-to-face interaction, the ratification of identities is accomplished with the same moves as the summons–answer sequence. This is especially true when people know each other ('Bill!' → 'John!') or when they are playing recognizable roles, as in service encounters ('May I help you?' → 'Yes'). When people do not know each other, or are not playing clearly recognizable roles, the participant who issues the summons generally needs to issue what Sacks (1972) calls a 'ticket' to the interaction, some justification for beginning the interaction. It might come in the form of an identification sequence (such as, 'Hi, I'm Mary's brother. You're Claire, right?'), a request ('Excuse me, I wonder if you can tell me how to get to the Louvre?'), or some kind of 'announcement of trouble relevant to the other' (such as, 'Pardon me, your pants are on fire.' [Sacks 1972: 345]). Utterances such as these often blend the task of ratifying identities and the task of topic introduction into the summons–answer sequence. The same is true for service encounters in which opening the channel, identification and topic introduction are often collapsed into a single sequence ('What can I get you?' 'I'll have a Coke'). For people who know each other, however, topic introduction can be far more complicated, since the purpose of having the conversation is not always immediately clear. Of course, the purpose of most of our conversations with friends is really just to have a conversation in order to maintain our relationship. Nevertheless, we still must work together to settle on something to talk about. This is often the purpose of formulaic greeting sequences (such as 'how are you?'), to give one party (usually the person who has issued the summons) the opportunity to introduce a topic.

Consider the following conversation between two people in a bookstore. One (A) is a customer, and the other (B) works in the shop.

```
51   A   (turns and notices B)
52       oh hi:: ↑↓ how's [it going↑↓
53   B                   [how's it goin'↑↓ (0.2)
54   A   great↑↓ (.) just got standing room for um (0.2) It's Only
55       a Play (0.1)
56   B   ye[ah:::^
57   A     [I'm absolutely] thrilled (.) so happy. (0.2)
```

In this example, the summons–answer sequence and the identification sequence are performed in the same moves, moves which are not just mediated through spoken words, but also through paralinguistic and non-verbal cues. When A turns towards B and looks directly at him, she both invites him into an interaction and makes a claim that she is a legitimate person for him to interact with. She does the same thing with her utterance ('oh hi:: ↑↓'): both the addition of the word 'oh' and the intonation and lengthening of the 'hi' serve to communicate a kind of familiarity (Pillet-Shore 2012). This is immediately followed by the first part of a greeting sequence ('how's it going↑↓'), which B immediately completes with the preferred response ('how's [it going↑↓'), giving A the opportunity to introduce a topic ('great↑↓ (.) just got standing room for um (0.2) It's Only a Play'). B's response ('how's [it going↑↓'), can be said to do three things: it completes the opening of the channel; it communicates mutual recognition, and it opens a slot for A to introduce the topic.

What's interesting about this short excerpt, then, is that it demonstrates how the different tasks necessary for opening a conversation can be combined into single sequences, and also how accomplishing these tasks often depends on complex combinations of modes (such as posture, gaze, intonation and spoken language). What's even more interesting, however, is the way in which the machinery of conversation allows us to manage the task of ratification of identities, a task which is often much more complex than it might seem on the surface. Sometimes, for example, ratification of identities requires specific acts of identification ('Hello, I represent the Obama for President campaign'). Most of the time, however, identification is done tacitly. You do not have to reintroduce yourself to your friend every time you meet her (though you do need to somehow display that you *recognize* her), and in most service encounters, people's identities are signalled by things like the way they are dressed or where they are standing (e.g., behind a counter). What's interesting about the conversation above is that although A clearly recognizes B, she probably does not know his name. She likely recognizes him as 'that guy who works in this bookstore'. And although B displays recognition of A, he actually does *not* recognize her (as revealed in a subsequent interview). Given the circumstances, however, (the fact that she is a customer and he's in the business of selling books) it would probably be inappropriate for B to interrupt the interaction with an utterance like, 'Excuse me, do I know you?' In fact, even in many other situations, this would be difficult to do due to the conversational inertia set into motion by this opening. It is difficult to answer 'oh hi:: ↑↓ how's it going↑↓' with anything other than 'how's it going↑↓', and once you've done that, you are, in a 'sense, 'stuck' in the conversation. Many of us no doubt have the experience of being 'stuck' in conversations with people whose identities we were uncertain of.

Of course, openings are very different for interactions that are mediated through technologies like telephones, mobile chat apps and video calls. What makes telephone calls special, for example, is that they tend to be more bounded than other sorts of interactions: there is no opportunity for gradual approach, no 'halfway' between being present to each other and interacting as there often is in face-to-face interaction (Hutchby 2001). Once the presence has been established, there is no easy way not to have an interaction. There is also, in many phone calls, no easy way for participants to ratify each other's identities during or before the summons–answer sequence (as there is in face-to-face communication), though, with caller identification technology now available on most phones, this is changing. Because of these constraints, the three different 'tasks' I identified above must usually be done in a more explicit fashion, often through a series of distinct exchanges. Schegloff (1968) notes that, in order to be 'anchored', phone calls must usually begin with a distinct summons–answer sequence (in which the ring of the telephone constitutes the summons and the verbal response of the recipient of the call constitutes the answer), an identification/recognition sequence (done either through explicit identification or voice recognition), and sequences involving greetings and initial inquiries. Even when participants have access to caller identification technology, they must still somehow manage identification/ recognition: the recipient of the call, for example, having read the caller's identity on his screen, might answer with 'Hello, Charles', not just by way of answering the summons or greeting Charles, but to let Charles know that he has been identified. Consider, for example, the beginning of the conversation between Randy and his father:

```
34  (phone ringing)
35  Dad:   hello? (0.4)
36  Son:   hey daddy↑↓
37  (1.0)
38  Dad:   hey bu::d↑↓
```

In this example, the first sequence, consisting of the ring of the telephone and the father's answer, constitutes the summons–answer sequence, the father's 'hello' functioning not as a greeting, but as a response to a summons. The second pair consists of the two parties establishing their respective identities. In conversations between strangers, this usually has to be done more explicitly: the caller might have to say something like, 'Hello, I'm calling from the Drama bookstore.' In conversations between intimates, however, voice recognition is usually sufficient to achieve mutual identification. In fact, declining to explicitly identify oneself itself constitutes a kind of expression of intimacy, what Schegloff (1968: 1078) refers to as an 'intimacy ploy'. What usually follows in phone conversations is a greeting sequence, consisting of the caller uttering a ritual phrase like 'How's it going?' or 'What's up', which is usually followed by a ritual reply such as 'not much', which opens up a slot for the caller to introduce the topic (the reason for the call).

Other media, such as messaging applications, involve still different forms of conduct when it comes to opening conversations, conduct which is affected by the affordances and constraints of the media for accomplishing the tasks of summoning, identifying participants, and regulating topic introduction. Not long ago, for example, my partner sent me a voice message on WhatsApp asking, 'hey↑↓ Baby. what's for dinner,' to which I replied by sending him a link for a recipe for kale and quinoa salad. This exchange is different from the two examples above in several important ways. First, there is no separate summons–answer sequence needed to open the channel before my partner can send his message. In fact, I am summoned (by a notification on my phone) *after* his message has been sent, and I 'answer' the summons simply by listening to the message, which creates an acknowledgement on his phone in the form of tick (□) next to the icon representing his recording. My sending him the link, of course, is also a kind of answer, though not necessary to establish that the message has been received. Second, there is no need for an identification sequence. His message is delivered to me as part of an ongoing 'chat' in my WhatsApp application which contains messages going back many months: when I open that chat his name and photo appear on the top of my screen, and when he receives my message, my name and picture appear on his. This is perhaps the biggest difference between WhatsApp conversations and the kinds of conversations that I discussed above: there seem to be no boundaries around them: they don't really need to be opened because participants are perpetually available to each other, with each having an equal right to propose a new topic at any time.

Once people find themselves in a 'state of talk', whether it be in a face-to-face conversation, a telephone conversation, or a WhatsApp chat, they normally adhere to a set of conventions designed to help them make their contributions in an orderly way and work together to manage the topic of the conversation. As with openings, these conventions are different for conversations mediated through different material technologies, but one rule seems to apply fairly universally across media, the rule that people take turns when talking and that only one person talks at a time. Although this seems like a simple enough rule, what's interesting is that people are able to pull it off so consistently. As I have mentioned in previous chapters, a wide range of technologies contributes to helping people to manage turn taking in conversation, including pauses, intonation, gaze, gestures and proxemics (see, for example, Goodwin 1980, 1981; Kendon 1990). One of the main ways we make turn taking orderly, however, is the way we 'package' our turns in what Sacks and his colleagues (1974) call 'turn constructional units'. A turn constructional unit is any utterance which can function as a complete turn by virtue of the fact that it accomplishes some complete conversational move (such as greeting, asking a question, giving an answer, or making a statement of some sort). An example of a turn constructional unit would be, 'Daddy, I'm gay.' Although this statement could be combined with other turn constructional units to make a longer turn, it can also stand by itself, and when a speaker, pauses at the end of such a unit, as Randy does after he says this to his father, this constitutes an invitation for the other party to take the floor (which Randy's father does, reacting to the statement with one word: 'gay?', an utterance which, despite its length, also constitutes a turn constructional unit: a complete conversational move).

It is possible, however, to utter a turn constructional unit like this and not relinquish the floor, by, for example, using the resources of grammar along with pausing and intonation to signal that there is more to come. This is what happens in the example from Kitzinger (2000) that I discussed in the last chapter:

```
15   Linda:  =It does, it does have an effect on you because (0.2)
16           If you've thought of yourself as heterosexual (1.0)
17           and you (.) >suddenly find yourself attracted to a woman
18           °it happened to me, < (0.2) a few years ago°
19           it's very (0.8) disturbing, [in a] way it's=
20   CK:     [mm]
21   Linda:  =it's (0.2) makes you very anxious (.)
22           because you then don't know how you're supposed to respond
```

In this example, the unit that serves a function similar to 'Daddy, I'm, gay' occurs in line 18 (°it happened to me, < (0.2) a few years ago°). But since it is grammatically embedded in a longer unit, it does not invite an immediate response from the audience the way Randy's revelation does. The important point here, and the point that Kitzinger makes, is that the way people manage turn taking in conversations can also have an effect on the *function* of utterances: Randy's revelation functioning as a 'coming out' because, along with revealing information about his sexuality, it also invites a response from his interlocutor, whereas, since it does not invite a response, Linda's utterance does not fulfil this function in the same way.

Of course there are other places in Linda's turn that have the potential to serve as 'transition' relevance places, such as the end of the main clauses in lines 15 and 19 ('It does, it does have an effect on you' and 'it's very (0.8) disturbing, [in a] way'). She avoids being interrupted at these points, however, by immediately beginning new clauses without pausing. When she does pause (such as at the end of line 15 and the end of line 16), the pause occurs after she has already signalled that there is more to come (the pause in line 15 coming after the word 'because', and in line 16 coming after a subordinate 'if' clause). What this shows is that people are good at designing turns so that listeners are able to *project* whether the turn will end or not (Liddicoat 2004). This helps people to hold the floor, even when they pause in the middle of a thought.

Turn constructional units constitute the *form* contributions take. But for a conversation to be coherent, participants must also pay attention to the *content* of turns so that one turn follows another in a meaningful way. In order to do this, they usually endeavour to make what they say 'fit' with what the speaker before them has said. One way they do this, which I discussed in the last chapter, is by offering what is clearly the second half of an adjacency pair – answering a question with an answer, for example, or an invitation with either an acceptance or a refusal. Another way is to try to make one's contribution conform *topically* to what was being discussed in the previous turn. In the event that the topic they want to bring up does not 'fit' with the previous turn, people will often wait for the conversation to reach a place at which the introduction of the new topic can 'occur naturally', 'that is, can be fitted to another'(Schegloff and Sacks 1973: 78). Abrupt shifts of topic are liable either to cause confusion or to create implicature, indicating, for example, that the topic being discussed makes the listener uncomfortable or is considered 'out of bounds'.

> Son: I'm gay, Mom.
> Mother: So, how's the weather over there?

When people wish to change topics in conversations, they have two ways of going about it. They can, as I said above, either try to somehow link their new topic with the one currently being discussed, or they can explicitly announce that they want to introduce a new topic using a 'discourse marker' (Schiffrin 1988) such as 'by the way', or 'I don't mean to change the subject, but …', or they can somehow announce that they are finished discussing the topic at hand by issuing topically empty contributions like 'okay' and 'so' (Schegloff and Sacks 1973), and leave it to the other person to begin a new topic if they wish, as Randy does in the excerpt below:

```
120  Dad:   … I had my suspicions there for a lil' while^
121         (4.2)
122  Son:   yeah?
123         (3.2)
124         well other than that everything's great. (0.7) so^
125         (3.8)
126         um:^
127         (2.2)
128         uh [huh^
129  Dad:      [ (inaudible)] (4.6) I will say this ( ) y'know (2.3) you'll never
130         get bored^ (4.1) right? (0.2)
```

In this case, his father opts not to bring up a new topic and persists in discussing matters related to his son's coming out until the conversation finally ends about three minutes later. This is, perhaps, not surprising. Some topics are difficult to change; they dominate encounters and come to define those encounters so that, even if they are left temporarily, they are often returned to before the end of the conversation. This is, of course, typical of many business or professional conversations in which a single topic might stand out as the 'reason' for the conversation. Conversations between friends and intimates are less often 'mono-topical', typically involving participants traversing multiple topics, many of these topics functioning more to increase solidarity between parties than to exchange information. The exception to this is, of course, conversations involving the delivery of important or delicate news such as Randy's 'coming out' to his father.

Conversations about delicate topics are not just hard to get out of. They are hard to get into as well, evidenced by the way Randy's phone call to his father begins. In telephone conversations, it is usually up to the caller to introduce the (first) topic of the conversation, an obligation that Randy delays by first asking his father a series of questions:

39	Son:	hey waddayu doin.
40		(1.1)
41	Dad:	waddum I <u>doin</u>?=
42	Son:	=$ye yeah.$
43		(0.7)
44	Dad:	I'm listenin t'my <u>son</u> thinkin (inaudible) cuz I ain't heard his
45		voice in a long ti:me
47	Son:	well wedup (.) waddayu doin right <u>now</u>.
48		(1.3)
49	Dad:	jus (inaudible) sittin up<u>sta:irs</u>^ (0.3)
50	Son:	oh who's <u>with</u> you.
51		(1.5)
52	Dad:	Sherry^ (0.5)
53	Son:	oh
54		(2.2)
55		ah::
56		(0.6)
57		hey canna tell you somethin?
58		(2.6)
59	Dad:	y'what?
60		(0.6)
61	Son:	can I <u>tell</u> you somethin?
62		(0.8)
63	Dad:	yeah
64		(0.8)
65	Son:	willya love me? (.) Period?

```
66          (1.1)
67  Dad:    yes.
68          (0.7)
69  Son:    like you you'll always love me^ (0.5)
70          As long as I'm [ah
71  Dad:                   [don't worry
```

In Chapter 1, I referred to this part of the conversation as the *preparation*, noting that such preparatory exchanges are typical of the speech genre of 'coming out'. As I said above, Schegloff (1980, 2007) refers to such exchanges as *preliminaries*, which he defines as: 'various types of talk that ... [are] produced by speakers and understood by recipients as talk not only "in its own right" but also "on behalf of," and specifically preliminary to, other talk that might follow, contingent on the response' (Schegloff 1980: 113). Many kinds of talk involve preliminaries. The questions that preface Randy's coming out to his father might be seen as constituting a 'pre-announcement' (Terasaki 2000) or, more specifically, a 'pre-delicate' (Maynard 2003; Schegloff 1980), a sequence that prepares hearers for receiving some potentially delicate news. As I noted in the first chapter, such pre-announcement sequences can serve multiple functions. Here, for example, it serves the very practical function of establishing that the father is in a situation (with regard to other involvements and other participants) in which he is able to receive the news. It also serves, as I said in Chapter 1, to elicit a promise from the father about how he will react. The most important function, however, is to signal to the father that the topic that will be introduced is potentially delicate by delaying its introduction. In other words, it serves as a kind of *metadiscourse* (see Chapter 3). As such, it plays a role both in the present interaction – signalling to the father that he and his son are engaged in a special kind of conversation – and in the wider 'Big C' conversation about homosexuality in the society in which the conversation takes place, contributing to the *technologization* of the speech genre of 'coming out': Every time someone uses a 'pre-delicate' to precede this kind of announcement, they are reinforcing the cultural notion that announcements of this sort are, by their nature, delicate, and that 'coming out' necessitates interactional conduct that is different from other kinds of (less 'delicate') announcements. Although the sort of lengthy preliminaries seen in this example are particularly associated with announcements of some weight, the use of preliminaries can occur in many different kinds of exchanges, especially those that involve the possibility that the listener might give a dispreferred response to a particular move. Thus, for example, invitations are often prefaced with pre-invitations ('Hey, what are you doing tomorrow?').

Closings are among the most difficult accomplishments in conversation. The first reason for this is because moving to end an interaction with someone is an inherently 'face threatening act' (Brown and Levinson 1987), and second because the turn taking mechanism of conversation, in which utterances typically function to create slots for new utterances, is difficult to stop once it has been put into motion. In order for an interaction to end, this conversational inertia must somehow be disrupted. As Schegloff and Sacks (1973: 294–5) put it, the initial problem concerning closings is 'how to organise the simultaneous arrival of the conversationalists at a point where one speaker's completion will not occasion another speaker's talk'.

Just as with other potentially delicate conversational moves, closings are usually managed through the use of preliminaries, specifically what are referred to as *pre-closings*. Pre-closings may consist of non-verbal cues like checking one's watch or putting on one's coat. But the most common form they take are 'topically empty objects' (ten Have 2007: 22) such as 'so', 'well' and 'okay' which serve the purpose of, on the one hand occupying the turn of the person who utters them with a contribution that neither continues an old topic nor introduces a new one, giving to the other party the option of either continuing the conversation (with the same or a different topic), or moving to terminate it. Sometimes this trading of 'empty objects' can go on for several turns before both parties are satisfied that it is safe to end the conversation.

Of course, some kinds of conversations are more difficult to end than others, partly because some topics are particularly hard to discontinue without threatening the other person's face, even after that person has given 'permission' to discontinue the topic through the issue of a topically empty object. This is why conversations between lovers are hard to end (for an example, see Channell 1997). It's also why it takes Randy and his father so long to get off the phone after he has accomplished his 'coming out'.

178	Dad	... <u>alright</u>:
179		(0.6)
180	Son	alright
181		(0.7)
182	Son	[okay^
183	Dad	[(inaudible)] (0.3) Bud <u>I</u> still love you (.) and I will <u>always</u>
184		love you (2.0)
185		and I will (.) uh always be proud of you (0.4) okay?
186	Son	yeah^
187		(2.6)
188	Dad	alright (.) aunt Sherry (inaudible) good to hear your voice
189		[(inaudible)

190	Son	[heh h.] (0.6) alright (0.1) thanks <u>dad</u>:
191		(1.0)
192	Woman	(inaudible)
193	Dad	and (inaudible) both miss you <u>terribly</u> (0.3)
194	Son	I know: (0.2) hel<u>lo</u>'m:
195		(1.3)
196	Dad	I won't (.) I'm not gonna say nothin' to anybody I'll let you
197		(1.1)
198		(inaudible) you feel like (inaudible)=
199	Son	= um:: (0.3) mh (0.2)
200		you can tell whoever you want:
201		(1.8)
202		everybody <u>here</u> knows: (0.2) Dad
203		(2.9)
204		so: (.) 'n it's all been great (0.3)
205		like nobody's (0.2) givin' me any <u>shit</u> about it
206		(1.0)
207		so:^
208		(3.6)
209		yeah [and
210	Dad	[alright Bud=
211	Son	= you can tell Sherry 'n the gir umm (0.1)
212		well you can tell Sherry
213		(2.5)
214		so^
215		(0.7)
216		alright.
217		(0.4)
218	Dad	I'll <u>tell</u> them
219		(0.5)
220	Son	alright well I <u>love</u> you Daddy:: (0.3) thanks for
221		everything=
222	Dad	=when are you comin' home.
223	Son	I'll be home before too long:
224		(0.9)
225	Dad	o<u>ka</u>::y you be <u>care</u>ful now=
226	Son	= alright (.) I love you
227		(0.8)
228	Dad	love you <u>too</u> Bud (0.1)
229	Son	alright (.) bye

There are several places in this extract where the conversation between Randy and his father could reasonably come to a close, the first being the exchange of potential pre-closings that begins at line 178, when Randy answers his father's 'alright' with his own 'alright'. This exchange does not result in a closure, however, because the father uses his open slot to continue the topic of how much he loves Randy. A similar move towards closure using offers of 'topically empty objects' occurs in lines 207–10 (so:^ (3.6) yeah and → alright Bud), but this time the move towards closure is interrupted by Randy, who begins a new sub-topic regarding who else his father can tell about his revelation ('you can tell Sherry 'n the gir umm (0.1) well you can tell Sherry'). The final move towards closure comes in line 220 when Randy says 'alright well I love you Daddy:: (0.3) thanks for everything'. Although his father chooses to use the slot opened to introduce a new topic ('when are you comin' home.), it is the sort of topic that typically occurs at the end of a conversation (making plans for future interactions). This is followed by two formulaic exchanges, 'you be careful now' → 'alright' and 'I love you' → 'love you too' before Randy finally closes with 'alright (.) bye'. All in all, it takes Randy and his father 21 turns from the beginning of the first pre-closing sequence in this extract to extract themselves from the conversation.

What this extract illustrates is that rather than seeing closing a conversation as a 'routine' that participants follow, it is better to see it as part of a negotiation of possibilities for ending the conversation or continuing it that are opened up at various points in the conversation (Schegloff and Sacks 1973: 324). How the parties manage this negotiation has to do with many factors, including their relationship and the topic of the conversation, and in some cases, the way in which one handles these points of possible closure can itself be exploited as a resource for communicating something about the relationship or topic: Randy's father pulling back from the brink of closing with a reminder to his son that he will always love him gives that reminder a slightly different meaning than it had when it appeared earlier in the conversation.

Finally, it needs to be remembered that in most conversations endings do not actually constitute true endings, but only temporary suspensions of interaction until some future time. One of the most important things that people do in closings is opening up possibilities for future interactions, not just by offering contributions that explicitly project future encounters such as 'see you next Tuesday' or 'I'll be home before long', but also by endeavouring to leave the conversation on 'good terms'.

Conversations in some media, however, do not require the same kind of delicate management of closings. My WhatsApp conversation with my partner about what we are having for dinner, for example, involves no pre-closings or even closing; it just abruptly ends. One reason for this might be that, because of the perpetual presence afforded by media such as WhatsApp, conversations are never really seen to end, but rather to only enter temporary abeyance until some future time when one or the other party has something new to say. This also, of course, has something to do with the topics that tend to be discussed using such media: conversations about topics like what to have for dinner are a lot easier to end abruptly without a closing than conversations involving weighty topics like 'coming out'.

Participation

Along with norms governing conversational conduct, interaction orders also consist of norms governing who can participate in conversations and in what capacity. As I noted above, participating in an interaction requires that people be somehow 'present' to each other, and that there be some opportunities for them to mutually monitor each other. Such opportunities are determined both by the technologies of talk they have available to them, and by the ways participants negotiate their roles according to various social norms. ATM machines, for example, are designed to make it difficult for more than one person to interact with them, featuring recessed screens and barriers that extend out on the sides that shield what customers are doing from passers-by and other customers waiting in the queue behind them. Goffman (1963: 38–42) refers to such barriers as 'involvement shields'. But another thing that makes interactions at ATM machines possible is the social norm that proscribes the person in the queue directly behind the person operating the machine from standing too close and peering over his or her shoulder at the screen. One of the main purposes of the interaction order, therefore, is to give people ways to manage the mutual monitoring possibilities afforded by particular environments, to modulate the type and amount of information available to others, and to regulate which participants are able to monitor what, and when they are able to do so.

Clearly, Saussure's diagram of the 'circuit of speech' that I discussed in the first chapter, in which there are only two participants, a 'speaker' and a 'hearer', does not come close to describing the multiple forms of participation people engage in in situations like queuing up at an ATM machine. Most situations, in fact, involve a complex matrix of participants 'with different sorts of rights and obligations for speaking, differential access to the speech of others, and different sorts of statuses – whether recognised, ratified, authoritative, or the reverse' (Haviland 2009: 308). These 'matrices' can be very different for different sorts of 'speech events' (Hymes 1974), such as service encounters, family dinners, university lectures, protest rallies, and performances broadcast over YouTube. Furthermore, sometimes people participate in more than one kind of event at a time, and take up different participant roles in these different events (as when my students engage in WhatsApp chats during my lectures). As Hymes (1974: 54) warns, 'The common didactic model of speaker and hearer which is still so central to much linguistic analysis specifies sometimes too many, sometimes too few, and sometimes the wrong participants.'

The most important thing about participant roles is that they are hardly ever fixed: participants have all sorts of opportunities to alter the way they are participating in interactions in both obvious and subtle ways. Goffman (1981) refers to the dynamic processes through which people manage their participation in interaction as 'footing', which he defines as the 'alignment we take up to ourselves and others as expressed in the way we manage the production and reception of ... utterances[s]'. He explicitly relates footing to the concept of 'framing', which I discussed at length in the previous chapter; changes in footing are often associated with changes in the way participants contextualize their conversational actions. But whereas framing has to do with 'what we are doing', footing has more to do with the roles we are playing in these doings.

Footing can be said to have two components, one related to participants' rights to contribute to interactions and to monitor the contributions of others, which Goffman calls 'participation frameworks', and the other related to their status relative to the words they are uttering and to other people (both present and not) who may have a role in the production of those words, which he calls 'production formats'.

The idea of participation frameworks is that different interaction orders make available different structures for gaining access to and partaking in social situations. Participants might be 'ratified' participants, that is, recognized by others to have rights to partake in the interaction, and within that category, they might take on roles such as 'speaker', 'hearer', or 'addressee'. Or they might be 'non-ratified' participants of various sorts such as 'eavesdroppers' or 'bystanders'. They might function as a group (with various degrees of affiliation), as with an audience at a play or a 'team' (Goffman 1959) that works together to participate in an interaction, or they may function as individuals.

As I said above, these frameworks are affected by the technologies of talk that participants have available to them at different 'sites of engagement'. Randy's YouTube videos provide a dramatic example of this. In one of them[1] he apologizes to his audience, saying 'um sorry I have to <u>whi</u>sper (.) but I'm actually kinda in a bunker^', reminding us that he is actually inhabiting two overlapping sites of engagement, one defined by the physical space from

---

[1]Available at https://youtu.be/0XGcmbMxvLQ.

which he is speaking, in which participation is regulated through things like the volume of his voice and the walls of the bunker he is in, and the 'virtual' site of engagement in which, no matter how softly he speaks, he can be heard by potentially millions of people.

Production formats have to do with the alignment that a speaker takes up to the words he or she is speaking. A person might present him or herself as the author of the words being spoken, as the *principal* (the party responsible for the content of the utterance), the *animator* (the person actually producing the words), a *character* or figure in some event being narrated, or some combination of these roles. In the story about Randy reading the newspaper which I discussed in the last chapter, Randy takes the role of animating the words of the individual who asks him, 'did you write that?' (but he is neither the author nor the principle of these words). In the same story, he also animates his own words ('I said$ No↑↓ (0.4) Jodie Smith wrote it he's a much (0.3) better writer than I am'), playing a character in his own story.

Production formats are an important part of interaction orders for two reasons. First, they provide resources for participants to strategically position themselves in relation to what they are saying and to other speakers (both present and non-present). Second, they play an important role in helping people to link one site of engagement to other sites of engagement and one social encounter to other social encounters (see Chapter 4).

We got a good sense of how complicated issues of footing can be in the example with which I began this book: what seemed at first to be an intimate conversation between two participants – a father and a son – was soon revealed to be, at the same time, a broadcast event involving all sorts of different kinds of participants. Although this example appears to be rather unique (not everyone videos their private conversations with their parents and uploads them onto YouTube), similarly complex participation frameworks and production formats are often at work in what may seem like much simpler interactions. Consider the following conversation, which takes place between two employees working at a busy bookshop in a large American city:

```
1   Roy      Waddya doin' for New Year::s^
2            (0.9)
3   Sylvia   hh (0.5) ahmm::^ hhh (0.3) that's one of those things
4            where there are a variety of possibilities and none of
5            them:: (0.5) is like (0.3) speaking to my soul right now^
6            (0.6) argh[m::
7   Roy               [that's usually how it goe:s.
8   Sylvia   (0.4) and so the [best
9   Roy                        [the best is just to follow the wind on
10           New Years I think (0.4)
```

```
11   Sylvia   I think so cos when you try to plan too much (0.5) tha
12            (.) which I havn't done in year:s it's: (.) inevitably
13            disappointi^ng=
14   Roy                      =always disappointing (0.3)
15   Sylvia   an::d eh^
16            (1.4)
17   Roy      yeah (0.2)
18   Sylvia   I sort of feel like it's (.) partially abou:t (0.5) who:: (0.6)
19   Roy      (sniff)
20   Sylvia   (0.6) you want to (.) be with (.) cuz I'm not (.) really
21            like (0.1) I hate crow:ds^ (1.1) so that's the other thing
22            is:: (0.6)
23            but some crowds aren't that bad like (.) the Restless Bar
24            mm: (.) was where I was at last year and I was
25            bartending^ (0.1) till seven a.m.^ (0.7) umm (.) and that
26            was pretty fun because I was (.) like (0.5) given a
27            fo::cus^ 'n I was behind the bar so my (.) area wasn't
28            crowded=
```

At first, this may seem to be a pretty straightforward example of a conversation conforming to the dyadic model of speaker and hearer that Hymes was so sceptical about in the quote that I gave above. But there are a number of features to this conversation that complicate this assumption. First is the fact that, although it seems that Roy and Sylvia are taking turns assuming the role of speaker, what is really going on is that Sylvia is giving an extended answer to Roy's question, and Roy's turns at speaking seem to be more about helping her to do this rather than taking back the floor himself. This is particularly clear in line 14, when Roy basically repeats what Sylvia has just said ('inevitably disappointi^ng' → 'always disappointing'), and line 17, where the 'yeah' seems to be not just an agreement but also a way of encouraging her to keep going. The point I wish to make is that the assumption that, in a two-party conversation, at any one moment, one party is the *speaker* and the other is the *listener* and that these roles switch from utterance to utterance (Schober and Brennan 2003) is far from cut and dried. There are different ways of being a speaker – one can, for example, be speaking for oneself or for someone else, answering a question, an accusation, or a request, telling a story, giving a lecture, or any other of a number of things – and there are also different ways of being a listener – one can, for example, take on the role of a collaborator, an audience member (see Goodwin 1984) an adversary, or any number of other roles. In the excerpt above, when Roy is speaking – what he is doing with his speech is actually *listening*.

But the most complicated thing about this conversation in terms of participation is that it does not take place in private. As I said above, Roy and

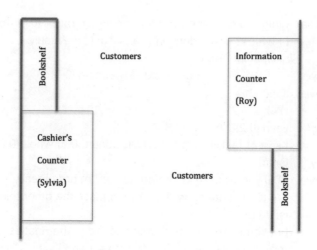

FIGURE 5.1 *Layout of the bookshop.*

Sylvia are employees at a crowded bookshop. They are sitting across from each other at two separate counters, Roy at the information counter and Sylvia at the cashier's counter (see Figure 5.1), and as they are talking, customers are walking back and forth between them. Although their conversation is fully audible to the passing customers, none of them are displaying any indication that they are listening, nor, of course, are they making contributions. Instead, they are displaying what Goffman (1971) calls 'civil inattention'.

In other words, although Roy and Sylvia are the only *ratified* participants in the conversation, it is available to be monitored by any customer close enough to hear it. Whether they are only bystanders (so engrossed in their own business that they do not even 'hear' what Roy and Sylvia are saying), overhearers (who hear and listen to the conversation but do not attend to it), or eavesdroppers (who are actively listening to the conversation, perhaps only pretending to browse the shelves near the counter in order to remain close enough to hear what is going on) is anyone's guess, since none of them openly react to what Ray and Sylvia are saying. We can assume, though, that the ability for the conversation to be monitored by strangers must have some effect on Roy and Sylvia. They may not feel like they are 'performing' for the passers-by, but at least the presence of others may put some constraints on the kind of topics they are willing to discuss and the kind of language they are willing to use.

This interaction could, of course, go on for some time without the fragile social barrier that separates this private conversation from the public context that surrounds it from being breeched. But it does not. Immediately after the last utterance by Sylvia in the excerpt above, a female customer approaches the cashier's counter where Sylvia is seated, and the participation roles change dramatically:

```
29  Roy                         = yeah
30  Sylvia      I had space to myself^ (0.6) uhm (0.3) hello::^
31  Customer    hi
32  (Customer places a book on the counter in front of Sylvia along with
33  her bank card.
34  Sylvia scans the barcode of the book,
35  inserts the customer's card into a mobile keypad,
36  and hands the customer the keypad.
37  The customer enters her PIN
38  and hands the keypad back to Sylvia.
39  Sylvia waits for a moment,
40  removes the receipt from the keypad
41  and hands it to the woman along with her card.
42  The woman takes the receipt and the card, puts them in her wallet,
43  and then picks the book up off the counter and puts it in her bag.)
44  Customer    Thank you (0.1)
45  Sylvia      Thanks
45  Customer    Thank you so much (.) sorry it sounded like an
46              interesting conversation (.) [ca ]continue on=
47  Sylvia                                   [oh]
48  Roy                                                 = he he he
49              [he he
50  Sylvia      [ha ha [ha
51  Customer    (Customer turns to face Roy)
52              [oh hi:: ↑↓ how's [it going↑↓
53  Roy         [how's it goin'↑↓ (0.2)
54  Customer    great↑↓ (.) just got standing room for um (0.2) It's Only
55              a Play. (0.1)
56  Roy         ye[ah:::^
57  Customer      [I'm absolutely] thrilled (.) so happy. (0.2)
58  Roy         Enjoy↑↓
59  Customer    bye (customer begins to leave but stops to browse some
60              SALE books on a table near the entrance)
61              (7.9)
62  Sylvia      yeah I guess well um (.) my brother:: is a chef and he
63              works at (.) eh:: (0.1) this restaurant where he was
64              like^ (0.5) if you:: wanna com'n hang out (0.3) at (.)
65              my (.) rest::rant::^ (0.1) then you can get (0.7) cheap or
66              free drinks 'n food all night °an I'm like:^° hm: that
```

67		sounds good=
68	Roy	= heh [he he
69	Sylvia	[ha ha
70		sss: 'n um::^ (.) 'n I <u>don</u>'t think it'll be that <u>crowded</u> (.)
71		cuz it <u>just</u> opened (.) <u>this</u> year^ (0.7) so::^ it's on the
72		Metropolitan (inaudible) (0.2) °I'm like° (0.3) an::d
73		it itsa good lo<u>ca</u>:tion^ (0.3) ah::m (1.1) but I (0.9)
74		you know I <u>don</u>'t think it'll be tha::t^
75		(1.6)
76	Roy	stop'n grab some food and a drink'n (0.5) go elsewhere
77		(0.2)
78	Sylvia	'n then it's <u>also</u> I just remembered it's like Frank Grady's
79		<u>birth</u>day:^ (0.2) °hmm° (0.4) he always does <u>some</u>thing
80		but I'm not sure::^ (0.6) if he was gonna go
81	Customer	(Calling from the entrance as she leaves) thanks=
82	Roy	=have
83		<u>fu:n</u>
84		(0.6)
85	Sylvia	if he was gonna go (.) <u>out.</u> (.) out^ or if he's gonna have
86		People <u>o:</u>ver^ (0.7) ah::m^ (0.7) then my friend <u>Cindy</u>
87		Is <u>doing</u>::^ (1.5) a <u>slum</u>ber party::^ (1.2) I said like
88		<u>right</u>^ (.) <u>yeah</u>. (0.7) which <u>also</u> be really <u>fun</u> (.)
89		but it's one of those things too where I only know her
90		and her <u>boy</u>^friend^ 'n I don't really know their <u>other</u>
91		friends^ (0.2) 'n so I'm like ( ) (high pitched) °eh::
92		eh::° (1.0) I don know (.) but^ wadda<u>you</u> doing.

What occurs in the initial moves of the excerpt above is that the customer interrupts the conversation between Roy and Sylvia by standing directly in between them. Her intention is not to join the interaction, but rather to begin another interaction, one involving purchasing a book. This, of course, is perfectly natural given Sylvia's role as a cashier and the customer's role as a customer, roles that, in this situation, override Sylvia's relationship with Roy. The interaction the customer is initiating is, in fact, immediately assumed to be more legitimate than the conversation between Sylvia and Roy, to the extent that the customer, initially, sees no need to apologize for the interruption. In this new interaction, the customer and Sylvia are the ratified participants, and Roy becomes a bystander.

Notably, the interaction between Sylvia and the customer takes place in almost complete silence. In fact, it is not very different from the silent conversation between me and the ATM that I described above, one involving such a clear sequence of moves that neither Sylvia nor the customer feels the need to comment on them until the termination of the interaction is singled by an exchange of 'thank yous'. And just as the other customers in the queue behind me at the ATM are not expected to become involved in my interaction with the machine, Roy and the other customers in the shop do not attempt to involve themselves in the interaction between the customer and Sylvia, displaying the same kind of civil inattention that they afforded Roy and Sylvia in their earlier interaction.

But then something very interesting happens. At the end of her interaction with Sylvia, the customer suddenly acknowledges the fact that she has interrupted the conversation between Roy and Sylvia, and even remarks on the quality of that conversation, identifying herself not just as a bystander to the conversation, but as a kind of eavesdropper ('sorry it sounded like an interesting conversation (.) [ca]continue on'). This is an extraordinary remark for a number of reasons, not least of which is that it violates the normal expectations governing interaction orders of this kind, especially those regarding civil inattention. Further evidence for the unusual nature of this remark comes from Sylvia's interjection ('oh') and Roy's laughter. Suddenly, Roy has become a ratified participant in the interaction between Sylvia and the customer, chiefly by virtue of the fact that the customer has identified herself as a participant of sorts in the interaction between Sylvia and Roy.

At this point, however, yet another shift in footing occurs. Just after Roy laughs, the customer turns to him and, as if recognizing him from a previous encounter, begins an entirely new interaction, complete with a greeting sequence ('[oh hi:: ↑↓ how's [it going↑↓' → '[how's it goin'↑↓ (0.2)'], an exchange of small talk, and a closing sequence ('Enjoy↑↓' → 'bye'). In this conversation, it is Sylvia who has been 'frozen out' to some extent, partly because the way the customer begins this interaction seems to claim with Roy a certain shared past experience that Sylvia is not privy to, and partly because the woman physically turns her back on Sylvia to face Roy. It's important to remember, of course, that the woman has not just made herself a participant in a 'private' interaction with Roy, but also a participant in a public performance for other customers who, might actually be eavesdropping in the same way she was eavesdropping on Sylvia and Roy.

Finally, after this conversation ends, and the customer walks away, Sylvia and Roy take up their conversation where they left off, as if they had never been interrupted, with Sylvia continuing to elaborate on her answer to the question about her New Year's Eve plans.

The point I wish to make with this analysis is that participation frameworks in interactions can be incredibly fluid, and the rules governing who is qualified to be a 'ratified' participant can be rather flexible. In other words, rather than seeing interaction orders as imposing strict frameworks for participation onto those present, it is better to see interaction orders as providing for people at particular sites of engagement various affordances and constraints for the *negotiation* of participation. This is in line with Kang's (1998: 140, emphasis mine) definition of the participation framework as a 'conceptual notion that *emerges* in interaction where participants display a shared knowledge of their relationships to one another (i.e., in terms of who is being addressed by whom, who is engaged in conversation, who is expected to respond, etc.)'. At the same time, some interaction orders (and the participation frameworks associated with them) have been technologized to the extent that there is much less room for negotiation. As a cashier in a shop, for example, Sylvia has very little leeway to negotiate her participation with the customer: she would not, for example, be able to ignore her and carry on with her conversation with Roy, at least if she wishes to continue in her job. There are also broader, cultural dimensions to interaction orders. Readers from the United States might, for instance, recognize the customer's insinuating herself into Sylvia and Roy's 'private' conversation as a typical 'involvement strategy' (Scollon, Scollon and Jones 2012), whereas readers from elsewhere might consider it unusual or even 'rude'.

A wider point I wish to make, however, is that in nearly every conversation we engage in, there are always more participants than may be immediately apparent to us. Not only are the customers in the store part of the conversation between Sylvia and Roy, but their boss, who is implicitly present in the form of various rules of workplace conduct that Roy and Sylvia are careful to observe, and might also be more explicitly present in the form of the security camera that watches them from the ceiling. Furthermore, if we examine the conversation more closely, we can identify a whole cast of people who, while they are not present as physical participants, are nevertheless 'speakers' of a sort in the conversation. There is Sylvia's brother, for example, whose words Sylvia animates when she says, 'he was like^ (0.5) if you:: wanna com'n hang out (0.3) at (.) my (.) rest::rant::^ (0.1) then you can get (0.7) cheap or free drinks 'n food all night'. There's also Frank Grady, whose birthday is on New Year's Eve, and Sylvia's friend Cindy and her boyfriend who are having a slumber party, whose invitations to Sylvia become part of her conversation with Roy.

Widening the circumference even more, one might even consider the ticket seller who sold the customer, her ticket to *It's Only a Play*, and those who did not manage to get tickets, members of the 'theatre going community' who recognize the difficulty of getting tickets to this show, and the 'community' of people who frequent bookstores such as this, all to be participants of sorts in this interaction. Bakhtin (1986: 95) considers the range of people that might be considered participants in a conversation (or addressees of an utterance), writing:

This addressee can be an immediate participant ... a differentiated collective of specialists in some particular area of cultural communication, a more or less differentiated public, ethnic group, contemporaries, like-minded people, opponents and enemies, a subordinate, a superior, someone who is lower, higher, familiar, foreign, and so forth. And it can also be an indefinite, unconcretised other. ... All these varieties and conceptions of the addressee are determined by that area of human activity and everyday life to which the given utterance is related.

In Bakhtinian terms, then, footing has to do with how one situates himself or herself in the web of discourse that converges in any interaction involving the words of participants who are present in various ways, and the words of those who are not. From this perspective, participation is not just a matter of participating in a single conversation, but participating in multiple conversations: some occurring at the same time, some having occurred in the past, and some yet to occur.

This complex vision of participation is rendered even more complicated if we consider the effects of various electronic media, which allow people to be present to each other over vast expanses of space and time, and which allow individuals to be present to vast, often undifferentiated audiences. One of the main ways new communication technologies alter the way we manage footing is by creating new kinds of interactional accessibility involving new ways of being present and monitoring others' presence (Jones 2004). In these circumstances, as Katriel (1999: 97) suggests, 'rather than talking about separate interactions, we might talk about an "interactional field" that may encompass both focused interactions and secondary involvements of various kinds'. Another way they alter how we manage footing is by making available new ways of *entextualizing* discourse and of 'replaying' or recontexualizing it in other sites of engagement involving other participants, who can take up various stances in relation to it.

A good example of this can be seen in a story Randy tells of coming out to his colleagues in the Air Force, in which he describes leaving the room to allow them to watch his YouTube channel, and then returning to receive their assessment[1]:

66 ah one day^ at <u>wor:k</u>↑↓ (0.3) ah (.) here in the desert^ we had (0.5) a
67 ban:d (.) come through^ and they wanted to (0.3) play us little private
68 show and I did not want to <u>go.</u> (0.6) ah I had (0.2) more (0.5) I had not
69 more im<u>port</u>ant things^ but I I had things that I wanted to do^ (0.5) and
70 everybody said <u>no:</u>↓↑ () they came out^ (.) they're only gonna be here

---

[1]Available at https://www.youtube.com/watch?v=gNrTdIMFLys.

71 for a little bit^ (.) go listen to em (1.0) so they played↓↑ a show for
72 about (0.6) twenty five of us they played like <u>six</u> songs^ (0.3) um:: (0.2)
73 I $took my ipod$ out and I caught the first song^ (0.3) and it was
74 rolling in the deep video (0.4) an:d ah: I put it up (0.2) ah on my
75 YouTube channel^ coz I hadn't put up a ba y'know in a few weeks^
76 and I was like <u>I'll</u> just y'know put something kinda off subject↑↓ (0.5)
77 I put it up^ (0.3) ah the next morn↑↓ing I wake up^ and it has like^
78 <u>seven</u> (.) <u>tee:</u>n (.) <u>thou</u>sand views↑↓ (0.5) ah:: in about <u>eight</u> hours^
79 (0.4) and I was like that (0.4) $tssss heh heh $ that's crazy^ but
80 im<u>me</u>diately my my <u>sto</u>mach just kinda knotted up and (0.4) coz like
81 man this is tha ohah people've <u>seen</u> this↑↓ you know a lot of people^
82 (1.0) have watched this. (0.3) um:^ (0.4) and so I was like (0.2) I was
83 like (.) <u>really</u> nervous^ I was I was kinda stressed out^ (0.5) and ah:^
84 (0.3) $.hhchaa$ (0.4) so:: ↓↑ (0.3) everybody started realisin like the
85 video was getting <u>bi::g</u>↓↑ (0.4) an:d um:^ (1.0) the next (0.2) <u>night</u> at
86 work^ (0.4) um: : (0.5) aaa:: (0.5) $hhhhh$ it it'd been mentioned on
87 Carson Daily's blog^ (0.5) and somebody^ (0.2) ah: (0.6) at work was
88 actually on a computer and they <u>saw</u>^ that it was on Carson Daily's
89 blog^ (0.5) an::d (0.5) and the caption was y'know (.) spawned off a
90 (0.2) a channel kinda focus around don't ask don't <u>tell</u>↑↓ (1.5) an:d^
91 (0.3) ah (0.8) so she's (.) she was like^ don't ask don't <u>tell</u>↑↓ and I was
92 like^ (.) <u>ye:ah</u> (0.3) it's like $don't worry$ 'bout it (0.3) don (.hh) (0.6)
93 don don^ (0.2) and she was like (.) I wanna <u>watch</u>↑↓ and so she clicks
94 on^ (0.3) the the the music video^ (0.4) an:d ah:^ (0.1) and then: you
95 know (.) of <u>course</u> all my links are in in the side^ and I was like no.
96 (inaudible) (.) it was like watch em <u>later</u>↑↓ watch em y'know when
97 you go home^ and she's like no no I wanna want (.) watch it now. (0.5)
98 an:d ah^ (1.0) it's like no don't don't she was like <u>yeah</u> <u>yeah</u> yeah yeah::
99 I really wanna watch. (0.5) and ah: (.) I said^ (0.3) Okay: um:^ (0.4)
100 and $prob$ probably like six or eight people gathered around that that
101 really wanted to see. (0.5) an:d I was like^ I'm gonna go and take out
102 the trash↑↓ (0.6) I'll be back in:^ fifteen minutes^ (0.5) um:^ (1.0)
103 you're gonna (.) find out eventually just go ahead and I (0.8) pulled
104 one video up and I push play^ (0.5) and I walked out. (1.3) come back
105 like fifteen minutes later:^ and everybody's like (claps hands) (0.5)
106 yeah::eh you know um:^ (0.3) $aha I remember$ I did <u>not</u> wanna I
107 wanted to (0.3) take the trash out forever I did not wanna come back
108 in↑↓ (0.2) and ah: (0.3) I was like^ (.) you know^ if like^ (0.6) <u>less</u>
109 than <u>fifty</u> percent of the people are pissed off I'll be happy I was like^
110 (0.5) if fifty percent^ (0.4) ar: ar: pissed off^ and fifty percent are
111 okay^ (0.2) I will be (0.2) um (0.2) pretty happy with this (0.3) an:d it
112 was <u>not</u>. (.) it was like (.) a lotta people^ (.) were okay with it^ (.) and a

113 lotta people (0.3) were more:↑↓ than okay with it they were like <u>oh</u>
114 y'know^ (.) con$<u>gra</u>tulations$ (0.4) I am not that I <u>did</u> anything^ (0.2)
115 it's like tellin' somebody like congratulations for being (0.5) y'know^ (.)
116 red headed or somethin (.) and it's I I <u>did</u> nothing but (0.9) the fact that
117 I kinda stepped out↑↓ (0.9) $had some <u>really</u> kinda private videos out
118 there^ (0.4) um they were like^ (0.5) y'know ya you're out↑↓ (.) and
119 so^ (0.9) it was (.hh) it was a <u>lot</u> <u>easier</u>^ (0.2) ah a lot <u>smoother</u>
120 process^ and it was <u>not</u> at <u>all</u> how I ever dreamt this this channel
121 would've helped me^ (0.4) ummm (1.0) but I was just^ (0.9) <u>pushed</u>
122 out of the closet I was just^ (0.6) thrown <u>out</u>.

What is interesting about this 'coming out' is that it takes place at the convergence of multiple sites of engagement occurring at different times and in different places. There is the immediate interaction in the office, when one of Randy's colleagues discovers that he has a YouTube channel devoted to 'Don't Ask, Don't Tell'. But this interaction is only made possible by a series of previous interactions, including the ongoing interactions between Randy and his YouTube audience that go back over many months, the interaction between Randy and the musicians in the band that he videos when they come to his base for a concert, the interaction between this video and the thousands of people who viewed it which brought the video (and Randy's channel) to the attention of various bloggers, and then to Randy's colleague sitting in the office.

Each of these overlapping sites of engagement also involve complex participation frameworks, with people variously playing roles as speakers, listeners, performers, audiences, overhearers and evasedroppers. It is Randy's participation as an audience member at the concert, for example, that transforms him into an 'accidental' performer for his colleagues. His previous entextualization of his performances of coming out to a different audience (his YouTube followers) allows him to assume the role of a 'speaker' in the speech act of coming out to them without actually having to speak (or even be in the room). And his colleagues are simultaneously ratified recipients of this speech act and overhearers of it, watching videos of Randy coming out that were filmed months before. What is interesting is the way they react ('I walked out. (1.3) come back like fifteen minutes later:^ and everybody's like (claps hands)' and 'they were like <u>oh</u> y'know^ (.) con$<u>gra</u>tulations$'), reactions more characteristic of an audience appreciating a performance than friends reacting to some delicate news. That is because what they are reacting to is *both* his 'coming out' and his *performance* of coming out.

This convergence of interactions, participation frameworks and production formats is, of course, then further entextualized into a *new* performance – the story that Randy tells in the context of this new video, which he uploads onto YouTube to be watched and commented on by yet other participants, and which, no doubt, has been appropriated in one form or another in interactions involving people Randy does not know and will never meet.

While this example highlights some of the affordances of new media like YouTube to make available new kinds of participation frameworks and production formats, it also illustrates important features that are common to all interactions. All interactions, in fact, take place at the convergence of multiple conversations involving all sorts of people which come together in ways that make certain forms of participation possible at particular sites of engagement. All interactions also in some way involve the appropriation of entextualizations of past discourse, if not in the form of durable texts like digital videos, at least in the form of stories about, references to, and quotations from past interactions. And finally, all conversations are, in a sense, performances of the larger conversations, or what Gee (2011) calls 'big C Conversations', that define our societies. Whether Randy is coming out to his father over the phone, his friend in the front seat of a truck, his millions of followers over YouTube, or his colleagues at work, he is contributing to the larger debates in his society about what it means to be gay, what it means to be a military man, and what it means to 'come out', and in doing so, helping to create for himself and others new opportunities for producing discourse and new frameworks for participation in interactions which, in the past, were not available to him. Here we begin to see more of the 'ethical' dimension of interaction orders that I discussed above; interaction orders are not simply sets of rules that govern how we treat each other, but also sets of opportunities to figure out how to treat each other better.

6

Talk and identity

'Dad, I'm Gay.'

Nobody would dispute that the purpose of this utterance is to claim a particular social identity: the identity of a 'gay man'. But that is not the only identity being claimed. The speaker is also claiming the identity of a son (by identifying his interlocutor as 'Dad'). Moreover, he is claiming an identity as a certain *kind* of son, the kind who has the courage to be 'honest' to his father, and imputing on his father the identity of a certain *kind* of father, one who is potentially able to accept his son's 'real' identity. When this statement is uttered by Randy Phillips in the context of the YouTube video I analysed in the first chapter, other identities also became relevant, such as his identity as a member of the US military, and his identity as a native of Alabama, and his identity as a YouTube celebrity. In fact, the way the identity of 'being gay' works in this and Randy's other videos depends crucially on how it interacts with these other identities. In other words, we rarely claim a single identity in interaction. Instead, we mix together different identities, and these different identities interact and affect each other. A gay son is different from a gay uncle. A gay soldier is different from a gay priest.

At the same time, when you think about it, none of these identities represent who Randy 'really is'. They are simply tools with which he makes relevant certain aspects of himself for the purposes of this interaction. In other interactions he might identify himself as a Christian, a backgammon player, or the owner of a tee-shirt business. Furthermore, no matter how 'honest' he is being in appropriating the identity of a gay man in this conversation with his father, or how accepting the father is of it, the real source of this identity is not his 'true self'; it is his society, which has in many ways 'prefabricated' this identity for him to use to label a combination of feelings, behaviours, dispositions and affiliations that are much more complicated than this label can express. The label is merely a convenient 'peg' (Goffman 1963) onto which to hang these things. As Wortham (2003: 189) puts it, 'Just as any speaker has to "rent" the words he or she uses from the already-used set of words available in a community (Bakhtin 1981), the categories that identify individuals [also] come from the community.' These categories are *technologies of talk*, with their own sets of affordances and constraints regarding what speakers can do with them, and who they can *be* with them.

Like all technologies, however, identities depend on how people use them; not just how individuals construct themselves by appropriating and deploying different identity labels, but how this is done in *collaboration* with other people. Others may choose to ratify the social identities we claim, or challenge them, celebrate them or denigrate them, and often they come to interactions with their own sets of identity labels that they would like to pin on us. When a son 'comes out' to his father, for example, the father may affirm this identity ('I always had my suspicions'), he may deny it ('That's impossible! What about your girlfriend?'), or he may even refuse to recognize it as a legitimate identity at all, calling it a 'phase' or a 'lifestyle'. He may also respond to this identity claim by either ratifying or challenging other identities, saying something like 'You're my son, and I'll always love you' or 'You're no longer a son of mine!' And so this seemingly stable category of being 'gay', as well as categories that seem even more stable, like being someone's 'son', still need to be worked out in interaction. Randy doesn't get to be 'just gay' – in every interaction he enters into, he must work with whomever he is with to construct a particular *way* of being gay. This is not just true for 'coming out' situations. All interactions involve participants negotiating various claims and imputations of identity, trying to work out with each other who they get to be in this particular interaction.

In this chapter, I will approach the problem of identity in spoken discourse, exploring how identities can be simultaneously seen as relatively stable *technologies* that we 'bring along' to interactions in order to accomplish particular social actions, *interactional accomplishments* that we 'bring about' anew in every interaction, and lifelong *projects* that result in the formation of what the Scollons (Scollon 2001; Scollon and Scollon 2004) refers to as our 'historical bodies', the collections of experiences, physical and mental dispositions, and competencies with different technologies of talk that we build up over our lives.

Identity is both wave and particle

In the last chapter, I discussed how social interactions are populated by *participants* who take up roles as different kinds of speakers and listeners. These participants, however, are more than just speakers and listeners of various sorts with various kinds of rights and responsibilities in the interaction order. They are also *social beings* – gay men, fathers, sons and soldiers – people who take up particular roles with various kinds of rights and responsibilities in the social world beyond the interaction order. As Malone (1997: 43) puts it, 'Conversations are populated with a cast of actors, present and absent, whose explicit characterizations and implicit known identities give shape and meaning to the talk.'

Although the notion of identity seems absolutely fundamental to so many social actions involving spoken discourse, from attending a job interview to 'coming out' to your parents, the term 'identity' is actually relatively new in the social sciences, first made popular in the 1950s through the work of psychoanalyst Erick Erickson (1950, 1968, 1975), who invented the idea of the 'identity crisis'. For Erickson, identity is a *psychosocial* construct, the product of the interaction between people's internal sense of a coherent self, their ability to assume the various roles that society makes available for them in the particular 'historical moment' in which they live. An 'identity crisis' occurs when they have difficulty matching up these prefabricated roles with their sense of their 'real' selves.

Those interested in spoken discourse have traditionally taken a less psychological and more sociological perspective on identity. Among sociolinguists there have traditionally been two main ways of understanding identity. One way has been to see it as a matter of fairly fixed demographic categories having to do with things like gender, race, class and profession. This is the perspective that dominated much of the early work in variationist sociolinguistics (see e.g., Labov 1972b; Trudgill 1974), which began with the assumption that 'people talk the way they do because of who they are' (Cameron 2001: 49). Another way to view identity has been to see it as something that is created in and through interaction, a perspective influenced by the work of microsociologists like Goffman and postmodern thinkers like Butler (1993a), Foucault (1976) and Giddens (1991). According to this perspective, identities are socially constructed and 'marked by indeterminacy and irreducible situational contingency' (Androutsopoulos and Georgakopoulou 2003: 1); even seemingly stable social categories like 'man', 'woman', 'gay' and 'straight' are seen as attributes that we 'perform' rather than possess (Butler 1993a).

Most of those researching language and identity today subscribe to neither of these extreme views. For them, identity is 'both wave and particle', both a matter of assuming fairly stable roles and category labels, and of interactionally 'creating ourselves' as we go along. One example of this more 'hybrid' position can be seen in the work of Bucholtz and Hall (2005: 585), who write:

Identities encompass macro-level demographic categories, temporary and interactionally specific stances and participant roles, and local, ethnographically emergent cultural positions; ... identity may be in part intentional, in part habitual and less than fully conscious, in part an outcome of interactional negotiation, in part a construct of others' perceptions and representations, and in part an outcome of larger ideological processes and structures. It is therefore constantly shifting both as interaction unfolds and across discourse contexts.

This position is, in fact, not inconsistent with that staked out by the sociolinguist Robert le Page more than thirty years ago. 'A person's identity is', wrote le Page and Tabouret-Keller in *Acts of Identity* (1985: 316), their seminal work on language and ethnicity, 'a heterogeneous set made up of all the names or identities given or taken up by her. But in a lifelong process, identity is endlessly created anew, according to various social constraints, social interactions, encounters, and wishes that may happen to be very subjective and unique.'

A simpler way of saying this is that identity is fundamentally a matter of social action – a matter of *doing* rather than *being*, or, as le Page and Tabouret-Keller (1985: 14) put it, 'a series of *acts of identity* in which people reveal both their personal identity and their search for social roles'. Like all social actions, acts of identity depend crucially on the kinds of tools – the inventory of roles and the 'equipment' for playing them (Goffman 1959) – that are available in particular sociocultural settings. Like all technologies, those which we use to perform 'who we are' in social life have affordances and constraints. Identities can grant or deny access to particular kinds of cultural tools and other social goods. They can be used to claim the right to participate in certain kinds of interactions in certain kinds of ways, or to avoid participating in other kinds of interactions. They can give us power over other people, or make us the subjects of others' power.

Also, like all technologies of talk, social identities are always situated in complex intertextual relationships with other tools that make up Discourses, and because of this it is possible to assume identities in rather indirect ways, simply by employing some other tool (such as a social language) that is also part of that Discourse. More importantly, though, whether social actors appropriate explicit identity labels, by, for example, declaring 'I'm gay', or implicit ones, by deploying some other tool that *indexes* that identity, they are aligning themselves to the ideologies and agendas of some Discourse.

At the same time, as with the other technologies of talk that I have discussed in this book, the affordances and constraints of social identities are not determinative of the actions that people can take with them. Identity is also something that is open to negotiation, dynamically constructed by people as they appropriate different tools (including identity labels like 'gay' and straight, social practices like 'coming out', and various ways of talking, acting, dressing and using objects and social spaces) into specific social contexts (sites of engagement), mixing and adapting them in sometimes unpredictable ways.

One useful way of understanding the relationship between identity and spoken discourse, then, is to think of identity as having two dimensions: the dimension of identity that we 'bring along' to our interactions (as cultural tools), and that dimension that we 'bring about' by the way that we use those tools (Zimmerman 1998; see also Baynham 2014). Agha (2007: 236) refers to these two kinds of identity as 'enregistered' identities and 'emergent' identities. He writes:

> A person's enregistered identities often create default perceptions of that person among those acquainted with the relevant stereotype. But a person's emergent identities depend on text-in-context relations between signs that occur in their actual behaviours in particular encounters.

Of course, these two kinds of identities are inextricably intertwined: whatever identities we are able to 'bring about' are partly the result of the technologies of talk we have 'brought along'. Although identities like 'gay' and 'straight' may not constitute our 'real selves', we often need such labels in order to make ourselves recognizable to other people. At the same time, these identities are themselves the result of countless efforts by individuals and groups to 'bring about' their social selves in particular circumstances through the appropriation of particular cultural tools and the association of those tools with other tools and with certain bodies of knowledge about tool use, a process that I referred to in Chapter 3 as *technologization*.

Rather than speaking of identities, Hall (1996) suggests that a more productive way of understating this relationship between what is brought along and what is brought about is in terms of *identification*, the ongoing process through which social actors claim and impute identities and position themselves within the systems of meaning of their cultures. Identification is not always a straightforward or easy process. First of all, it is often just as much a matter of rejections, refusals or disavowals as it is a matter of claims and imputations (Kulick 2003b). That is to say, one common way of identifying who we are is by identifying who we are *not*. Second, the repertoire of identities we have available to claim for ourselves and to impute onto others is never freely chosen by us, but rather provided (and constrained) by the dominant Discourses circulating in the sociocultural environments in which we happen to find ourselves (De Fina 2015; Gee 2011), Discourses within which 'some kinds of identifications are authorized, legitimate and unmarked, and others are unauthorized, illegitimate, and marked' (Kulick 2003b: 149). At the same time, these Discourses themselves are not stable, but always in flux, so that identities that were perfectly legitimate in the past might now be illegitimate, and those that in the past might have been marked (like 'gay') are increasingly less marked. Finally, claims and imputations only work if they are *recognized* (Gee 2011) by others, and even after they have been recognized, they are always subject to challenge, negotiation and revision.

Identities that are 'brought along'

For identities to be 'brought along' into interaction requires two things: that there is an inventory of 'technologized' identities (or, as Wortham [2003: 193] calls them, 'metadiscourses of identity') available to social actors, and second, that there exists some means by which to signal or 'invoke' them. These identities and 'means of identification' together constitute what Gee (2012, 2014) refers to as 'identity kits'. 'The workings of society and history', he writes (2014: 153),

> have given rise to innumerable kits with which we can live out our social lives as different and multiple kinds of people, different for different times and places ... as men, women, workers, students, gamers, lovers, bird watchers, environmentalists, radicals, conservatives, feminists, African-Americans, scientists, bar members (lawyers or drinkers) of different types, and so on and so forth through an endless and changing list.

These identity kits circulate through societies, becoming available to different individuals based on a variety of circumstances and criteria, and individuals develop their own individual identities as a result of the range of identity kits that they have access to and the ways they adopt these kits to identify themselves, or others adopt them to assign identities to them. It is these identity kits that allow individuals to negotiate acts of identification across interactions and over time, and as they do so, they also contribute to the ongoing technologization of these identities (Wortham 2003).

In one sense, this notion of 'identity kits' is similar to Goffman's (1959) idea of personal 'fronts', the 'expressive equipment' that social actors have access to to perform different roles in their lives, rather like the costumes, props, scripts and stage sets that actors use. Like 'fronts', identity kits include not just semiotic tools, but physical ones as well, such as badges and uniforms, stethoscopes and picket signs. In speaking of 'fronts', however, Goffman, has little to say about the social or ideological nature of this expressive equipment, nor about how different pieces of equipment might be related. What distinguishes 'identity kits' from 'fronts' is the idea that the tools in an identity kit are related to one another in a coherent way as parts of Discourses. The intertextual relationships between tools in an identity kit also make it possible for users to mix the tools from different kits in such a way that these tools can both retain their ability to index the Discourses from which they come and contribute to the construction of new or 'compound identities', (such as 'gay Southern Baptist airman') and eventually, perhaps, new identity kits.

The way in which identity kits are used, then, is often a complex business. It rarely involves just pinning a label on oneself or another person, dressing in a certain way, or speaking a particular social language. Typically, performing social identities involves deploying multiple tools in a particular identity kit together in ways that 'work' in particular social circumstances. As Ochs (1993) points out, the relationship between language and identity is not 'a straightforward mapping of linguistic form to social meaning'. Rather, she says, identity is 'constituted and mediated by the relation of language to stances, social acts, social activities, and other social constructs' (Ochs 1993: 336–7). While indexing identities is sometimes simply a matter of deploying some semiotic or material tool from a particular identity kit that directly 'points' to that identity, more often than not, it involves making more indirect indexical links. One might use a tool that enacts a particular stance towards others in an interaction, or performs some kind of recognizable social practice, or indexes another identity altogether, and these stances, practices and other identities may indirectly point to the original identity. In other words, identity kits are rarely self-contained; they are linked in complex intertextual relationships to other identity kits and to sets of social practices, social relationships and social groups and institutions.

Identity kits can develop around all sorts of different types of identities: types based on attributes like gender, race and sexuality; on political affiliation; on profession and other group membership of various kinds; on where one lives or comes from; on dietary choices; or on one's participation in particular types of activities (like birdwatching), attraction to particular types of sexual partners ('rice-queens'), or preoccupation with particular kinds of cultural products (Lady Gaga Fans). Many of these identity kits include some kind of explicit label associated with the identity that we can use in acts of identification (e.g., 'I'm gay', or 'she's conservative'), but not always, and sometimes these labels change or become matters of contention between different groups who may want to use them for different purposes or may wish to police the way they are used (as is the case with what has become known in the United States as the 'N word'). Other tools typically found in identity kits include social languages, speech genres and other ways of speaking associated with certain kinds of people, social practices and norms of behaviour, and various kinds of physical objects and physical spaces. Agha (2007: 4) refers to these tools as 'enregistered emblems of identity'.

Obviously, not all identity kits are available to everyone. Some kits are only available to people of a particular gender or age or from a particular place. Others – like those of doctors, lawyers and university professors – require some kind of institutional credential as a prerequisite to using them. But the issuing of credentials is really just a means of making explicit something that is true of all identity kits – the fact that just having access to a collection of tools is not enough; one must also have attained some degree of *mastery* over those tools, mastery that typically comes through long interaction with other users of the same tools.

Among the most important kinds of identities that we bring along to social interactions are those based on social relationships. All identities, of course, are in some way relational. Teachers depend on having students; salespeople depend on having customers; soldiers must be parts of armies; and presidents must have countries or organizations to lead. But for some identities, the relational aspect is central, identities such as 'father' and 'son', for example. People often use relational labels in acts of identification, such as 'Hi Daddy', and 'I love you, Son,' or they might use labels which call attention to some aspect of the 'face system' (Scollon, Scollon and Jones 2012, see below) associated with these relationship, terms of address such as 'honey' or 'sir'. Other means of identification commonly used for relational identities are what Goffman (1971) refers to as 'tie signs': tools such as wedding rings, school uniforms, hand-holding practices, and shared objects which communicate to others that two or more people are somehow 'together'.

In many societies, relational identities, especially those around kinship, are among the most thoroughly technologized, and the act of identifying oneself or someone else as, for example, someone's son, wife, sister or father, is a way of claiming and imputing a very clear social status and set of rights and obligations (Enfield 2013). Often, in fact, appropriating labels, terms of address or other tools which index such identities is a way of asserting these rights and obligations. This can be seen in the following exchange between Randy and his father:

    Dad   yer my son:: (1.5) 'n I'm very <u>proud</u> of you: (1.1) okay?
          (0.8)
    Son   <u>yes</u> sir:
          (2.5)
    Dad   'n I will always love you:
          (2.3)
    Son   thanks (0.3) thanks Dad (1.0) I wasn't sure <u>what</u> you'd say:

In this example, the identity label 'son' is being used by Randy's father as a tool not just to ratify a relational identity but also to communicate acceptance.

In a sense what he is saying is that the rights and obligations associated with this identity essentially supersede any threats to the relationship that Randy may imagine his being gay might bring. By responding to his son's invocation of a 'gay' identity by imputing the 'son' identity, he shifts the terms of the conversation from the rather uncertain ground of what he might think of homosexuality to the more certain ground of what obligations a father has to his son, and Randy cooperates in this shift, ratifying his 'son' identity by calling his father 'sir' and 'Dad'.

Another example of the utility of using explicit labels for relational identities comes from Sacks (1992a: 711):

A kid comes into the parents' bedroom in the morning and says to his father, 'Can we have breakfast?' His father says, 'Leave Daddy alone, he wants to sleep'

What's interesting about this example is that the father combines his use of this identity label with his assumption of a particular 'footing' in the interaction (see last chapter). By referring to himself in the third person ('Daddy') rather than the first person ('I'), he is able to invoke his 'father' identity (and the rights associated with it, including the right to be 'left alone') without having to say straight out something like: 'I'm your father and I have the right to tell you what to do.'

Other identities that often have labels and particular terms of address attached to them are what van Leeuwen (1996) calls functional identities, identities based on things that people *do* like occupations ('police officer', 'senator', 'doctor', and 'sergeant'), pastimes ('mountaineer', 'bird-watcher'), or social practices associated with political or economic orders ('insurgent', 'asylum seeker'). Still others are based on things like the place where one lives or is from ('American', 'Southerner'), physical or psychological attributes ('extrovert', 'diabetic'), or political or philosophical beliefs ('Christian', 'conservative', 'existentialist').

Among the most widely invoked identities in most contemporary societies are those based on race, gender and sexuality, One thing that makes these categories special is their perceived *embodied* nature. Many of the identities mentioned above (like those associated with professions, social practices and political beliefs) are, to a large degree, seen as voluntary identities (Scollon, Scollon and Jones 2012), identities that people choose to take on. The categories of race and gender, on the other hand, are generally seen as involuntary – identities that we are 'born with'. That is not to say that these identities are not socially constructed or that they do not need to be 'performed' anew in every interaction. It is just that these identities have been so thoroughly technologized by most societies, so intimately associated with certain physical traits, that people born with these traits who do not wish to take on the labels and other forms of expressive equipment in the 'culturally approved' identity kits associated with these categories are bound to have a hard time. Of course, what counts as 'culturally approved' racial and gender identities is always changing and varies from society to society.

Sexuality is different. While race and gender have a long history of being seen as embodied identities, sexuality has only recently come to be seen in this way, and, at least in the society in which Randy lives, there are still some who refuse to regard homosexuality as an identity you are 'born with'. I have already described in previous chapters Foucault's (1976) description of how Western constructions of homosexuality changed from treating it as a practice to treating it as a 'species'. Whether or not one regards being gay (or any other identity) as voluntary or involuntary, or, to use van Leeuwen's (1996) words, as a matter of 'doing' or a matter of 'being', of course has serious consequences for how social actors are able to use these identities to perform social actions. Gays, lesbians, bisexuals and transgendered people who manage to have these identities regarded as embodied, for example, are in a much better position to argue that they be treated in the same way that gender and racial identities are. This struggle over whether sexual identities get defined in terms of 'doing' or in terms of 'being' is something that plays out not just in 'Big C Conversations' on issues such as same sex marriage and non-discrimination laws, but also in small c conversations like that between Randy and his mother in which they negotiate the legitimacy of the identity that he claims:

```
77  Mom   (2.0)
78        yeah ↑↓ (0.5) so when did this come about ↑↓
79  Son   (1.2)
80        prolly when I was about five^
81  Mom   (5.5)
82        why? (0.6)
83  Son   I've I've always known Mom (.) I've always (0.3)
84        (0.4) always always known (2.2) I've always known
85        (0.6) I've always known
```

In this excerpt, Randy's mother frames his gay identity as something that has 'come about', and which, presumably, can change again in the future. In response, Randy frames it as something that he has discovered, not decided upon, and something that he was been aware of since early childhood. In the excerpt below, he similarly argues that this identity is an essential part of his self in response to his mother labelling it a 'concept':

217		I may not under<u>stand</u> that <u>concept</u>^
218		(0.5)
219	Son	well^=
220	Mom	=but that doesn't mean I don't <u>love</u> you
221	Son	(4.5)
222		it's not a concept (0.9) it's it's who I <u>am</u> (0.9)
223		it's it's why^ (0.9) you like who you like^ (0.3)
224		and it's why::^ (0.1) my sisters like who they like^
225		(1.0) a::nd^ (1.6) I've (.) <u>a</u>lways been that way Mom↓↑
226		(0.6) it's not something I just de<u>cided</u> (0.7) this
227		weeken::d^ or last yea::r^ or^
228		(1.6)
229		<u>a</u>lways (0.4) ana (.) ap (.) um (0.3) I <u>knew</u>^
230		(2.9) a <u>long</u> time ago Mom↑↓

Randy's strategy in this conversation is a local version of a broader identity strategy adapted by the LGBT community over past few decades which Spivak (1987) calls 'strategic essentialism', a strategy of presenting gay and lesbian identity as an inviolable 'social fact' (Mehan 1993). The strategy that his mother is using is also a version of a broader strategy practised by those opposed to equal rights for gays and lesbians which we might call 'strategic de-essentialism', a strategy of framing gay and lesbian identity as a matter a 'choice', a 'lifestyle'. What this conflict illustrates is that sometimes the same identity label can be associated with very different identity kits and be used to take very different kinds of social actions. Another thing it highlights is the fact that deploying tools from a particular identity kit is only half the work of claiming an identity. That identity and your right to assume it must also be *recognized* and regarded as legitimate by others.

Gee (2011: 31) calls the discursive processes we use to claim identities that others will *recognize as legitimate* and genuine as 'recognition work'. Sometimes recognition work is accomplished explicitly using credentials like diplomas, licences, badges or identification cards. More often however, recognition work involves displaying our ability to deploy different technologies of talk (ways of speaking, acting, valuing and using various objects and symbols) in ways that others view as competent (Gee 2011; Hymes 1971). Claiming to be a skateboarder, at least in many skateboarding communities, involves not just being able to skateboard, but also being able to talk in certain ways, dress in certain ways, and interact with other skateboarders in certain ways (for details see Jones 2011). Gee gives an example, based on the work of Wieder and Pratt (1990), of the ways native Americans recognize each other as 'real Indians'. Being a 'real Indian' is not just a matter of kinship or genetics. It involves being able to perform a whole host of discursive practices related to when to speak and what to speak about, when to keep silent, how to treat different kinds of people, and how to move one's body and direct one's gaze. The main point that Gee (and Wieder and Pratt) make is that 'doing being a real Indian' is not something that one can do alone. 'One cannot be a "real Indian"', writes Gee (2014a: 145) unless one appropriately recognizes other 'real Indians' and gets recognized by others as a 'real Indian'. Bucholtz and Hall (2005) refer to these same processes under the label of 'authentication', arguing that claiming social identities always involves claims about the authenticity or genuineness of those identities. Of course, as Randy's conversation with his mother illustrates, it is even more difficult to get someone to recognize your claim to an identity as legitimate if they don't recognize the identity you are claiming as legitimate.

Struggles over which identities can be claimed and imputed by different people, what these identities mean, and how they can be used are a common part of many interactions, particularly those involving what Goffman calls 'people processing' in which those with some kind of institutional authority – 'priests, psychiatrists, school teachers, police, generals, government leaders, parents, males, whites, nationals, media operators, and all the other well-placed persons' (Goffman 1983a: 17) – are put in the position of identifying others as particular kinds of people. What is important in such situations is the fact that the ways people are labelled is dependent on the kinds of identities that gatekeepers themselves have available to them. In his study of the labelling of a student as 'learning disabled', for example, Mehan (1993) examines how the various people involved – the student's teacher, his parents, the school psychologist, and a medical officer – contributed differently to this identification based on the different identity kits that they themselves brought to the process, with some (like the psychologist) able to exercise more control over the process than others (like the child's parents).

Another example – which is historically relevant to Randy's struggle with the military's 'Don't Ask, Don't Tell' policy – is the role that psychiatrists have played in screening practices to weed out potentially gay military recruits starting from the beginning of the Second World War. Prior to that time, the US military had no policy of excluding homosexuals. Instead, what was prohibited was the *act* of 'sodomy'. In 1941, however, psychiatric testing was introduced into the Selective Service process, in part, argues Bérubé (2010), as a result of efforts by powerful people in the psychiatric profession, such as Harry Stack Sullivan (ironically a gay man himself), to show how psychiatry could contribute to the war effort. These new screening procedures, along with the various practices of 'diagnosis, hospitalization, surveillance, interrogation, discharge, administrative appeal, and mass indoctrination' (Bérubé 2010: 2) associated with them not only served to institutionalize the identity of the homosexual as a 'certain kind of person' within the military, but also served to institutionalize the identity of the military psychiatrist as the main person in charge of managing this new administrative apparatus.

Both of these examples illustrate, first of all, that acts of claiming identities for ourselves and imputing them onto others always involve the exercise of power. They always involve differential access to particular identity kits and the technologies of talk associated with them, and they always involve some people having more power than others to *identify* or, to use Althusser's (1971: 174) term, to 'hail' people into subject positions.

Further complicating our understanding of 'brought along' identities as cultural tools is the fact that identity labels can take on different meanings and serve different purposes in different situations and for different communities. Sometimes, individuals or groups may appropriate identity labels in ways that are only loosely associated with the actual people they are usually used to label. An example of this can be seen in the practice of adolescent boys in the United States regularly calling one another 'fags'. In her study of 'fag discourse' in a American high school, Pascoe (2005) describes how the young men she studied appropriated the label 'fag' for a variety of social purposes, including creating group solidarity, excluding certain people from the group or from an activity, enforcing norms of behaviour, and, most importantly, claiming their own masculinity. While 'fag discourse' undeniably indexes homosexuality and, more generally, non-masculine behaviour, to call someone a fag in this context is not the same a calling them 'gay'. 'The "fag" identity,' writes Pascoe (2005: 339) 'is a fluid one, certainly an identity that no boy wants, but one that a boy can escape, usually by engaging in some sort of discursive contest to turn another boy into a fag'. 'Few boys are permanently identified as fags; most move in and out of fag positions ... the term can be invested with different meanings in different social spaces' (342). 'Fag' may be used as a weapon with which to temporarily assert one's masculinity by denying it to others, or it can be taken on temporarily as an identity performance, as when a boy imitates a 'fag' in order to show that he is not one. In such situations then, claims of identity like 'I'm gay' and imputations of identity like 'you're a fag' rarely invoke 'real' gay identity. In fact, most of the boys whom Pascoe interviewed said that they would actually never use the term fag to refer to an 'actual homosexual person' (337).

What this example highlights is the fact that identities are always *situated*, and that different enregistered emblems of identity can have different meanings and different uses in different situations. That's not to say that when high school boys use the word 'fag' it is not offensive to 'actual homosexual persons'. What it means is that 'brought about' identities have a wide range of social purposes apart from simply identifying people, purposes such as joking, challenging people and enforcing group norms.

Identities that are 'brought about'

As the discussion above makes clear, claims and imputations of identity are never solely individual acts. Instead, people produce their social selves 'through processes of contestation and collaboration' with others (Bucholtz 1999a: 12). Simply having access to tools from a particular identity kit is not enough to successfully 'pull off' an identity in social interaction. As Auer (1992: 22) points out, 'A "doctor" is not a doctor because he or she holds a diploma and a "patient" isn't a patient because s/he has entered a "doctor's office"; but both become incumbents of the complementary roles of "doctor" and "patient" because of the way in which they interact, taking on the rights and obligations of the partners in this unequal relationship.' In fact, it is these 'situationally emergent identities' (Erickson and Schultz 1982) that affect how people are able to use the identities that they have brought along, and how things like unequal power relationships ultimately play out.

Among the strategies people use to manage the moment by moment emergence of identity are strategies of *impression management*, (Goffman 1959), involving various practices of revealing and concealing certain aspects of ourselves to others, *politeness strategies* (Brown and Levinson 1987), the ways in which we encode our relationships with those with whom we are interacting in discourse, and *positioning strategies* (Davies and Harré 1990), the ways in which we use the identities we have 'brought along' to construct socially coherent 'stories' out of our interactions.

In this book, I have been using the example of 'coming out' in the context of the military's 'Don't Ask, Don't Tell' policy to illustrate various aspects of spoken discourse. But all interactions, even those that involve more mundane practices like buying a book in a bookstore or chatting about what you are going to do on New Year's Eve, involve questions of 'asking' and 'telling', decisions about what information and how much of it we are willing to reveal to our interlocutors. Goffman compared impression management to a card game (1967: 32). A hand may be played in a variety of ways, and opponents have only a limited idea of the hand itself from seeing how the player plays it. Each play is a partial result of what cards have already been played and of what the player is planning to do in the long run. Thus some plays may be attempts to get an opponent to play a particular card or see how he or she will react, to fish for information on what an opponent intends.

This analogy reminds us that claims to identity may not be explicit or straightforward, that often they are partial, implicit, hedged, and contingent on the kinds of claims that other people make or the ways they respond to indirect emblems of identity that we have offered. The practice of 'coming out' as it is engaged in by many LGBT people is a good illustration of the complexity of the 'information game' involved in claiming and imputing social identities. As we have seen from Randy's experiences (discussed in the last two chapters), coming out is not simply a matter of telling someone you're gay; it often involves a range of strategies of concealment and disclosure that play out across time with various audiences. Psychologists interested in the way gays and lesbians manage their social identities have spoken of 'coming out' as a practice that usually occurs in stages, including 'passing', 'covering', being implicitly 'out', being explicitly 'out' to selected people, publicly 'affirming' one's identity, and becoming integrated into the 'gay community' (Griffin 1992; Croteau 1996). Within any of these stages, however, they might engage in various creative acts of masking and displaying their sexual identity to, as Liang (1999: 18) puts it, 'protect themselves from the dangers of homophobia while locating themselves in solidarity with listeners who are familiar with these strategies'. Orne (2011) refers to the way gays and lesbians produce and reproduce different, sometimes ambiguous, versions of gay identity as 'strategic outness', a term which highlights the essentially partial and contingent nature of being 'out'.

At the same time, however, strategies of identity management often raise issues of recognition and authenticity (see above). In some circumstances, for example, a person who is seen as being unwilling to 'own up' to a particular identity might be seen as inauthentic or cowardly. In fact, one of the consequences of the technologization of the social practice of 'coming out' is the creation of a new set of identities, those of the 'out' and the 'closeted' gay or lesbian (Rasmussen 2004). In other circumstances, however, one might be seen as inauthentic for 'flaunting' a particular identity.

As is obvious from Randy's experiences with his YouTube channel, the kinds of media one has available with which to play this 'information game' (Goffman 1959) can also have a dramatic effect on the impression management strategies one can use. Media can make available 'involvement screens' which allow people to be much more selective about the kinds of information they 'give off' to others, as we saw with Randy's early videos in which his face was invisible (see Chapter 3). At the same time, they can also limit people's ability to control the way information about them is circulated, as occurred when Randy was 'exposed' to his colleagues when a video on his YouTube channel went 'viral' (see Chapter 5).

Another important set of strategies that people use to manage the moment by moment emergence of identity involves what is referred to by linguists and discourse analysts as 'politeness' (Brown and Levinson 1987; Leech 1983). What is meant by politeness in this context is not 'being nice' to other people or obeying the rules of etiquette associated with different situations (although such behaviours might, in certain circumstances, constitute 'politeness strategies'). What it means is the way we use language and other technologies of talk to negotiate our relationships with others in interaction, especially relationships of intimacy (how close we are to them) and relationships of power (the degree to which one person is able to exercise power over another). Since all social identities are essentially relational, a big part of negotiating claims and imputations of identity involves negotiating signals of intimacy and power. Part of being a parent, for example, might be communicating a certain amount of closeness towards one's child, and part of being a teacher may involve communicating a certain amount of power over one's students. But politeness strategies provide ways not just of ratifying the social relationships associated with certain social identities, but also of modulating and modifying them, so one can, for example, enact identities of a 'strict parent' or a 'friendly teacher'.

Politeness strategies are sometimes called 'face strategies', because they give participants in conversations a way to work together to protect each other's 'faces'. 'Face', in Goffman's definition, is 'the positive social value a person effectively claims for himself by the line others assume he has taken' in an interaction (1967: 41). In other words, face has to do with getting the identities that we are claiming recognized by others. But for politeness theorists, it is much more complicated than that, having to do with two fundamental needs that people experience in social life: the need to be 'liked'(sometimes called *positive face*) and the need to be 'respected' (sometimes called *negative face*). In many ways, these two needs are contradictory – showing too much intimacy towards a person who has a higher status than you can be seen as disrespectful, and showing two much respect to someone you are close to can be seen as cold. In every interaction we need to negotiate and sometimes adjust the degree of intimacy and respect we show to the people with whom we are interacting, depending on who we trying to be, and who we think they are trying to be. We use politeness strategies, however, not just to show what kind of relationship we think we have with other people, but also to negotiate and sometimes even change those relationships.

Strategies used to show intimacy are known as 'involvement strategies' (or *positive* politeness strategies) (Scollon, Scollon and Jones 2012; Tannen 1984). They include things like using informal forms of address (such as first names or nicknames), claiming common opinions, interests, knowledge and/or group membership, expressing interest or concern, using common social languages or speech genres, and being talkative. Strategies used to show respect are called 'independence strategies' (or *negative* politeness strategies), and they include using formal titles like 'mister' or 'professor', avoiding making assumptions about others, trying to avoid imposing on people and apologizing when you do, using formulaic or ritualistic language like 'please' and 'thank you', and being taciturn. When we use these different strategies we communicate not just closeness or distance (with close friends using more involvement strategies and strangers using more independence strategies), but also power: people who are more powerful are freer to use involvement strategies to those who are less powerful, but the less powerful are usually obliged to use involvement strategies to the more powerful.

Since power and distance are relative rather than absolute, and because interaction often involves some negotiation of power and distance, people usually employ both independence and involvement strategies, mixing them tactically depending on the situation and what they are trying to accomplish in the interaction. Although in most interactions that we enter into, we have a pretty good idea about what sort of relationship we have with the people with whom we are talking, we can also use these strategies to negotiate changes to the relationship. A good example of this can be seen in the conversation in the bookstore which I discussed in the last chapter:

```
44  Customer  Thank you (0.1)
45  Sylvia     Thanks
45  Customer  Thank you so much (.) sorry it sounded like an
46                 interesting conversation (.) [ca ]continue on=
47  Sylvia                                   [oh]
48  Roy                                                  = he he he
49                 [he he
50  Sylvia     [ha ha [ha
51  Customer  (Customer turns to face Roy)
52                 [oh hi:: ↑↓ how's [it going↑↓
53  Roy        [hows it's goin'↑↓ (0.2)
```

In the beginning of this excerpt, both Sylvia and the customer are using independence strategies: having maintained a respectful distance from each other during the transaction, they are closing the transaction with a ritual exchange of 'thank yous'. After this, however, the customer executes a pivot from independence to involvement, first by injecting a degree of enthusiasm into her final 'thank you' ('Thank you so much'), and then by revealing that she has been listening to their private conversation, behaviour that would only be expected from an intimate. Interestingly, she couches this show of involvement in the language of independence, an apology, and then goes on to use language that (half mockingly) asserts her power over them, giving them 'permission' to 'continue on'. The effect of the complex mix of independence and involvement strategies in this utterance is to transform the identities of the people involved from 'shop clerks' and a 'customer' to 'friends' (or at least friendly acquaintances), a transformation that is completed when the customer turns to Roy and greets him like an intimate: 'oh hi:: ↑↓'.

This example demonstrates that politeness strategies are not simply used to ratify existing identities and relationships, but also to claim and impute new identities and relationships. Since different social identities like 'customer' and 'teacher' come with certain expectations about how people claiming these identities should treat others and be treated by them, politeness strategies can be a way of indexing certain identities (Ochs 1993). This is even true for gender identities. Holmes (1988, see also Ochs 1993), for example, shows how femininity can be indexed by using politeness strategies like paying compliments, and Pascoe (2005), whose work I discussed above, shows how, among groups of adolescent boys, ritual insults like calling someone a 'fag' can be a way of showing solidarity and indexing masculinity.

Even in interactions in which the relationship between the parties is very clear, social actors can use independence and involvement strategies strategically to orient towards different aspects of their relationship. This type of oscillation between independence and involvement is especially apparent in relationships between parents and children, as can be seen in the following exchange between Randy and his father:

Dad   yer my son:: (1.5) 'n I'm very proud of you: (1.1) okay?
       (0.8)
Son   yes sir:

What Randy accomplishes through his use of the more formal 'yes sir' in this exchange is not so much to create distance between him and his father as to frame his father's previous utterance of acceptance as 'authoritative' and to ratify the hierarchal father–son relationship that his father is orienting to.

A third important set of strategies that people use to manage the emergent nature of social identity is known as 'positioning strategies'. Davies and Harré (1990: para 18) define positioning as

the discursive process whereby selves are located in conversations as observably and subjectively coherent participants in jointly produced storylines. By giving people parts in a story, whether it be explicit or implicit, a speaker makes available a subject position which the other speaker in the normal course of events would take up.

The concept of positioning is based on the idea that whenever we interact with others we are basically composing 'stories' in which we and the people we are talking to play 'characters'. The 'storylines' of particular interactions, such as the phone call between Randy and his father, on the one hand tend to constitute coherent 'stories' in and of themselves (which is one reason why issues like closing an interaction, which I discussed in the last chapter, are so important). On the other hand, each interaction is also part of the longer storyline of the relationship between the people who are interacting (Randy's ongoing relationship with his father, for example), and also draw upon larger cultural or societal storylines (such as the more general 'story' of sons coming out to their fathers or the more specific 'stories' of gay rights in America or the history of the 'Don't Ask, Don't Tell' policy). Often, of course, multiple storylines converge at a single site of engagement, and participants discursively orient towards these different storylines and position themselves and the other person in them by saying things like 'yer my son:: (1.5) 'n I'm very <u>proud</u> of you', or 'do you know what it says in the Bible about that?'

One of the important things about discursive positions and the storylines which they promote is that they often provide the context in which speech acts are interpreted (see Chapter 4). 'Your my son, and I'm very proud of you' has a different illocutionary force when uttered by a father whose son has just 'come out' and one whose son has just gotten a good grade on an arithmetic test, and 'Do you know what the Bible says about that?' has a different meaning when uttered by a mother to a gay son and when uttered by a parishioner to a priest. Identifying speech acts requires an understanding of the storylines within which the acts occur and the kinds of discursive positions that those storylines make available. Just as storylines and characters help to create speech acts, however, speech acts also help to create storylines and position participants in them. Utterances like 'I'm gay', 'I do', and 'Stop in the name of the law!' all invoke well-worn cultural storylines and position their utterers as a gay man 'coming out', a bride or bridegroom getting married, or a police officer in pursuit of a suspect, respectively.

Positioning doesn't just involve collaboratively composing stories, but also managing our 'footing' in relation to those stories, communicating how much responsibility we wish to take for their authoring. Bamberg and his colleagues (2011) for example, examine how positioning relates to footing in the following conversation, which takes place among a group of fifteen-year-old boys and an adult moderator (Mod) about the existence of gay boys at their school.

```
1   Ed:     there ARE some gay boys at Cassidy
2   Mod:    do they – (-T-) – do they suffer in eh at your schools
3           do they are they talked about in a way//
4   Ed:     I don't think there are any -I – don't – think there are any
5           openly gay kids – at – school
6   James:  Ah yeah there are
7   Ed:     wait there's one
8           – there's one I know of
9   James:  actually (.) I know a few of them
10          I don't KNOW them but I've SEEN them
```

```
11  Ed:      how can you tell they're gay
12  Alex:    yeah you can't really tell
13  James:   no (.) like how do I know they're gay <rising voice>
14  Ed:      yeah
15  James:   well (.) he's an 11th-grade student (.) the kid I know
16           I'm not gonna mention names
17  Ed:      all right (.) who are they <both hands raising>
18  James:   okay um and I'm in a class with mostly 11th-graders
19  Josh:    and his name is <rising voice>
20  James    ah and ah and um a girl
21           who is very honest and nice
22           she has a locker right next to him
23           and she said he talked about how he is gay a lot
24           when she's there (.) not with her
25           like um (.) so that's how I know
26           and he um associates with um a lot of girls
27           not many boys.
```

The point that Bamberg and his colleagues make about this interaction is that by positioning himself as a character in his story of a gay boy in his school, James also manages to position himself as *not gay* in a larger cultural storyline of masculinity that has currency among him and his friends. At first he does this by shifting his position from somebody who 'knows' gay people to someone who has only 'seen' them, marking his association with them as more distant. This, however, creates for him a new, potentially undesirable position as someone who, while he many not know these particular gay people, is someone who knows enough *about* gay people to be able to recognize them by sight. In order to distance himself from this position, he invokes another narrator – 'a girl who is very honest and nice' who is revealed as the source of the information. This 'girl' serves as a kind of buffer between James and the 'dangerous' position of being too closely associated with this gay boy. Furthermore, she herself is also insulated from being too closely implicated in 'gayness' because of her gender, and by not having spoken to the gay boy directly, but instead learning the news from overhearing his conversations with others. By the end of the story, then, James has transformed himself from someone who 'knows a gay boy' to someone who 'knows a girl' (who just happens to have a locker close to that of a gay boy), chiefly by repositioning himself from the position of the 'author' of the story to the position of someone who is only 'animating' a story that someone else told him.

This example dramatically illustrates what Davies and Harré (1990) refer to as the 'moral' dimension of positioning. When we manage the ongoing emergence of identity in interaction by invoking various storylines and positioning ourselves as characters in these stories, we also reproduce the 'moral orders' which these stories promote. In the case of James, he is not just distancing himself from this particular gay boy or attempting to assert his heterosexual identity to his friends. He is also reproducing a moral storyline in which gay people are considered the 'dangerous other' from whom 'normal' boys ought to keep their distance. And it is such storylines being reproduced over and over in casual conversation that help to make government policies like 'Don't Ask, Don't Tell', not to mention social practices like 'gay bashing', seem to some to be normal and acceptable.

Identity projects

In this chapter, I have outlined a view of identity that has particular currency in contemporary discourse studies in which, rather than seeing the person as *having* an identity, sees the person as a strategic actor who works with others to construct his or her identity anew in every interaction using the discursive tools that are available. Useful as this perspective is in highlighting the contingent and strategic nature of social identity, it runs the risk of ignoring the fact that we do not enter interactions as 'blank slates'; we bring to every conversation a long history of claiming and imputing identities and of mastering different identity kits. A professor does not have to 'recreate' his identity as a professor every time she walks into a lecture hall, and Randy and his father do not have to renegotiate their relationship every time he calls on the phone. In fact, the identities that we are able to claim and impute in a given interaction depend on those that we have claimed and imputed in the past, and if we diverge too much from the expectations set up in these past encounters, we run the risk of being accused of not acting like 'ourselves'.

So, despite the socially constructed and contextual nature of identity, successful interaction still depends upon our engagement in longer-term 'identity projects' (Harré 1983) through which we both build the public images or 'reputations' that we carry into interactions, and we internalize the social practices and dispositions (Bourdieu 1977) that define us personally and allow us to credibly assume particular 'brought along' identities. Of course, these longer-term projects are themselves made up of countless individual, situated acts of claiming and imputing identity and negotiating our identities with others. Holland and Lave (2001) refer to this process as the 'thickening' of identity. They argue that, although the ways people might position themselves or get positioned by others in particular interactions might be unpredictable, over time identities often 'thicken' as people come to increasingly think of themselves and be thought of by others as particular kinds of people. In fact, they point out, both psychological stability and cultural stability depend on the creation of these stable, 'thickened' identities.

There are obvious affordances to having 'thickened identities'. When interacting with people who don't know us, we can use these identities (entextualized in documents like ID cards and passports) to do things like cash cheques and pass through immigration check-points. When interacting with people who do know us, we have an immediate way of recognizing our shared histories. These stable personal identities, as Goffman (1971: 189) puts it, provide 'a framework of mutual knowing, which retains, organizes, and applies (our) experience(s)' with other people. On the other hand, personal identities can also constrain us. They place limits on what we can say and do and still be 'ourselves' (Simons 1995), and over time these 'thickened' identities might turn into stereotypes, or caricatures, or 'reputations' that might be taken up and used by other people in ways that could be either beneficial or harmful to us (Collins 1981).

Wortham (2003) argues that identity projects can be seen to take place on three 'timescales': the scale of the individual social interaction, in which social actors take up and make use of 'threads' of identities that they have constructed in previous interactions, the scale of a person's lifetime, which is made up of various trajectories of identity claims, and the scale of the sociocultural histories of various social identities themselves as 'technologies of talk'. He writes (206):

> In order for an individual to be socially identified, processes at three time scales must interact. Circulating sociocultural categories of identity must be taken up into the ontogenetic trajectory of an individual, such that a recognizable category comes consistently to identify that individual across many interactional events of social identification. Each of these three processes depends on the others: Sociocultural categories of identity exist only through the individuals whom they identify and the events in which they actually circulate; individuals' developing identities become recognizable only through sociocultural categories and exist empirically only in actual events; and events of social identification presuppose both sociocultural categories and individuals to be identified.

Given the variety of identities that people may potentially claim throughout their lives, what sorts of discursive mechanisms exist to help them to build and maintain relatively stable social identities across different contexts while at the same time maintaining the flexibility to modify existing identities or to claim new ones as the need arises? One answer to this question lies in the affordances that different technologies of talk provide for *entextualizing* identities in coherent ways. Chief among these technologies is the speech genre of the narrative (Ochs and Capps 2009; Schiffrin 1996). Many different contexts create occasions for us to tell stories about ourselves and how we came to be the way we are, from casual chats around the dinner table like when a husband asks his wife how her day went, to more formal occasions when oral narratives are elicited such as medical examinations, psychiatric treatments, and courtroom cross-examinations. The genre of the narrative helps to link the three timescales across which Wortham says identity projects are carried out: the immediate context of the interaction in which such stories are told, the longer biographical timescale across which the present self is linked to past selves through narrative, and longer sociocultural histories within which these identities are rendered recognizable to others who share the same culture. Wortham (2003) calls such forms of discourse 'participant-denoting discourse', discourse in which 'a participant both gets represented and enacts a particular identity' at the same time (193). An example can be seen in the story that Randy tells about coming to the realization that he is gay in a video entitled 'When I realized I was different'.[1]

```
15   prhh (1.0) I realized I was different like rea::lly early (0.1)
16   probably::^ (0.6) um:^ (0.3) elementary school ↓↑ (0.2) uh (0.2)
17   I (.) didn't know what it was^ (0.9) but I (.) knew it was different^
18   um:^ (1.2) probably (.) the very very (0.6) en:d of high school I
19   actually^ (0.9) realized it (0.2) an::d (0.7) um:: (1.2) figured out what
20   it was^ (0.8) but it was it was definitely at least until my senior year
21   before I realized that^ (0.7) kinda did a little bit of stuff^ (0.8) at the
22   very end of high school (.) very very (0.8) very little bit^ (0.8) and^
23   (0.2) I thought it was a phase↓↑ (0.3) uh^ (2.2) prolly a year^ after I
24   graduated high school I went into the military^ (0.4) I was:^ (0.4)
25   um: (1.6) went into basic training^ (0.9) no (0.8) no problem^ (0.5)
16   I went to school after that^ (0.7) no problem^ I got to my first duty
17   station^ (0.5) I was over:^ (0.4) I was at my first duty station for over
18   a year ↓↑ (0.4) I was actually stationed on the east coast which^ (0.7)
19   uh: (0.4) I guess is is (0.2) prolly bigger:: ↓↑ (0.4) y'know gay↑↓
20   (0.2) scene ↓↑ (0.6) um sorry I have to whsper (.) but I'm actually
21   kinda in a bunker^ (1.0) um: ↓↑ (1.5) and so^ (0.6) didn't really
22   bother me^ (0.6) um:^ (1.1) then I (0.2) I (.) moved. (.) to↑↓ (0.8)
23   Europe ↑↓ (1.1) uh and I I thought it was completely a phase^
24   (1.3) didn't really think anything of it^ (0.5) I move to Europe
25   where it's: (.) it's completely different than America^ and it's
26   I would (0.1) say^ (0.6) more accepted ↓↑ (0.6) uh: (1.2) and that
27   kinda when it hit me. I wasn't not there but a couple weeks^ (0.9) and
```

---

[1]Available at https://youtu.be/0XGcmbMxvLQ.

28   realized (.) when you see things^ (1.2) uh (1.2) you know↑↓ (0.5)
29   you just realize it it about yourself^ (0.5) and you kinda see where
30   you fit^ (1.3) into society^ (0.2) and^ (.) so I definitely discovered
31   that^ (0.7) and that's what it took^ (1.4) I was prolly (0.4) I'm twenty
32   now^ (.) I'm just about to be twenty-one^ (0.8) so^ (0.3) but it^ (.) it
33   took me that long ↑↓

The important thing to note about this story is that it functions both as a 'window' on the narrator's understanding of himself and an active attempt by him to *perform* this self by linking up all of these various periods in his life and and events during those periods into a story (Bamberg, De Fina and Schiffrin 2011). Through the narrative frame imposed on it, Randy's sexuality becomes something that has emerged over time in a coherent way rather than a collection of disconnected feelings and incidents. Most important, the form Randy chooses to entextualize his gay identity not only ties that identity to his personal experiences, but also contributes to its technologization as a particular kind of identity, one that is *discovered* rather than *acquired* (see above). The stories he might tell about other identities such as being an airman or a backgammon player would likely construct these identities more as acquired than discovered.

In other words, personal identity projects both reflect and reproduce the collective identity projects of communities, partly because it is these communities that provide the technologies of talk that individuals use to entextualize their personal experiences. Randy's project of 'being gay' is not just a personal project, but it is linked to a broader social project (which Butler [1993b] half factitiously refers to as 'the professionalization of gayness') through various conventionalized speech genres and social practices like 'the coming out story' (a version of which he tells above), and the practice of 'coming out' itself. It is in this way that our societies provide us with the tools by which to become our 'real selves'. As Leap (1999) argues, 'coming into gayness' is not a status achieved through biology, or through the 'speech act' of announcing 'I'm gay', but rather through the acquisition of culture-specific strategies of entextualization through which personal identity projects can be accomplished.

In the next chapter, I will further explore the role of different social groups or 'communities' in providing individual social actors with the technologies of talk that they use to conduct interactions, form relationships and claim social identities, and in helping members to master these technologies. I will also explore how technologies of talk, as they are deployed by individuals in situated interactions, also contribute to the transformation of communities into 'social artefacts' or 'cultural tools' that can be moulded, refabricated and mobilized by individuals to take specific social actions.

7

Talk and communities

I began Chapter 4 by discussing the practice of handing and how people use it to perform different kinds of actions. Specifically, I discussed how the actions of a student handing a university president a yellow umbrella and the university president *not* handing the student his diploma during a graduation ceremony that took place in the wake of mass pro-democracy demonstrations in Hong Kong were construed as different kinds of 'speech acts' by participants and witnesses. I'd like to begin this chapter with another example of handing, this one also associated with the 2014 pro-democracy protests in Hong Kong. This example of handing, however, did not take place in the context of a 'solemn' event like a university graduation. Rather, it took place in the fractious context of the demonstrations themselves at a point when police officers and student demonstrators were facing off along cordons set up by authorities. Some days earlier, police and protesters had clashed in violent incidents in which the police had used tear gas and pepper spray, and, as the occupation of key areas of the city continued, the polarization between the police (and those who supported them) and the protesters (and those who supported them) became more pronounced. People in the city began wearing symbols to advertise their loyalties, yellow ribbons for those supporting the protesters, and blue for those supporting the police (and government). The following transcript comes from a video that went viral on social media at that time of a police officer handing a protester a bottle of water during a tense moment at the police cordon.[1] Interestingly, this is the same officer who, moments before, had uttered the 'threat': '對住禁多人打人，我都唔想禁樣做' ('I don't want to use force in front of all of these people') (see Chapter 4).

1 Protester 有冇少少水？
            (Do you have a little water?)
2 Police   (handing a bottle of water to protester) 我依方面都唔

---

[1]Available at https://youtu.be/zhEes9IslSU.

3   係得番幾多。喂留返 小小比我。唔好咁玩喎，大佬
          *(I don't have much left. Hey, leave some for me. Don't mess
          with me, man.)*
4   喂，大家都係兄弟，唔好咁樣好唔 好呀！
          (Hey, we are all brothers. Don't act this way, okay?)

What is interesting about this act of handing is the way it became, on the social media pages where it was shared and re-shared, more than just the action of one person handing a bottle of water to another person, but of one *group* of people reaching out to another *group* across a seemingly unbridgeable ideological chasm. Some promoted it as a demonstration that, despite their differences, protesters and police could still get along if they remembered that they were, in the end, members of the same group: Hong Kongers. This is, in fact, the interpretation that the police officer himself gives to this act when he says: '喂, 大家都係兄弟，唔好咁樣好唔 好呀！' (Hey. we're all brothers. Don't act this way, okay?). Others, however, sought to use the video to draw group boundaries even more sharply, to insist that this particular police officer was the exception rather than the rule, and to subdivide the police into two kinds: cops who use force and cops who show kindness to citizens (despite the fact that this video shows that moments before this exchange this particular cop was also threatening to use force).

In this chapter, I will explore how people speak as members of different groups (families, communities, organizations, institutions and cultures), how different technologies of talk affect and often come to characterize interactions within and between particular groups, and how group membership is used as a mediational means in spoken discourse. The traditional way of looking at the relationship between talk and social groups among those who study discourse has been to try to understand how membership in different groups affects the way people talk, and how speakers claim group membership by using particular registers (Agha 2004) or genres (Swales 1990). While I will also be considering such questions, I will mostly focus on how groups themselves are used as 'technologies of talk' in order to perform certain social actions such as convincing a group of protesters to move back or arguing for or against a government policy, and on how these groups come to be *technologized* as groups in the first place.

Imagined communities

We all belong to multiple groups. Some are groups that we join voluntarily, such as the fan club for our favourite singer or the company where we work. Others are groups in which our membership is usually considered less voluntary, our families, our nation and what people refer to as our 'culture'. It is difficult to have an interaction without doing so as a member of some group (and often, of multiple groups), though which memberships we orient to vary from interaction to interaction. The fact that I'm president of my local chapter the Lady Gaga fan club may not be something that I bring up at important faculty meetings at my university, and my status as a professor at my university may not be something I orient to when I'm dancing at a Lady Gaga concert. Nevertheless, every conversation that we have involves claims and imputations about group membership, whether these claims and imputations are explicit, as when the police officer above says to the protester, 'we are all brothers', or implicit, as when the customer in the bookstore in the conversation I analysed in Chapter 5 says to the shop clerk, 'I just got tickets to *It's Only a Play*', claiming for herself and imputing onto her interlocutor membership in a group of people who like to go to the theatre, or at least who are 'in the know' enough to know that *It's Only a Play* is a play, and that getting tickets to it is a big deal.

Sometimes these claims and imputations are part of a struggle that we engage in with those with whom we are interacting to manage the membership we have in these multiple groups and to define the terms of such membership. In one of his videos, for example,[2] Randy responds to a question regarding the seeming contradiction between his membership in the 'gay community' and his membership in the US military:

```
32   (0.9) uh (0.3) shh (0.5) this one^ I::^ wasn't really sure what to think
33   about. (0.3) but^ (.) do you ever struggle^ (0.1) with the concept^
34   (0.7) that^ (.) you are fighting for a country^ (0.5) that's treating
35   you as a sub human. (0.5) no (0.2) never thought of it that
36   way^ ever. (0.3) I think I'm treated pretty good (0.5) I (0.5)
37   get three meals a day^ (0.2) actually it's prolly more like four or
38   five. (0.6) ah I've I get all my shots^ (0.6) haven't missed a
39   a paycheck yet^ (0.4) uh (0.2) I am well taken care of (1.0)
40   so I've never really been in any^ (1.2) horrible danger^
41   oh and thanks (.) thanks for the Seals by the way^ (0.7)
42   I don't want this to be political^ (.) bu:t^ (0.5) some people need
43   to die sometimes (0.6) an::d (0.7) and we got that taken care of
```

The interesting thing about this example is not so much about how Randy actually reconciles being gay with being a member of the armed forces, but how he *manages* his membership in these different groups by claiming loyalty to the nation and its actions through his reference to the killing of Osama bin

---

[2]Available at https://youtu.be/8D81LjveyN8.

Laden as something '*we* got taken care of'. In doing so, he claims an identity as a 'patriotic American' who orients to the positive aspects of the nation, in contrast (he implies) to people like the questioner, who orients towards negative aspects of the nation by, for example, accusing it of treating some people as 'sub human'.

Randy's membership in the 'nation', in fact, is, apart from his membership in the military and in the 'gay community', one of the most important tools that he uses to build his identity and to manage his 'coming out', as well as to define the boundaries of these other communities and manage how they intersect and interact with one another, as can be seen in the example above. In a similar example,[3] he relates his membership in the nation to his practice of posting videos on YouTube:

31   happy Memorial Day^ (0.8) uh
32   (0.2) I know:: I know I know (.) I'm a <u>week</u> late. (0.5) but there are
33   so many people that've given^(.) <u>so:</u> much↑↓ (0.7) um^ (0.4) just
34   so we can do: (0.5) sstupid things and have freedoms y'know^
35   (0.4) stuff like make YouTube videos^ (0.7) uh:: (0.2) so. We gotta
36   tellum thanks: ↓↑ (0.8) so if we set a (.) aside one day↑↓ (0.3) ah (.)
37   outta the year I <u>think</u> that's fair. (0.9)

In this chapter, I will be using the word 'community' to refer to these different kinds of groups. The notion of 'community' is both extremely popular and highly contested among sociolinguists and discourse analysts, who speak, among other things, of 'speech communities' (Gumperz 1972; Labov 1972a), 'discourse communities' (Swales 1990), 'communities of practice' (Eckert and McConnell-Ginet 1992; Lave and Wenger 1991), and 'imagined communities' (Anderson 1991). I will using the word in a very broad sense to include both close-knit groups of people like families which have developed their special ways of talking and communicative rituals, and broad disparate groups like 'YouTube users' who, while they may share some communicative practices only rarely think of themselves as a coherent 'group'. For me a community is less an actual group of people than it is a *tool* that people use to take action in the world. Being a 'YouTuber' or an 'American', a 'theatre goer' or member of the 'Jones family' are essentially technologies of talk that people appropriate in different situations. Of course, not all groups that share communicative practices come to be technologized as 'communities'; we don't, for example, regard users of semicolons or telephones as recognizable groups. So the important questions for students of spoken discourse are (1) how do communities come to be technologized as cultural tools? and

---

[3]Available at https://www.youtube.com/watch?v=FXBJawOILwk.

(2) how do people appropriate and use these tools in social interaction and what affordances and constraints do they introduce into those interactions?

In addressing the first question, the notion of 'imagined communities' introduced by the famous student of nationalism Benedict Anderson (1991) is useful. For Anderson, what makes an 'imagined community' is not how big or small a group of people is or even how much actual interaction they have with one another, but their capacity to think and *talk* of themselves as a community. His prototype for the imagined community is the nation-state. Nations are imagined communities, he writes, 'because the members of even the smallest nation will never know most of their fellow-members, meet them, or even hear of them, yet in the minds of each lives the image of their communion' (6).

In many ways, this conception of community is very much at odds with models that dominate sociolinguistics and discourse analysis such as that of 'speech communities', which focus not just on people who speak the same language, but also who have 'consistent, repetitive, and predictable interactions and contact' with one another (Gumperz 1972: 220), 'discourse communities', which are characterized by 'mechanisms of intercommunication among its members' (Swales 1990: 25), and 'communities of practice', defined by Lave and Wenger (1991) as a group of people who do things together. Anderson's notion of imagined communities, on the other hand, focuses not on people who are in physical contact, but on people who are *discursively* and *ideologically* joined. In his study of nationalism, he argues that what made it possible for people to begin to imagine themselves as members of nations was the development of new discursive technologies like the printing press. Such technologies make it easier for semiotic tools like slogans, holidays (like memorial day) and narratives of the nation (like the narrative of the killing of Osama bin Laden) to circulate through groups of people (regardless of whether or not they have ever met), and to be appropriated and used for concrete actions (like showing that a gay airman can still be patriotic). Now, of course, new technologies like YouTube are facilitating extended forms of textual circulation that help people who are physically and temporally distant from one another to imagine themselves as members of communities.

As I said above, sociolinguists and discourse analysts have a variety of ways of conceptualizing communities including speech communities, discourse communities and communities of practice. In a sense, these three different kinds of communities represent different kinds of technologies of talk that people use to imagine themselves as communities (and that analysts use to imagine them as objects of study). Not only do these technologies come to function as emblems of membership in such communities, but as members use them they play a role in the ongoing technologization of these communities. Through these processes, imagined communities become *cultural artefacts* (Anderson 1991: 4) that people can take up, independent of the other technologies associated with them, to use as technologies of talk in their own right.

Speech communities, discourse communities and communities of practice, then, are terms we use to describe the way in which people congregate around particular technologies of talk, develop norms for using them, and develop metadiscourses for talking about them. What these different concepts represent is not so much different social entities as different *processes* through which groups of people imagine themselves as communities using different kinds of discursive resources (Wertsch 1998b). The idea of speech communities focuses on how people imagine communities using varieties of language and registers (social languages). The idea of discourse communities focuses on how people imagine communities using genres, recognizable forms of discourse used to fulfil the shared goals of the group. And the idea of communities of practice focuses on how people use social practices and social identities to imagine communities, and how they define membership in terms of participation in these practices. In actual interaction, people might at different moments orient themselves towards communities based on how they talk, how they use different forms of discourse, and how they do things together, and groups of people who are imagining themselves as members of particular imagined communities like Americans, gay men and theatre goers might use any of these technologies to accomplish that imagining. Finally, the way one person might imagine America or the gay community is always very different from his or her fellow Americans or fellow gays. Communities ultimately get imagined in multiple ways on multiple 'scales' (Blommaert 2005, 2010): They get worked out in short timescale conversations, and also through longer scale historical processes involving the kind of circulation of textual artefacts which Anderson focused on.

In what follows I will consider these three types of 'communities' – speech communities, discourse communities, and communities of practice as the building blocks of 'imagined communities'. I'll trace a little of the history of these concepts and summarize the intellectual debates surrounding them, and I will demonstrate some ways these kinds of communities facilitate the formation of imagined communities like Pittsburghers, YouTubers and gay soldiers. But before doing so, I need to deal with what is perhaps the most pervasive and most contentious category for talking about different groups of people – the category of 'culture'.

'Culture' and 'intercultural communication'

Despite its frequent use in both academic work and in everyday life, 'culture' is a word with many contradictory definitions. Some speak of it as a set of 'rules' or 'customs' or 'habits' that define a group of people, others focus on the material artefacts that bind groups of people together, still others define it as a body of knowledge one needs to function in a particular society, and others see it as the collection of symbolic forms through which groups of people make meaning. Most of these definitions portray culture as a characteristic of communities, but the more frequent use of the word in popular discourse is to describe actual groups of people themselves as cultures, as in 'American culture', or 'Chinese culture' – groups that are defined primarily not by habits, artefacts, knowledge or symbolic forms, but by political boundaries and ethnicity.

A number of students of spoken discourse have devoted considerable energy to understanding the relationship between culture and language and, in particular, to studying what they call 'intercultural' or 'interethnic communication'. This has been a focus for researchers of the ethnography of communication (see e.g., Kiesling 2012), for whom a priority is understanding the kinds of communicative tools and knowledge that people need to be in possession of in order to show themselves as competent members of their cultures. Interactional sociolinguists (see e.g., Gumperz 1982; Tannen 1984, 2005) have also explored how different communicative patterns and repertoires (including ways of structuring information, taking conversational turns and using contextualization cues) that people from different places, such as New York and California (Tannen 2005), or from different 'ethnic groups' – such as white Alaskans and Athabaskans (Scollon and Scollon 1981) – bring to conversations that sometimes result in miscommunication. Perhaps the most widely cited study of this kind is Gumperz's (1982) examination of the communication problems between Anglo-British baggage handlers at an urban airport and the Indian and Pakistani women who served them in the cafeteria. The servers were perceived both by their supervisor and the cargo handlers they served as surly and uncooperative. After tape recording and analysing interactions between the servers and customers, Gumperz concluded that one source of difficulty was the way the servers used intonation. When asking customers whether they wanted gravy, for example, the servers often spoke the word with a falling intonation ('gravy'.), rather than the rising intonation that is usually used for questions in British English. As a result, the customers interpreted the servers' utterances to mean something like 'this is gravy', which they took as rude. The problem was solved, Gumperz relates, after time was spent in English teaching sessions discussing differences in intonation patterns in different varieties of English. Notably, what made things better in this situation was not just that the women learnt to say gravy 'correctly', but that they were given a metalanguage to understand and account for feelings of discrimination. As Gumperz (1982: 174) puts it:

It seemed that the Indian workers had long sensed they had been misunderstood but, having no way of talking about this in objective terms, they had felt they were being discriminated against. We had not taught the cafeteria workers to speak appropriate English; rather, by discussing the results of our analysis in mixed sessions and focusing on context bound interpretive preferences rather than on attitudes and stereotypes, we have suggested a strategy for self-diagnosis of communication difficulties.

The point that Gumperz and other interactional sociolinguists make is that people of different 'ethnic' or 'cultural' groups learn to use various kinds of technologies of talk and to interpret how other people are using them differently, and that since this learning is largely unconscious, we are often not aware that other people who are using the same or similar technologies might have learnt to use them in very different ways. Obviously, the theoretical and practical contributions of work done to describe the discursive sources of miscommunication between people who use language differently have been considerable. Where work like this becomes problematic is in how researchers often imagine these different users of language as members of 'cultures' or 'ethnic groups', and interpret communication problems as a result of participants' membership in these groups, often not considering other factors such as the differences in power that are often features of intergroup contact, the ways people sometimes 'use differences (or beliefs about differences) in strategic ways' in conducting their social interactions (Eckert and McConnell-Ginet 1992: 467), institutional constraints on communication, membership in *other* groups such as those that form around things like gender or occupation, or *actual* prejudice and discrimination based on things like race or religion. As Gerd Baumann (1996: 98, emphasis in original) observes, 'there is something deeply problematic ... about the equation between "ethnic" *cultures* and self-evident *communities* upon which' dominant discourses about intercultural communication are based.

    That is not to say that, as in Gumperz's study, people usually thought of as being from different 'cultural' groups might not use language in different 'culturally conditioned' ways which they may not be completely aware of, but a better way to explain these differences might be in terms of other labels for these groups like speech communities (a term Gumperz himself uses elsewhere), discourse communities, or communities of practice, that is, labelling them based on the phenomenon we are observing (speech, discourses or practices) rather than on some extra-situational category ('culture' or 'ethnicity'). Even though studies of intercultural communication 'may apply these categories correctly', they often don't 'take into account the *relevancy* of these categories in each interaction' (Nishizaka 1995: 301).

    Another way of understanding the relationship between culture and spoken language is to focus on the way in which cultures are *imagined* by participants themselves in situated interactions, and how certain configurations of tools and practices come to be technologized as cultures. Among the work taking this perspective is that by conversation analysts, who regard culture as emergent in interaction and resist assigning people membership to a particular culture prior to analysis (see e.g., Antaki, Condor and Levine 1996; Antaki and Widdicombe 1998). Their argument is that whether or not an interaction should be treated by analysts as an intercultural encounter depends chiefly on whether or not participants themselves orient towards the category of culture and make it contingently relevant to their interaction (Sacks 1992a; Schegloff 1972).

This approach can be seen, for example, in Nishizaka's (1995) examination of how, in conversations between 'Japanese' and 'foreigners' on a radio programme, the 'cultural identities' of participants are interactively constituted and made contingently relevant, either through explicit reference to a particular category, or by references to social relationships or 'category bound activities' (Sacks 1992a). A similar example can be seen in Mori's (2003) study of how American and Japanese students orient towards interculturality and use it as a resource for organizing interaction in classroom conversations by, for example, presuming knowledge or activities associated with students of foreign languages or cultures or using certain forms of address to members of one category and not another. Students of Bateson's (1971) 'natural history method', like Erickson and Schultz (1982), also point out how participants in interactions use categories in strategic ways. In their examination of 'intercultural' interactions between counsellors and students, for instance, they show how students orient away from cultural identities to more 'situationally emergent' identities (such as a common interest in wrestling) in order to get better treatment.

This practice of strategically orienting away from cultural categories and even contesting them is dramatically illustrated in a conversation which Ron Scollon (2002: 5–6) relates in which his wife, Suzanne, a Chinese-American, encounters a stranger walking a dog that happens to be a Japanese breed:

SS: Hello.
Man: Are you Japanese?
SS: (looking at the dog) No.
Man: He is; he eats with chopsticks.
SS: (silence)
Man: Are you Chinese?
SS: I'm American.
Man: I mean, what's your background?
SS: My grandparents were from China.

By trying to place Suzanne Wong Scollon into a cultural category based on her appearance, then placing his dog in the same category, and finally, assigning to the dog a practice stereotypically associated with people of this category (using chopsticks), this stranger attempts to use the *idea* of Japanese culture to create solidarity with Suzanne Scollon (through his dog) and to thus open up an opportunity to begin a conversation. Scollon, on the other hand, resists his orientation not just to Japanese culture, but to ethnically defined cultural categories altogether, first by refusing to accept the alternative category he offers ('Are you Chinese?') by claiming another category ('American'), and then even resisting placing her grandparents in that category saying they were 'from China', rather than 'Chinese'.

For mediated discourse analysts such as Scollon, whether or not an interaction is intercultural depends not just on the perspective of the participants, but also on the perspective of the analyst. Many interactions, he says, which when viewed through a narrow circumference, might not be considered intercultural, might be found to exhibit traces of interculturality when viewed through a wider circumference in which the heterogeneous trajectories of people and technologies is revealed (see Chapter 4). 'Every action', he writes (2002: 2), 'occurs at an intersection of multiple lines of actions, discourses, material and biological life trajectories and is therefore inevitably culturally complex.' Thus, he argues (1), 'the relevant question is not: Is this or is this not a moment of intercultural communication? The question that needs to be asked is: What interests does it serve to discursively construct this moment as one of intercultural communication?'

Speech communities

The notion of 'speech communities' represents a way of understanding how people (and analysts) use linguistic codes and varieties to imagine themselves (or those they are analysing) as members of communities and use these communities as resources for social action. The idea of speech communities has a long history in sociolinguistics. Like the concept of culture, it can be treated both as an empirical category and as a cultural tool. As Durante (1997: 6) puts it, 'speech communities ... [are] simultaneously real and imaginary entities whose boundaries are constantly being reshaped and negotiated through myriad acts of speaking'.

Earlier understandings of speech communities focused chiefly on the linguistic resources that different groups of people have available to them. Perhaps the most canonical definition from this perspective is that of Leonard Bloomfield (1933: 29) who defined a speech community as 'a group of people who use the same set of speech signals'. This definition reflects both the focus of many early scholars of descriptive and structural linguistics on language as a *code*, as well as the presumption of monolingualism that characterized their work. Later definitions took into account the fact that what is shared by the members of a speech community may not be a single language, but a repertoire of variant codes. Regardless of whether or not a speech community is characterized by one or multiple codes, though, in this earlier definition it is primarily a 'language based unit ... not connected to any larger social theory' (Bucholtz 1999b: 203–7).

Later definitions of speech community, however, focused not just on linguistic resources, but also on the norms that people have for using them and the ways these resources are brought together in specific kinds of 'speech events'. This wider definition is the one used by ethnographers of communication and interactional sociolinguists. Hymes (1972: 54–5), for instance, defines a speech community as: 'A community sharing rules for the conduct and interpretation of speech, and rules for the interpretation of at least one linguistic variety', and argues that 'the basis of description' of the speech community should be 'as a social, rather than a linguistic, entity'. Similarly, Gumperz (1972: 114) defines speech community as 'any human aggregate characterized by regular and frequent interaction by means of a shared body of verbal signs and set off from similar aggregates by significant differences in language usage', elaborating on this definition by noting that (116) 'the speech varieties employed within a speech community form a system because they are related to a shared set of *social norms*' (emphasis mine). Labov (1972) also emphasizes shared norms in his definition of speech community, arguing that 'the speech community is not defined by any marked agreement in the use of language elements, so much as by participation in a set of shared norms' (1972: 120–1) which assign to different language elements different sorts of *values* in different contexts.

More recent conceptualization of speech communities chiefly expand upon and elaborate this notion of value, focusing on the ideological nature of language and language use within communities (see e.g., Schieffelin, Woolard and Kroskrity 1998). The emphasis of these later perspectives is not just on linguistic resources or on the norms people adopt for using them, but on the knowledge that members of speech communities share about 'the way language choice, variation, and discourse represents generation, occupation, politics, social relationships, identity, and more' (Morgan 2006: 4). In other words, the focus of this perspective goes beyond how people use linguistic resources to communicate to the way they use them to *imagine* speakers of these varieties as certain kinds of people, and how these varieties themselves are *enregistered* (Agha 2005, 2007) as emblems of social groups in day-to-day interaction and in public discourse. As Johnstone and her colleagues (2006: 79) put it:

Imagined 'languages', 'dialects', and 'speech communities' ... arise in local social and discursive practices that are enabled and constrained by larger-scale political and economic conditions. According to Michael Silverstein (1998: 408), 'users of languages in essence construct culturally particular concepts of [linguistic] normativity that bind subsets of them into "language-bearing groups"'. That is to say that 'languages' and 'dialects' are cultural constructs, produced by a group of people using, or orienting to and/or talking about, a particular set of linguistic features, in a process that also constructs the group itself. (Gal and Irvine 1995)

Such 'language-bearing' groups are imagined through the circulation of metadiscursive representations and evaluations of how people from different places talk. Another factor that influences these processes of imagining, Johnstone and her colleagues point out, is migration, which puts people accustomed to speaking in one particular way in contact with those who speak differently, so that features of talk that previously went unnoticed 'because everyone in a speaker's social network used them, become noticeable in contrast with new forms emanating from elsewhere' (Johnstone, Andrus and Danielson 2006: 89).

The example which Johnstone has devoted considerable attention to is 'Pittsburghese', a regional dialect which, until recently was associated chiefly with working-class speakers in the US city of Pittsburgh (see Johnstone 2007, 2009; Johnstone, Andrus and Danielson 2006; Johnstone and Kiesling 2008). What is interesting about this speech community is that there was little sense among speakers of this variety that their way of speaking was special until the industries they worked for closed or moved away, leading many to migrate out of their city to places where their accent became something that marked them as special. Gradually, Pittsburghese became an emblem of pride among communities of diasporic Pittsburghers, as well as the subject of newspaper articles, books, stories and humorous tee-shirts sold as 'souvenirs of Pittsburgh', further 'enregistering' the dialect in the minds of locals and out-of-towners. What is interesting about this example is that it shows how, over time, the way a speech community is imagined can change dramatically, as, in Pittsburgh, linguistic features that once indexed socioeconomic class gradually came to be regarded as emblems of the city as a whole.

Speakers of Pittsburghese, or any other regional dialect, of course, also speak other varieties, registers and social languages, and appropriate these different varieties into different interactions for different purposes. Each individual belongs to and transverses multiple speech communities, and, as le Page and Tabouret-Keller (1985: 181) have pointed out, regularly alters his or her linguistic patterns to 'resemble those of the group or groups with from time to time he [/she] wishes to be identified or so as to be unlike those from whom he [/she] wishes to be distinguished'. Many young middle-class

Pittsburghers, for example, may not speak Pittsburghese except when they are engaging in 'stylized performances of local identity' (Johnstone 2007).

At the same time, many speech communities are characterized not by a single variety, or even just by a repertoire of varieties, but by the characteristic ways that members *mix* varieties. This is a point illustrated dramatically by Barrett (1997) in his description of ways of speaking employed by African American drag queens in Texas bars. To claim membership in this speech community, he notes, members must be able to switch between a range of incongruous linguistic styles indexing groups as diverse as white women and African American men, at strategic moments.

Finally, sometimes people adopt the speech styles of speech communities of which they are *not* members as ways of positioning themselves in relation to different social groups, a phenomenon that has been documented by Rampton (1995), who describes the linguistic 'crossing' that takes place in groups of multi-ethnic London youth, as well as by Chun (2001) who examines the way Korean-American men adopt features of African American Vernacular English as a way of adopting a particular stance towards the dominant white speech community. Adopting speech styles associated with other groups can also function to mark someone as *not* a member of the group, as when the adolescent boys studied by Pascoe (2005, see Chapter 6) imitate 'fag talk' to inoculate themselves from being labelled fags. Work like this marks yet another stage in the evolution of sociolinguistic conceptualizations of speech communities, a shift from a focus on speech varieties, registers and styles to a focus on acts of 'stylization' (Coupland 2001) through which individuals, drawing on a range of technologies from both inside and outside their own speech communities, both play with and police the boundaries that separate social groups.

Discourse communities

Whereas speech communities are imagined around linguistic varieties and styles, discourse communities are imagined around genres, forms of language associated with different spheres of human activity. The term discourse community was coined by the applied linguist John Swales to describe groups of people who are united by a particular communicative agenda – a collection of things they want to get done with words – as well as a collection of genres designed to help them do those things. Although Swales was mainly concerned with written communication, spoken discourse, as I pointed out in Chapter 3, also has a wide variety of genres associated with it – some more general, such as stories and jokes, and others associated more specifically with particular communities, such as 'coming out stories' – that function in the same way the written genres that Swales described do, providing the means for groups of people with the same goals to achieve those goals. Although genres, and specifically for our purpose, speech genres, are usually thought of as particular forms of discourse defined by their structure, the most important thing about them is that they are 'forms of action' which are organized around 'moves' (Bhatia 1993).

Swales (1990: 24–7) says there are six features that characterize a discourse community: (1) it has a 'broadly agreed set of common public goals', (2) it has 'mechanisms of intercommunication among its members', (3) it has 'mechanisms … to provide information and feedback', (4) 'it possesses one or more genres in the communicative furtherance of its aims', (5) in addition to genres it also has 'specific lexis', and (6) it has a 'threshold level' of expert members.

One important aspect of discourse communities, which distinguishes them from the idea most people have of speech communities, is that they always involve a conscious process of adopting linguistic forms; people are not 'born into' discourse communities as they might be born into speech communities. In addition, these genres serve dual functions as both emblems of membership in the community and as concrete means to achieve social goals. Not only does relative competence in generic forms and usage separate expert members from novice members, but genres also create for members different roles and participation statuses: all members at a business meeting, for example, are equally engaged in using the speech genre of the meeting, but the genre designates different forms of participation for the chairperson and the other members present. Genres also serve a gatekeeping function, keeping out or exposing as 'inauthentic' those who do not know how to use them correctly.

One example of a discourse community is the collection of people who have participated in the It Gets Better project,[4] a YouTube movement started by the sex columnist Dan Savage in which gays, lesbians, bisexuals and transgendered people and their straight allies were called upon to make videos telling their own stories of how things 'got better' for them as a way of consoling and encouraging young people who might be contemplating suicide as a result of being bullied for their non-normative sexuality. Since its inception in 2010, over 50,000 user-created videos have been uploaded to the It Gets Better website, and around 100 of these stories were transcribed and compiled into a bestselling book (Savage and Miller 2011).

In line with Swales's (1990) criteria, the community was formed around a common goal: to 'give LGBT teens hope', and a set of principles underlying

---

[4]Available at http://www.itgetsbetter.org/.

this goal was articulated in the 'It Gets Better Pledge' that members are asked to take via the website:

> **THE PLEDGE:** Everyone deserves to be respected for who they are. I pledge to spread this message to my friends, family and neighbors. I'll speak up against hate and intolerance whenever I see it, at school and at work. I'll provide hope for lesbian, gay, bisexual, transgender and other bullied teens by letting them know that it gets better. (It Gets Better Project 2010)

It also has a set of clear mechanisms for intercommunication, participation and feedback among members, namely the It Gets Better website and related YouTube channels where viewers can leave comments and engage in discussions. Most importantly, it is imagined around a particular speech genre, the 'It Gets Better video' which employs a narrative format characterized by a number of distinctive discursive moves.

> Move 1: Introducing the purpose of the video (to tell viewers that 'it gets better').
> Move 2: Telling the speakers' story, which usually includes incidents of bullying and suffering, often culminating with a suicide attempt, and then followed by a resolution brought on by coming out and finding a supportive community.
> Move 3: Relating the story to the viewers' situation and giving the viewer advice and encouragement, usually involving exhortations not to attempt suicide and to have faith that things will get better in the future.
> Move 4: Repeating the purpose of the video and the catchphrase 'it gets better'.

This generic structure has become so conventionalized, in fact, that some have come see it as somewhat of a cliché. Mason (2011: 13), for example, offers the following parody of the genre:

> I was raised in a conservative small town and/or in a conservative family and/ or as part of a conservative religious community. I was bullied, sometimes violently, in school, felt isolated as a result, and contemplated suicide. I endured high school and moved to a big city and/or attended a college with a diverse campus. I found a community of like-minded queers, accepted my true self, and came out. Love, a successful career, and a family followed.

Finally, the community is characterized by expert and novice members. In fact, one of the main purposes of the community is to teach novice members (both other LGBT adults as well as young people) to tell their own stories using the template outlined above. In this process, tellers and listeners come to see each other as members of a kind of 'oral tradition'. Many of the videos by younger contributors, in fact, include accounts of their process of socialization into the community by watching other people's It Gets Better videos. One participant, who goes by the screenname Jaykounter, for example, begins his video like this:

Hello, my name is Jacob and I'm here to thank the *It Gets Better* project for all their love and support in helping me in my time of need. I know that it can be very hard growing up, you know, different and I would like to let any gay transgender lesbian or bisexual or anyone who's ever been bullied, to let you guys know that it does get better.

Although the genre of the It Gets Better video offers to users a conventional template to follow in telling their stories, as with all discourse communities, members do not always slavishly follow these conventions, but rather, adapt them to their own particular situations and life stories. In fact, the ability to not just reproduce genres, but to alter them in creative ways is the mark of an expert member of a discourse community. In the It Gets Better videos, part of this creativity has to do with the way speakers are able to weave the universal phrase 'it gets better' into their own personalized messages. Randy Phillips, the star of the YouTube videos I've been analysing in this book is a prototypical member of this community, and has, in fact, made his own It Gets Better video,[5] in which he follows most of the conventional moves of the genre, but also alters it too fit his circumstances and his story. First of all, as in his other pre-DADT repeal videos, he does not show his face. More important, he uses the imminent repeal of this policy as an illustration of how things are getting better.

1   what's↑↓ (.) up. Youtube↑↓(.) for those of you who have been (0.1)
2   following along^ (0.3) uh and (.) and know what's goin' on^ (0.5)
3   you know that we are within (.) the last week^ (0.5) of the: (.)
4   implementation of the repeal^ (0.4) of the:: (0.5) Don't Ask Don't
5   Tell^ (0.6) policy. (0.3) uh (.) for those of you who don't^ (.)
6   exactly understand what Don't Ask Don't Tell is^ (0.5) it's a
7   policy that's been around for about fifteen years^ (0.4) um:^
8   (.) that does not allow (0.3) gay lesbian and bisexuals (0.5)
9   to serve openly (0.4) i:n^ (0.5) the United States military. (1.2)
10 tsk (.) .hh um^ well^ (0.4) that's (.) that's all goin' away on the

[5]Available at https://youtu.be/ZBDZiMgcrVw.

11   twentieth and I think it's (.) it's a <u>huge</u> move (0.5) in American
12   civil rights^ (.) and uh you know there have been bigger things
13   like^ (0.3) abolishing slavery^ (0.4) um^ (0.3) giving women
14   the right to vote^ (.) ah getting (0.1) rid of segregation (0.5)
15   and those have all been great. But this is (.) this is <u>huge</u> (0.5)
16   for our generation: it's it's it's <u>our</u> (0.2) um (.) step of civil rights
17   (0.7) and uh^ (0.7) everybody's like (.) wo whata ya think. uh (.)
18   how doya feel about^ (0.2) about the twentieth. (0.4) and
19   honestly I (.) it's not^ (0.1) I'm not super excited about it do I
20   think it's important^ (.) yes. (0.5) um (0.6) but do I think life is
21   great right now^ (0.4) <u>ab</u>solutely.

Second, he gives to the catchphrase: 'it gets better' his own personal interpretation, using it to make the point that the best way to make things better is not to think that the future will be better, but to appreciate the good things in the present. In the final segment of his video, usually used in this genre for the move of 'advice giving', he offers the following advice:

99   don't feel like (0.5) you have anything to prove
100   to anybody (0.8) um (0.6) stay in there (0.9) it gets better (.) it
101   gets great↑↓ (0.4) and you'll know↑↓ (.) you'll know when it when
102   it gets better↑↓ (0.4) um when you're o<u>kay</u> with the time that
103   you're at. (0.5) right now when you can say^ (0.4) um^ (0.6)
104   that you know this (.) this is it. (1.2) I'm in my prime (.) I ha
105   $tomorrow's probably going to be a great day^$ (0.4) but I'm okay
106   with today. (0.7) and uh (1.2) that's (.) that's my words of advice.

Interestingly, this is not the video from Randy's channel that appears on the It Gets Better website, but instead the video that I began this book with of his successful coming out to his father, which, although it in some ways departs structurally from genre of the It Gets Better video, accomplishes all of the requisite moves indirectly by presenting viewers with a real-life example of things getting better.

One important thing about genres is not only that they define the discourse communities in which they are used, but also that they can help these communities to create links with other communities through the way in which genres draw upon and form connections with other genres. In fact, it is often because of these intertextual connections that genres are able to function as such effective technologies of talk. In my own analysis of the It Gets Better project (Jones 2015), for example, I argue that the ability of this discourse community to attract so many members and so much support from non-members lies in the way the stories told in It Gets Better videos establish intertextual links to more mainstream canonical narrative genres like the religious exemplum, the testimony and the confession. By blending these genres in a process which Briggs and Bauman (1992) call 'strategic interdiscursivity', members of the It Gets Better discourse community are able to claim 'textual authority' by linking their experiences with traditional storylines. They are also able to blur and reconfigure the boundaries that separate discourse communities, creating ways not just for LGBT adults and teenagers to participate, but also for straight allies, parents, politicians, corporate entities like Google, and even former bullies to join in with their own It Gets Better videos.

Communities of practice

While speech communities involve people building group identity around the distinctive ways they talk, and discourse communities involve them building group identity around distinctive speech genres and the shared goals these genres are designed to help them achieve, communities of practice involve people imagining group identity around shared social practices, practices like skateboarding, stamp collecting and recovering from alcohol addiction.

The idea of communities of practice was developed by the educational psychologists Jean Lave and Étienne Wenger (1991) to describe the set of relationships among people who are mutually engaged in a particular task and have a shared repertoire of resources to use in accomplishing it. Communities of practice can be large or small, formal or informal, long term or ad hoc. The important thing about communities of practice is that they involve people *doing things together*, and that those involved are able to think of themselves (and talk about themselves) as belonging to a group that is doing these things.

As educationists, Lave and Wenger are particularly interested in communities of practice as mechanisms for learning and the ways people come to be socialized into the particular practices around which these groups are imagined. The main ways communities of practice function, they say, is through providing to novice members opportunities for 'legitimate peripheral participation', chances to somehow engage in the practice of the community even before they become entirely competent in them. Through interacting with more experienced members in the context of social practices, newcomers gradually come to assume more central roles in the community. In other words, learning is not just a matter of acquiring skills or knowledge, but a matter of changing one's identity within a community. One example of this that they give is recovering alcoholics participating in Alcoholics Anonymous meetings. Members of the AA community, they point out, are united by a common practice – staying sober and helping others stay sober. It is a practice which involves mutual engagement at regular meetings (in fact, without regular mutual engagement one cannot be considered to be participating in the group). It also involves a set of shared resources which include written texts like the 'Big Book', slogans, norms of interaction governing who can say what when, and speech genres like 'the recovery story'. Most important, however, are the opportunities that Alcoholics Anonymous meetings provide for novice members to participate by listening to others tell their stories and, when they are ready, by trying to fit their own experiences into the narrative template for recovery that the organization provides (Cain 1991; Humphreys 2000). In the context of this community, then, recovery is seen not just as a matter of not drinking, but as a social practice that one actively performs with others.

What's particularly useful about this example in the context of the study of spoken discourse is that Alcoholics Anonymous is a community in which discursive resources, or 'technologies of talk', play a central role: the main thing that members do when they get together is talk, and one of the main things that distinguishes expert members from novices or non-members is their mastery of particular social languages and speech genres. What is stopping us then, we might ask, from labelling Alcoholics Anonymous a speech community or a discourse community? The answer is that *members* don't think of it that way. They don't think of themselves as people joined together by the fact that they talk in the same way, or by their ability to tell certain kinds of stories (like those who contribute to the It Gets Better Project), but rather by the *practice* of staying sober, of which talking in a certain way and telling certain kinds of stories form a part.

As a theoretical framework, the idea of communities of practice has gained considerable traction among sociolinguists and discourse analysts, mainly because it gives to analysts a way to understand the discursive behaviour of groups that cannot be accounted for by traditional models of either speech communities or discourse communities. The framework was first adopted into sociolinguistics by Penelope Eckert and Sally McConnell-Ginet (1992) to help them solve the problem of studying language and gender. It's no good, they reasoned, to study 'women' or 'men' as 'speech communities' or as 'discourse communities' since not all women or men talk the same as other women or men or use the same speech genres. Rather, it is better to focus on the ways particular groups of women and men talk when they are engaged in particular social practices. What makes language 'gendered' in this way of looking at things, is the fact that many social practices come with social norms about if and how members of different genders are expected to participate. 'Modes of participation available to various individuals within various communities of practice,' write Eckert and McConnell-Ginet (1992: 473) are often 'a direct or indirect function of gender', and 'these modes determine not only the development of particular strategies of performance and interpretation, but more generally access to meaning making and meaning-making rights'. Ways of 'talking like a woman' or 'talking like a man' 'emerge in the course of [these] mutual endeavour[s]' (464). This view provides a way to focus on how agency is constrained and enabled by the technologized social practices we are meant to engage in as members of our societies. It also reminds us that a person's ways of speaking (including their mastery of social languages and speech genres) are not a matter of simply 'belonging' to a particular community, but are developed through participation in myriad social practices of which those ways of speaking form functional components. As Eckert (2008: 110) puts it:

> A white working-class Italian-American woman does not develop her ways of speaking directly from the larger categories 'working class', 'Italian-American' and 'female', but from her day-to-day experience as a person who com-bines those three (and other) memberships. Her experience will be articulated by her participation in activities and communities of practice that are particular to her place in the social order. It is in these communities of practice that she will develop an identity and the linguistic practices to articulate this identity. Thus communities of practice are fundamental loci for the experience of membership in broader social categories.

Because it sees community membership as rooted in practices rather than speech varieties or genres, the community of practice model has been seen to offer analysts a way to overcome some of the perceived weaknesses of these other models, especially their tendency to marginalize non-linguistic aspects of social activity. From the point of view I am taking, however, which sees these different kinds of communities as technologies of talk that *social actors themselves* orient towards and take up to perform different social actions, what is important about these different models of community is the degree to which they enable social actors to do what they want to do in particular circumstances. In some situations, it might be more useful to identify oneself as a member of a speech community or a discourse community, and in others it might be more useful to identify oneself as a member of a community of practice. The important questions in thinking about communities of practice, then, as with speech communities and discourse communities, have to do with how they come to be 'imagined' as communities by their members, and what people can 'do' with them once they have been imagined.

   Throughout this book, I have been discussing the practice of 'coming out' and the various ways in which this practice can function as a 'technology of talk' which gay and lesbian individuals use to engage in certain kinds of interactions, manage their relationships with others and claim social identities. This practice has also proven to be an important political tool for the broader

'LGBT community', helping to create more 'visibility' for gays and lesbians and transforming them from passive victims into agents of social change (Armstrong 2002; Orne 2011; Shepard 2009). In fact, we might argue that the practice of 'coming out' has served as one tool through which gays and lesbians have been able to 'imagine' themselves as belonging to a coherent community. Given the variety of circumstances gays and lesbians face and the range of practices they participate in, however, it would be a mistake to see the 'LGBT community' as a 'community of practice' imagined around the social practice of 'coming out'. A better way, following Eckert and McConnell-Ginet (1992), would be to see gays and lesbians as engaging in multiple communities, each providing opportunities for mutual engagement in different practices, and each of these practices providing different ways for them to identify with other gays and lesbians.

A more appropriate example of a community of practice imagined around the practice of 'coming out' would be Randy's YouTube channel. On this channel, Randy and his followers are primarily engaged in managing their individual struggles with 'coming out' and giving one another advice. It is their mutual engagement in this specific practice that, from the point of view of members, gives to this channel its utility.

As Randy himself puts it:

```
24   pretty much (.) what I I
25   started this (0.2) this (0.3) YouTube channel for (0.7) was to: (.)
26   uh help me come out. (0.7) I know^ there's a lotta people that'll
27   benefit (0.5) from this (0.1) and I (.) I don't want to sound selfish^
28   (0.7) but I made this (0.1) f for me: (0.2) so (0.4) people can (0.7)
29   help me out (.) y'know^ (0.2) so every (inaudible) when I can push
30   me and say (0.5) alright (.) um (0.4) when are you gonna take the
31   next (.) next step when are you gonna^ (1.1) um (0.6) y'know tell
32   somebody⁶
```

Elsewhere in another video,[7] he explicitly resists using the channel to talk about topics unrelated to the primary practice of 'coming out':

```
1   ah sorry I haven't made ee eny
2   eh video for a while but I really didn't want to (0.6) make a video
3   just about nothing^ so: (0.4) this whole channel's pretty much (.)
4   focused on my whole (0.5) coming out process and (0.7)
5   I I didn't really just wanna make a (.) hey (0.8) what's up video
```

---

⁶Available at https://youtu.be/FXBJawOILwk.
⁷Available at https://youtu.be/-osYqoDJ4Tk.

And later in the same video he says:

44   I really just want this to be uh (0.2)
45   like a (0.8) a coming out channel

What makes this a community of practice is the opportunity that the medium provides for mutual engagement. The channel is not just a means for Randy to 'perform' his coming out to an audience. Randy's followers are active participants, responding to Randy's videos, giving him advice, and sharing their own experiences.

What is interesting about this community is that Randy, who is clearly it's most central member, presents himself, at least in the beginning, as a *novice* when it comes to the social practice of 'coming out', and relies on more 'expert followers' to give him guidance and encouragement. One example of such guidance comes from a follower named OSTRAEB4, who writes:

Good for you and your maturity and courage young MAN! Be true to yourself and what you are doing to set your soul and mind free from the mental prison of oppression. You're well spoken and convey your thoughts well. Just beware of disclosure to ppl you think are your friends and if they reject you then let them be. You don't need them because as I've always said, It takes a real man to stand up and be true to his realization of being gay. I disclosed to my family at age thirty a couple decades ago.

This contribution and others like it are designed not just to give Randy encouragement, but to offer evaluations of his performance of the practice so far and specific advice about the how to better participate in it in the future.

Along with such expert members, however, there are also other novice members, some of whom are less far along in their mastery of the practice than Randy, and for whom Randy functions as a role model, providing for them inspiration and ideas about how they can manage their own initial, peripheral participation. One (named flcb90) writes:

Hey Man I appreciate everything that you have done and everything you are doing. I actually just broke up with my 'girlfriend' because I have known that I am gay for quite a while. I was not raised in church but when I was around 12 a friend invited me and I got real big into the church thing to the point of wanting to become a pastor, or that was until the point that I realized that I was gay. Right now I'm working on doing the same thing you did when it comes to videos of your coming out The past couple of weeks I have just got to a point where I just couldnt keep living a lie and so I am hoping that doing videos will help give me the strength to come out.

Thanks for all of your videos, and you have diffenitly (sic) provided much help to me and have given me the strength to be myself

One thing that is particularly important about this community of practice is the way the material means through which people communicate provide enhanced opportunities for legitimate peripheral participation. As mentioned in Chapter 3, for example, one affordance of digital video is that it allows Randy to 'come out' (very publically) as gay, while at the same time, concealing his identity (i.e., not 'coming out' as himself). The opportunities for posters to contribute using pseudonyms provide for them similar opportunities to 'come out' without actually risking revealing their identities. It is not that participants see these anonymous revelations to strangers as a replacement to actually coming out to their friends and family members. Rather, they see them as opportunities to participate in the practice of 'coming out' in more peripheral ways as a prelude to a more complete mastery of the practice in the future. Randy himself puts it this way[8]:

```
6   why are you↓↑ (0.9)
7   doing this on YouTube. why are you coming out on YouTube↓↑ (0.6)
8   an::d ↓↑ (0.2) I really wanna say^ (1.6) cause I know how^ (0.4)
9   s:upportive^ (0.8) th (.) this kinda audience can be^ (0.6) an::d^ (1.5)
10  ninety-nine percent of everything I've gotten has said y'know^ (0.4)
11  good job go for it↓↑ (0.4) and it's a lot of encouragement that I can
12  get^ (0.7) ah (.) to build up to: ↓↑ (0.6) people closer to me. (0.3) it's
13  weird that you can come out to a stranger↓↑ (0.4) a lot easier than
14  you could ever come out to^ (0.7) your mom and your dad^ (1.1)
15  an:d people that you see everyday. (0.5) so that's exactly why.
```

Finally, an important aspect of this and other communities of practice is that they are not just means through which people are socialized into particular practices, but also places where, through the collective participation of members, these practices themselves evolve and change. As I said in Chapter 3, communities are essential engines for the technologization of cultural tools: social languages are technologized through peoples' interaction in speech communities; speech genres are technologized through their interaction in discourse communities; and social practices are technologized through their participation in communities of practice. Thus, Randy and his followers are not just collaborating in learning how to 'come out', but are also actively involved in debating what sort of practice coming out is and what sort of practice it might become in the future. One poster, for example,

[8]Available at https://www.youtube.com/watch?v=8D81LjveyN8.

questions the whole notion of 'coming out', declaring, 'Straight people do not have to make a public declaration that they are sleeping with someone of the opposite sex so why do we have to declare publically that we are sleeping with someone of the same sex?' (phillip fensom).

What then is the relationship between these more concrete communities, imagined around specific technologies of talk, and the more abstract communities I talked about at the beginning of this chapter such as the 'gay community' or the community of 'Americans'? These communities are, of course, not communities in the same sense, in that they do not involve mutual engagement, and often do not even involve shared languages, genres or social practices. Americans speak a whole range of language varieties from Pittsburghese to Valley Girl Talk, and members of the 'gay community' participate in a whole range of different social practices from 'coming out' to 'fishing' in public parks. What these imagined communities are, instead, are rhetorical artefacts which are made possible by the mutual engagement of people in these more concrete communities. What is important about these artefacts is that they allow people who may not share languages, or genres or practices to still rally around common goals and take collective actions. The potency of such artefacts can be seen in cases where, for example, members of a nation rally around a common cause in times of war or national disaster. Similarly, the idea of a 'gay community' has come to play an important role in the advancement of legal rights and social recognition for gays and lesbians, not to mention in collective responses to crises like the AIDS epidemic.

Movements built around such imagined communities provide people with the means of making sense of their individual experiences and managing their individual struggles with oppression by seeing themselves as part of a larger group (a nation, a race, a sexual orientation), even in cases where they have very little contact with other members of these communities. In fact, ideas like 'the gay community' exist in a dialectical relationship with the more concrete communities that form around specific technologies of talk. It is through the mutual engagement of members of these more concrete communities' that the imagining of these more abstract communities becomes possible. At the same time, the idea of these imagined communities is circulated back into these more concrete communities, becoming a part of the ways that members talk, of the genres they use to take social actions, and of the practices they participate in together.

8

Answerability and
the future of talk

I began this book with the example of 'coming out', a speech genre which I said involves two essential actions: revealing and responding. Both of these actions are extremely consequential, both for the parties involved in such conversations and for the societies in which these parties live. By revealing something about yourself which other people don't know, you are putting yourself on the line, testing the limits of what sorts of social identities can be accommodated in the context of your social world. And by the way people respond to such revelations, they are saying something about how people ought to be treated and what sorts of people should be included and excluded. Coming out is not just a conversation involving one person telling a secret to another. It is a conversation about what kind of society we wish to live in.

Throughout this book, I have been arguing that all conversations, even the most mundane ones, share with 'coming out' the same essentially ethical dimension. Every conversation we have involves issues of identity, agency, and group affiliation; every conversation involves us in some way 'putting ourselves on the line'; and every conversation demands from us that we *respond* to other people, not just in terms of what they are saying, but also in terms of who they are being.

At the core of the approach I have been outlining in this book is Bakhtin's (1986) notion of *dialogue*. Most people, when they think of the word 'dialogue' think that it is simply a conversation, usually between two people, often of the type you might find in a language textbook, but the idea of dialogue as Bakhtin explained it is much more complex, and much more profound. What he meant when he spoke of the *dialogic* nature of spoken discourse is that everything that we say (and everything that we '*do* with our words') is in some way a *response* to something that was said or done previously, and is an invitation for a subsequent response from someone else. As Bakhtin

(1986: 91) put it, 'Each utterance refutes affirms, supplements, and relies upon the others, presupposes them to be known, and somehow takes them into account. ... Therefore, each kind of utterance is filled with various kinds of responsive reactions to other utterances of the given sphere of speech communication.'

The 'dialogic' nature of spoken discourse, can be understood on several different levels. In the simplest sense, it can be seen on the level of the immediate conversation in which what one person says is always addressed to someone and creates the conditions for that person to respond in a particular way. If one person asks a question, for example, he or she is creating the conditions for the other person to give an answer. That's not to say that the other person always responds with an answer, but, as I discussed in Chapter 4, even *not* giving an answer or remaining silent is considered a kind of response.

But there's another way to think about this idea of dialogue that takes us beyond the boundaries of particular conversations. Rather than just seeing utterances as responses to what another person has just said, we can also see them as responses to things that may have been said in previous conversations. In fact, this is a central aspect of most of the conversations that we have with the people we know: so much of how we talk to them depends on the history of utterances that we have with them that has accumulated over our relationship. So one of the most important things about dialogue is how it works beyond the level of the bounded, situated interaction to link conversations with other conversations, and situations with other situations.

Taking this idea one step further, we start to see that we are always responding not just to the person to whom we are talking, but to all sorts of other people as well. If I'm talking to you about the president, for example, I'm not just responding to your opinions about the president, but also to what the president has said, what other people have said about the president, and a whole field of utterances about the presidency that have accumulated in my consciousness and in the cultural context which I share with you. And so our conversation about the president, no matter how private, is also part of one or more larger political/ideological conversations that are taking place in the society in which we live, what I have been referring to (following Gee 2011) as 'big C Conversations'. And this is not just true for conversations about such things as the presidency or gays in the military. It's true for every conversation. Even the most mundane exchanges we have link us to one or more 'big C Conversations' in our society.

Finally, we are not just responding to other people, but are also responding to *ourselves* – to those 'voices' inside of our heads, which have formed out of previous conversations that we have had. Vygotsky (1962) calls these voices 'inner speech'. The important thing about inner speech is that it is the result of being exposed to 'outer speech'; it is the internalization of what other people, our parents, our teachers, our lovers and friends, and the media have said to us, and our responses to those utterances. 'Our minds', as Morson (2009: 14) puts it, 'are composed of the listeners that inhabit us ... [and] we address them when we think.'

The key point of this idea of dialogue, then, is that everything we say is also connected in a web of discourse to people, places and practices that extend far beyond the present conversation. 'Any concrete utterance' says Bakhtin (1986: 91), is a 'link' in a 'chain of speech communication', and every conversation takes place at the intersection of multiple chains of utterances.

As I have been arguing throughout this book, what this view of spoken discourse inevitably leads us to is a way of studying conversation that cannot ignore its ethical dimensions. The word Bakhtin (1993) used to capture the ethical dimension of conversation is *answerability*. Whenever we engage in social interaction, he insisted, we become *answerable* for what we say and do. We are answerable, of course, to the people with whom we are interacting – we must respond to their contributions and provide contributions for them to respond to that conform to the rules of the *interaction order* that govern whatever site of engagement we find ourselves in. But we are also answerable to all of the other people who might be implicated in this conversation in one way or another and for the way we are contributing to the larger 'big C' Conversations of which this interaction may be a part. So whenever we interact, we are not only collaboratively authoring the 'story' of our interaction and the 'story' of our ongoing relationship with the people with whom we are talking, but we are also taking part in authoring the 'grand narratives' (Lyotard 1979) of our communities and societies. Finally, we are answerable to ourselves. Every conversation we have is an opportunity to decide what sort of person we want to become. 'The difference between humans and other forms of life', write Clark and Holquist (1984: 67–8) by way of explaining Bakhtin's notion of answerability, is that human life is 'a form of authorship ...'

> What the self is answerable to is the social environment; what the self is answerable for is the authorship of its responses. The self creates itself in crafting an architectonic relation between the unique locus of life activity and the constantly changing natural and social environment which surrounds it. This is the meaning of Bakhtin's dictum that the self is an act of grace, a gift of the other.

Throughout this book, I have been developing an analytical approach that focuses on the relationship between spoken discourse and the concrete *actions* we take with it. In this final chapter I would like to argue, following Bakhtin, that every social action is deep down an ethical act, and that the foundation of ethical action is answerability. What this means is that questions of ethics are not abstract, philosophical questions, but practical questions concerned with 'the individual's capacity for good or harm... through responsive acts of language' (Juzwik 2004: 537). As Haynes (2013: para 3) writes:

> The need to answer the other responsibly implies obligation. Such obligation is never solely theoretical, but is an individual's concrete response to actual persons in specific situations. Thus, for Bakhtin answerability is the name for individual responsibility and obligation that leads to action – for ourselves, of course, but also on behalf of others.

What this also means is that questions of ethics (including questions about power, agency, ideology and inequality) are not just questions reserved for critical discourse analysts and other scholars interested in the 'big D' dimensions of discourse – they are questions that anyone interested in spoken discourse must confront in one form or another. Just as people engaged in conversations are, in Bakhtin's (1993: 10) words, without 'alibi' – they must respond in some way to the people they are talking to and the social contexts in which their conversations take place – scholars of spoken discourse are also without 'alibi' – they cannot avoid considering the *consequences* of utterances for the people who are producing and receiving them and for the societies in which these people live. The study of spoken discourse is not just about how we use language and other 'technologies of talk' to act, interact, claim identities and imagine communities, but also about answering the question: 'how we shall live together?' (Nielsen 2012).

It is all well and good, of course, to insist that acts of speaking are ethical acts and that we are somehow answerable to one another, but the job of a discourse analyst is to try to explain *how* answerability is possible, how the technologies of talk that I have been discussing in this book provide for us concrete resources to address the ethical dimensions of conversation. The answer to these questions I will offer in this chapter is that discourse helps us to be answerable to one another through its essentially *reflexive* nature, the ability it gives us 'to constitute an utterance and its structure as object and situate it in a social situation' (Lucy 1993a: 2). As Lucy (1993b: 11) writes:

> Speech is permeated by reflexive activity as speakers remark on language, report utterances, index and describe aspects of the speech event, invoke conventional names, and guide listeners in the proper interpretation of their utterances. This reflexivity is so pervasive and essential that we can say that language is, by nature, fundamentally reflexive.

Reflexivity is the quality of discourse that allows us to turn back at look at what we have said and done and talk about it, to reflect upon it, to reformulate it, and to reframe it through what I referred to in Chapter 3 as *metadiscourse*.

In Chapter 3, I said that the affordance of language to allow us to talk about our talk plays an important role in the technologization of the tools we use to conduct conversations, including speech genres, social languages, social practices and social identities. All of these tools come about through processes by which people reflect upon and call attention to how they are talking, what they are doing, and who they are being. In fact, many of the conversations that I have analysed in this book involve people in some way talking about their talk. But metadiscourse is not limited to explicit verbal comments on what we are saying or how we are talking. Many of the other discursive processes that I have discussed in this book – entextualization, contextualization, indexing, framing, establishing footing, identifying and positioning oneself and others, using 'politeness strategies' to signal our relationship with others, and 'imagining' communities around different kinds of technologies of talk – are all essentially metadiscursive processes, because they involve people not just producing discourse, but organizing it, commenting upon it, taking some kind of stance towards it, and using it to signal their communicative intentions. They are examples of what Bateson (1971; Ruesch and Bateson 1951) called 'metacommunication'. It is through such metacommunicative strategies that the practices, identities and relationships that form the fabric of social life are made recognizable (Urban 1996). As Silverstein (1993: 35) puts it, metadiscourse is responsible for the 'contextually situated, interactional establishment, maintenance and renewal of social relations in societies'.

The reason metadiscursive strategies are so important in helping us to be answerable to one another is that they represent moments in conversations when aspects of 'what we are doing', 'who we are being', and 'how we are treating each another' become available for us to reflect upon, debate and revise. They are the moments in conversations in which we work together to construct the technologies of talk that we will carry into future interactions. And they are the moments that present us with opportunities to understand how our 'small c' conversations contribute to 'big C' Conversations. In a sense, the most important parts of the conversations in which Randy comes out to his father and his friend and his comrades in the Air Force that I discussed in the previous chapters are not the moments when he reveals his secret and his interlocutors react, but the moments following the 'coming out' when Randy and his interlocutors discuss and reflect upon his revelation and their reaction, because it is in these moments that they are talking about not just what it means to be 'gay', but what it means to be a father, a son, and a friend, and they are talking about not just 'coming out', but more generally what it means to reveal, and respond, and be answerable to others for those revelations and responses.

But metadiscourse is not always a good thing. It can also be used to make us *less* answerable, to silence debate, harden stereotypes, increase inequality and 'put people in their place' (Morgan 1995: 12). In a debate in the summer of 2015, presidential candidate Donald Trump was asked by Fox News reporter Megyn Kelly about the language he had used in the past to talk about women. 'You've called women you don't like "fat pigs", dogs and disgusting animals,' she noted. 'how will you answer the charge … that you are a part of the war on women?' Kelly's question is a good example of metadiscourse: an attempt to get Trump to be accountable not just for what he has said, but also *how* he talks. In response, Trump produced his own example of metadiscourse:

> I think the big problem this country has is being politically correct. I've been challenged by so many people and I don't, frankly, have time for total political correctness. And to be honest with you, this country doesn't have time, either.

Rather than answering Kelly's question, Trump uses metadiscourse to characterize the question as a certain type of talk – 'political correctness' – a type which has already been widely discredited among many of the voters that made up the debate's audience. What Trump does, then, is to use metadiscourse to discredit metadiscourse, to argue not only that it is 'unfair' to hold him accountable for his words, but that reflecting on words and their impact is what is distracting the country from taking the kinds of actions that we need to take, an argument that, of course, ignores the central premise of much of the work in discourse analysis that I have reviewed in this book: the fact that discourse and action are inseparable, that we do things with words, and mean things with actions, and that all actions are somehow dependent on discourse. In other words, just as the metadiscursive affordance of language can be used to make us more answerable to each other, it can also be used to make us less answerable.

Metadiscourse and accountability

On 10 July 2015 a 28-year-old African American woman named Sandra Bland was stopped for a routine traffic violation in Waller County, Texas by Texas State Trooper Brian Encinia. During the stop, a dispute occurred which resulted in Bland's arrest. Three days later, she was found dead in her jail cell as the result of an apparent suicide. Bland's arrest for what appeared to be a minor infraction, and her subsequent death, attracted considerable media and public attention and led the Texas Department of Public Safety to release the dashcam video of the arrest.[1] The conversation between Bland and Encinia recorded on this video became the object of intense public debate about the extent to which police officers should be answerable for their actions, especially in regard to their treatment of African Americans, an issue which was already in the news due to a spate of reports of unarmed African Americans (some of them children) being shot and killed by police officers. In some ways, this incident demonstrates the power of metadiscourse to connect 'small c' conversations like that between Bland and state trooper Encinia prior to her arrest to 'big C' Conversations about police conduct, citizen rights, and racism. At the same time, the conversation recorded by the dashcam also demonstrates the limits of metadiscourse, the way that metadiscourse can sometimes be used to escalate conflicts rather than resolve them.

The interaction begins like any routine traffic stop with Encinia asking for Bland's licence and registration and then radioing the details to the dispatcher:

1	Encinia	Hello ma'am. (0.8) we're the Texas Highway Patrol^ the
2		reason for your stop is because you didn't fail: (.) you failed
3		to signal (0.5) a <u>lane</u> change. (0.5) you got your drivers
4		license and insurance please?
5		(2.8)
6		what's wrong.
7		(22.5)
8		how long you been in Texas↑↓ (0.7)
9	Bland	got here yesterday^ (0.4)
10	Encinia	okay.
11		(10.7)
12		do you have a drivers^ license?
13	Bland	(inaudible)
14	Encinia	no ma'am↑↓
15	Bland	(inaudible)
16	Encinia	okay↓↑
17		(11. 4)
18		°okay°
19		(3.0)
20		where you headed to now↑↓ (2.0)
21	Bland	(inaudible) (0.8)
22	Encinia	o:kay↓↑ (1.3) give me a few minutes (.) alright↓↑
23		(4 min. 11 sec. elapses. Sounds of police radio.)

---

[1]Available at https://www.youtube.com/watch?v=CBh3wzXd3vg.

The encounter begins to get more complicated when Encinia returns to Bland's vehicle and comments upon her apparent irritation:

```
24  Encinia   you okay? (0.8)
25  Bland     I'm waitin on you you (0.4) this is your job. (0.3)
26            I'm waitin on you (.) when you gonna let [me go.
27  Encinia                                          [I don't know (.)
28            you seem very irritated=
29  Bland                              =I am. I I really am. I feel like
30            it's crap what I'm getting a ticket for (.) I was getting out
31            of your way. (.) you were speeding up^ (0.3) tailing me↓↑
32            (0.4) so I move over^ (.) and you stop me. (0.4) so^ (.) yeah↑↓
33            so yeah I am a little irritated [but^
34  Encinia                                  [yeah=
35  Bland                                          =that doesn't stop you
36            from givin me a ticket (.) so^
37            (4.4)
38  Encinia   are you done? (1.1)
39  Bland     you asked me what's wrong ↓↑ (.) and I told you. (0.6)
40  Encinia   okay.=
41  Bland          =so now I'm done (.) yeah.=
42  Encinia                                   =okay.
```

While Bland is obviously annoyed at being cited for a violation she thinks she did not commit, rather than addressing this objection, Encinia's response is to metadiscursively comment upon her explanation ('are you done?') in a way that implies that it is somehow inappropriate, even though he himself has just seconds before elicited it. The conflict further escalates when Encinia issues an apparently unrelated directive (in the form of a 'request') that Bland put out her cigarette. When she refuses to comply, questioning his right to issue such a directive, he orders her out of her car:

```
43            (3.7)
44            you mind putting out your cigarette please? (0.3)
45            if you don't mind↑↓
46            (2.9)
47  Bland     I'm in my car↑↓ I don't have to put out my
48            cigarette↑↓ (0.3)
49  Encinia   well you can step on out now↓↑
50            (0.8)
51  Bland     I don't have to step out of my [car
52  Encinia                                  [step out
```

```
53              of the car.
54              (2.6)
55   Bland      why am I^ (0.3)
56   Encinia    step [ out      of      the      car.
57   Bland            [ no you don't have (.) no you don't have the right.
58   Encinia    STEP [ out    of ] the CAR.=
59   Bland              [you do not.]
60                                           =you do not have the
61              right to do that=
62   Encinia                    =I do have the right^ (0.3) now step
63              out (.) [or [ I     will ] remove yout↓=
64   Bland              [inaudible]              =I refuse to talk to
65              you other than to identify my[self
66                                      [STEP out↑↓(.)
67              or I will remove yout↓=
68   Bland                        = I am getting removed
69              for a failure [ to signal↓↑
70   Encinia             [ STEP out↑↓ (0.4) or I will remove yout↓ (.)
71              I'm giving you a lawful order.
72              (1.6)
73              get outta the car (.) now. (0.3) or I'm gonna
74              remove you. (0.2)
75   Bland      and I'm calling my [lawyer
76   Encinia                     [I'm gonna get you outta here↑↓=
77   Bland      =okay you gonna get me outta my car?=
78   Encinia                                =get out.
79   Bland      okay↓↑ (0.4) alright.
80   Encinia    (on radio) twenty=five [ les (inaudible]
81   Bland                          [ let's do this (0.3)
82   Encinia    yeah^ (.) we're gonna (.) going [ to.
83   Bland                                [yeah? (0.3)
84              don't (.) don't touch me^
85   Encinia    GET outta [ the CAR.]
86   Bland               [inaudible] (0.3)
87              don't touch me^ (.) I'm not under arrest (.) you don't have
88              the right to touch [me
89   Encinia                      [you are under arrest. (0.2)
90   Bland      I'm under arrest for what↑↓ (0.3)
91   Encinia    (on radio) twenty-five [ inaudible ] send another unit.
92   Bland                          [for what↑↓]
93              (0.5)
94   Encinia    get outta the CAR.
```

95		(2.1) (radio sounds)
96		get out of the <u>CAR</u>. (.) <u>NOW</u>. (0.4)
97	Bland	why am I being apprehended. (.) you tryin to give me
98		a [ticket^
99	Encinia	[I said (.) get out of the <u>car</u>.=
100	Bland	= why am I being
101		apprehended.=
102	Encinia	=I am giving a lawful order. (0.4)
103		I am gonna <u>drag</u> you outta here=
104	Bland	=so you're gonna
105		drag me outta my own car↑↓
106	Encinia	GET <u>OUTTA</u> THE <u>CAR</u>. (0.5)
107		(Encinia draws Taser) I will <u>LIGHT</u> you <u>UP</u>. (.)
108		<u>GET</u> <u>OUT</u>.
109	Bland	wow.
110	Encinia	<u>NOW</u>.
111	Bland	wow.
112	Encinia	get <u>OUTTA</u> the <u>CAR</u>.
113	Bland	wow you doing all this for a failure to signal.

The important question here, from the perspective of understanding answerability, is how someone's refusal to put out her cigarette could have so quickly escalated into a situation in which a police officer threatens to electrocute an unarmed woman with a Taser. The answer lies in how the two parties use metadiscursive strategies to transform the conversation into one that is not about Bland's alleged traffic violation, but about who has the right to say and do certain things in the conversation. Encinia begins this transformation by noting that Bland seems 'irritated', implying that this is an inappropriate stance, and then replying to her explanation with 'are you done?' Even the request for Bland to put out her cigarette can be seen at the level of metadiscourse as an attempt by the officer to assert his authority over Bland. This 'request' is not so much a request as an 'order'. Bland, for her part, continually questions the officer's right to issue certain directives, asks him to clarify 'what's going on here', and asks him to reconcile the degree of force he is using with the severity of her alleged offence ('you doing all this for a failure to signal.').

Tannen (1992), drawing on the work of Bateson (1935), talks about a phenomenon in conversation known as *complementary schismogenesis* in which the metadiscursive strategies that two people use don't match to the extent that the more one person engages in a particular strategy, the more the other responds with the complementary strategy, so that each person's behaviour drives the other person to increasingly more exaggerated forms of the opposing behaviour. In this situation, for example, the more the officer attempts to assert his authority, the more Bland resists this authority, the more determined he becomes to assert his authority. The real key to understanding this dispute, however, is the fundamental inequality between the parties when it comes to their ability to use metadiscourse. Because of his position of power, the officer has the ability to assert his authority and question her failure to comply in more indirect ways ('are you done?'; 'you mind putting out your cigarette please?'). In other words, like the police officer in Hong Kong who said, 'I don't want to have to use force in front of all of these people,' Encinia is in the position of being able to threaten her 'without threatening her'. For Bland, on the other hand, questioning the officer's authority depends upon more explicit assertions of her rights and his responsibilities. She cannot afford to be subtle. But what she does manage to achieve with this strategy is to force him to be more explicit about his exercise of authority ('I am giving a lawful order'), thus bringing to the surface of the conversation his assumptions about his power over her.

What happens after this excerpt is less clear, since it occurs outside the frame of the video. Perhaps aware of this, however, Bland produces another form of metadiscourse by narrating the events. 'You just slammed me, knocked my head in the ground,' she says as Encinia is handcuffing her. She then informs him that she has epilepsy, to which he replies, 'Good, good.' In his account of the incident in the arrest warrant affidavit, Encinia wrote that Bland became 'combative and uncooperative' and that she was placed in handcuffs to protect the safety of the officer. He also wrote that Bland 'was placed under arrest for Assault on a Public Servant'. Thus, what began as a series of indirect threats by the officer, and escalated into more direct threats (I will <u>LIGHT</u> you <u>UP</u>) is transformed by the officer into a narrative in which Bland is portrayed as threatening him. Such is the power of metadiscourse in the hands of those with the authority to entextualize interactions.

But that's not the end of the story, because Encinia's report is not the only entextualization available of the incident. After inquiries from Bland's family as a result of her death, and pressure from the media, the Texas Department of Public Safety released the dashcam footage from which the excerpt above comes, footage which was immediately posted on YouTube and drew more than 1.2 million views within twenty-four hours. Because, the video so clearly contradicted Encinia's account, its release resulted in him, at least temporarily, being removed from active patrol duty.

The most important result of the entextualization of this event on video and its circulation over the internet, however, was that it helped to link this particular incident with a broader pattern of police abuse against African Americans, and to link the 'small c' conversation between Bland and Encinia to a 'big C' Conversation about racism and police brutality that was going on at the time. This 'big C' Conversation itself, was the result of a series of incidents involving

African Americans dying at the hands of police, including teenager Michael Brown in Ferguson, Missouri, forty-three-year-old Eric Garner in New York City, twelve-year-old Tamir Rice in Cleveland, Ohio, and fifty-year-old Walter Scott in North Charleston, South Carolina, who, like Bland, was stopped for a minor traffic violation.

Such incidents of violence against African Americans in the United States, of course, are not new. What is new is the prevalence of digital video cameras, either in the form of police dashcams or bodycams, or in the form of personal video cameras embedded in the cell phones of civilian witnesses, which allowed these incidents to be so efficiently *entextualized*, and the existence of social media sites like YouTube that allow these entextualizations to be shared, circulated and commented upon by the public. This perhaps is part of the promise of digital technology when it comes to spoken discourse, its potential not just to document incidents like this, but to link individual interactions to larger patterns of behaviour, and individual conversations to larger public debates about power, authority and inequality. Randy Phillip's public coming out on YouTube and the dashcam footage of Sandra Bland's arrest are both examples of how new technologies of talk are changing the nature of spoken discourse, blurring boundaries between public and private and in some ways forcing people to be more accountable – more 'answerable' for their talk and actions. Of course, there is also something disturbing about the pervasive recording of interactions, which often constitutes an invasion of people's privacy, and the 'culture of public shaming' that has developed on the internet around these technologies (Solove 2007). But the most dangerous thing about such practices of entextualizing interactions is that they entice us into thinking that these artefacts represent 'objective' versions of what actually happened. As I argued in Chapter 4, just as important as entextualization in conveying meaning and performing actions is the way discourse is *contextualized*. Although digital technologies have given us new ways to entextualize our words, what we are ultimately able to 'do with those words' still depends on many of the older technologies of talk that I have discussed throughout this book which we use to recontextualize and interpret them.

Technologies of talk as technologies of seeing

There is perhaps no better example of how these older technologies of talk can affect the way seemingly objective representations of social interactions are 'read' than the case of Rodney King, arguably first major case of police brutality against an African American documented on video. On 3 March 1991, an African American motorist named Rodney King was detained and beaten by four officers of the Los Angeles Police Department. The incident was captured on video from the balcony of a man who lived close by, and the man subsequently sent the tape to a local television station. The video showed the officers surrounding King's body and taking turns repeatedly striking and kicking him while the others looked on. The airing of the video sparked outrage among the public, and the four officers involved were charged with assault and use of excessive force on the basis of the seemingly inconvertible evidence of the video tape. When the case came to trial, however, the four officers were acquitted, based on an interpretation of the tape which portrayed the officers' actions as justified attempts to protect themselves against King, who was seen to pose a threat to them. The verdict resulted in widespread condemnation in the African American community and sparked the Los Angeles riots of 1992.

Goodwin (1994) provides an explanation of how the defence attorney and his 'expert witnesses' managed to transform what seemed to most people to be an objective representation of a black man being brutally beaten by four police officers into a representation of police officers protecting themselves against a violent criminal through the use of various *metadiscursive* strategies made possible by the technologies of talk they had available to them. Perhaps the most important of these technologies was the *speech genre* of courtroom questioning, which allowed the defence attorney to structure and present the video in a way that was very different from that experienced by viewers who had seen it on television. First, this genre enabled them to replace the soundtrack of the video (which contained the officers hurling racial slurs at King) with the commentary of expert witnesses, so that the 'evidence' consisted not just of the images, but of the images as narrated by the attorney and his experts. Second, they were able to, stop and start the tape, play it in slow motion, and capture moments from it as still images, decontextualizing them from the flow of events. This fragmented version of the tape had the effect of interrupting the narrative flow of the incident, turning what had been the 'story' of a man being beaten into a series of clips and images to be analysed in isolation. Finally, the question–answer format of the examination allowed the attorney to control the 'reading' of the tape so that certain parts of it were highlighted and other parts were pushed in the background. Of course, the prosecutors also had access to many of these strategies in their cross-examination, but were not able to use them as effectively because they were less prepared to engage with the micro-analytical reading of the tape that the defence attorney introduced.

Another important technology that the defence was able to deploy was the *social language* of police work with its terms such as 'escalation', 'de-escalation' and 'assessment period' and its way of labelling and dividing up phenomena that was likely unfamiliar to most of the members of the jury. In explaining the tape, for example, rather than using everyday terms like 'strike', 'kick' and 'beat', the expert witness explained the officers' actions in this way (Goodwin 1994: 617)

> Expert: There were,
> ten distinct (1.0) uses of force.
> rather than one single use of force.
> ...
> In each of those, uses of force
> there was an escalation and a de-escalation, (0.8)
> an assessment period, (1.5)
> and then an escalation and a de-escalation again. (0.7)
> And another assessment period.

Not only did this language have the effect of making the officers' actions seem like an 'orderly' and 'systematic' response to the situation, but it also served to portray their actions as a kind of 'professional craft' which requires a level of expertise that most people in the general public are unable to claim, and therefore unable to evaluate.

There were also important tools that Goodwin does not mention in his analysis but which for many other observers seemed to be central to the defence's ability to transform the victim, King, into a dangerous threat who had to be subdued. Most important of these was the *social identity* of the black man in contemporary American society, and the cultural storyline of violence and fear associated with this identity. Of course, neither this identity nor this storyline was explicitly deployed by the defence attorney or his witnesses. Rather, it was subtly indexed by the repeated *positioning* of King as a threat to the officers in the expert narrative, and the repeated attention paid in the visual evidence to King's black body as an object of suspicion. 'The visual representation of the black male body being beaten on the street by the policemen and their batons', as Butler (1993c: 16) puts it, 'was taken up by (a) racist interpretive framework to construe King as an *agent* of violence, one whose agency is phantasmatically implied as the narrative precedent and antecedent to the frames that are shown'. Within the framework of this cultural storyline, Butler observes elsewhere (Yancy and Butler 2015: para 6) black men:

> are perceived as threats even when they do not threaten, when they have no weapon, and the video footage that shows precisely this is taken to be a ratification of the police's perception. The perception is then ratified as a public perception at which point we not only must insist on the dignity of black lives, but name the racism that has become ratified as public perception.

Such observations lead us to see how, in this and many other situations, racism itself has become a pervasive 'technology of talk', a 'schema' through which reality is read.

The 'technologization' of racism as a cultural tool takes place on many different levels: On the level of the legal system that punishes African Americans more severely than whites for the same crimes, on the level of the media which portrays white outrage as protest and black outrage as rioting, and on the level of individual interactions between African Americans and police officers like that between Sandra Bland and state trooper Encinia. As this schema is continually deployed on all of these levels, the form of thinking that resulted in the acquittal of the officers who beat Rodney King and the treatment of Bland at the hands of state trooper Encinia becomes, as Butler (Yancy and Butler 2015: para 13) puts it, 'more and more "reasonable". ... In other words, every time a grand jury or a police review board accepts this form of reasoning, they ratify the idea that blacks are a population against which society must be defended.'

The point I wish to make in this discussion is not just a point about racism in America. It is a bigger point about the power of metadiscursive strategies to shape our perceptions of reality and our treatment of other people, either for good or for ill. As Goodwin (1994) observes, our understanding of reality is always filtered through the discursive resources and metadiscursive processes that we use to focus attention onto different aspects of our phenomenal and social environments. Seeing an event as 'meaningful' is not a transparent, psychological process, but is instead a socially situated activity accomplished through the deployment of a range of historically constituted discursive practices and technologies of talk.

Discourse analysis as mediated action

This observation should give heed, not just to African American motorists, police officers and members of juries, but also to discourse analysts. Our access to 'what's going on' in any particular interaction that we wish to analyse is similarly filtered through various technologies of talk, including both material technologies such as tape recorders and video cameras and written transcripts, and semiotic technologies such as theories, analytical frameworks, and the speech genres and social languages that we use to talk about and report on our work.

In the beginning of this book, I demonstrated how our perception of the conversation between Randy and his father changed as we adjusted the 'circumference' of our analysis, sometimes 'zooming in' on small details of the interaction like the pauses between turns, and sometimes 'zooming out' to reveal the larger context of the conversation, first revealing it to be part of a telephone conversation, then to be part of a YouTube video, then to be part of a larger historical moment in the United States when the 'Don't Ask, Don't Tell' policy was in the process of being lifted. What I was trying to show by doing this was how our understanding of what's going on in spoken discourse can change radically depending on the analytical circumferences that we draw around the people and the interactions we are studying. Throughout this book, I have attempted to further widen the circumference of my analysis of Randy's coming out, showing how individual conversations like this are always linked to broader ideological debates and power struggles in society.

The main point I have been trying to make is that it is impossible to really understand such conversations without widening our perception to take into account the broader social contexts of the societies in which such conversations take place, in the same way it is impossible to understand Sandra Bland's confrontation with state trooper Encinia without taking into account the longer history of confrontations between African Americans and law enforcement officials in the United States and the technologized racism that has often governed these encounters. At the same time, it is also impossible to understand these broader social contexts or to engage sensibly in debates about things like racism or homophobia if we are unable to see how these social contexts are created through the moment by moment technologization of the tools that we use for talking to each other that takes place in situated social interactions.

Being a good analyst of spoken discourse requires that we become adept at 'circumferencing', at continually adjusting our perception of phenomena so that we don't get 'stuck' either in the 'small d' discourse of the individual interaction or the 'big D' discourse of the social context. 'Circumferencing' is also the secret to being answerable to one another when it comes to how we use and interpret spoken discourse in our everyday lives. One way to avoid being answerable, as the examples above show, is to fix our view of reality into one particular circumference in a way that blinds us to what is occurring on other scales. This is what the defence attorney in the Rodney King trial does when he focuses the jury's attention onto the micro movements of the figures in the video in a way that distracts from the wider activity that was occurring and the broader social context in which it was occurring. It is also what people do when they respond to the cry of 'black lives matter' with the more universal phrase 'all lives matter', broadening the circumference in a way that deflects attention away from the specific dangers imposed on black lives by systematic police violence and institutional racism.

The purpose of analysing spoken discourse is not just to find out something interesting about language and communication. It is to make us better at it.

In a way, we are all discourse analysts. What Randy is doing when he discusses his strategies for coming out with his followers over YouTube, and what Sandra Bland is doing when she tries to make state trooper Encinia accountable for his actions, and what the defence attorney in the Rodney King trial does when he re-presents the video of the beating to the jury through the framework of the officers' 'professional vision', and even what the store clerks and customer are doing in the conversation in the bookstore I analysed as they negotiate their various rights and responsibilities in the interaction, is essentially discourse analysis. And it is through understanding how we engage in such everyday acts of analysis that we will be able to be more answerable to each other for what we say, for what we do, for who we are, and for the societies we live in. As Hymes (cited by Luke 1996: viii–ix) puts it:

> Discourse ultimately cannot change the inequalities that make it rational for centres and margins of power alike to combine in ecological destruction … nor change interests that find it reasonable to allow the destruction of habitat, even to continue to prepare for the destruction of us all; but discourse is everywhere, and scrutiny of our own and that of others is a lens that may sometimes focus light enough to illuminate and even to start a fire.

References

Agha, A. (2004), 'Registers of language', in A. Duranti (ed.), *A Companion to Linguistic Anthropology*, 23–45, Malden, MA: Wiley-Blackwell.

Agha, A. (2005), 'Voice, footing, enregisterment', *Journal of Linguistic Anthropology*, 15 (1): 38–59.

Agha, A. (2007), *Language and Social Relations*, Cambridge; New York: Cambridge University Press.

Alexander, J. C. (2003), *The Meanings of Social Life: A Cultural Sociology*, New York: Oxford University Press.

Alexander, J. and Losh, E. (2010), 'A YouTube of one's own? Coming out videos as rhetorical action', in C. Pullen and M. Cooper (eds), *LGBT Identity and Online New Media*, 37–50, London: Routledge.

Althusser, L. (1971), 'On ideology and ideological state apparatuses: Notes towards an investigation', in L. Althusser (ed.), *Lenin and Philosophy and Other Essays*, 121–73, London: New Left Books.

Anderson, B. (1991), *Imagined Communities: Reflections on the Origin and Spread of Nationalism*, London: Verso.

Androutsopoulos, J. K. and Georgakopoulou, A. (2003), 'Discourse construction of youth identities: Introduction', in J. K. Androutsopoulos and A. Georgakopoulou (eds), *Discourse Constructions of Youth Identities*, 1–25, Amsterdam; Philadelphia: John Benjamins.

Androstopholous, J. K. and Tereick, J. (2015), 'YouTube: Language and discourse practices in participatory culture', in A. Gerogakopoulou and T. Spilioti (eds), *The Routledge Handbook of Language and Digital Communication*, 354–70, London: Routledge.

Antaki, C., Condor, S. and Levine, M. (1996), 'Social identities in talk: Speakers' own orientations', *British Journal of Social Psychology*, 35 (4): 473–92.

Antaki C. and Widdicombe, S. (1998), *Identities in Talk*, London: Sage.

Armstrong E. (2002), *Forging Gay Identities: Organizing Sexuality in San Francisco, 1950–1994*, Chicago: University of Chicago Press.

Auer, P. (1992), 'Introduction: John Gumperz' approach to contextualization', in P. Auer and A. Di Luzio (eds), *The Contextualization of Language*, 1–37, Amsterdam: John Benjamins.

Auer, P. and Di Luzio, A. (1992), *The Contextualization of Language*, Amsterdam: John Benjamins.

Austin, J. L. (1962), *How To Do Things With Words*, Oxford: Oxford University Press.

Bach, K. (2006), 'Speech acts and pragmatics', in M. Devitt and R. Hanley (eds), *The Blackwell Guide to the Philosophy of Language*, 147–67, London: Blackwell.

Bacon, J. (1998), 'Getting the story straight: Coming out narratives and the possibility of a cultural rhetoric', *World Englishes*, 17 (2): 249–58.

Bakhtin, M. M. (1981), *The Dialogic Imagination: Four Essays*, edited by
    M. Holquist, translated by C. Emerson, Austin: University of Texas Press.
Bakhtin, M. M. (1986), *Speech Genres and Other Late Essays*, edited by
    C. Emerson and M. Holquist, translated by V. McGee, Austin: University of
    Texas Press.
Bakhtin, M. M. (2010), *Toward a Philosophy of the Act*, edited by V. Laipinov and
    M. Holquist, translated by V. Liapunov, Ausin: University of Texas Press.
Bamberg, M., De Fina, A. and Schiffrin, D. (2011), 'Discourse and identity
    construction', in S. J. Schwartz, K. Luyckx and V. L. Vignoles (eds), *Handbook
    of Identity Theory and Research*, 177–99, New York: Springer.
Bara, B. G. (2010), *Cognitive Pragmatics: The Mental Processes of
    Communication*, translated by J. Douthwaite, Cambridge, MA: MIT Press.
Baron, N. (2010), *Always On: Language in an Online and Mobile World*, New York:
    Oxford University Press.
Barrett, R. (1997), 'The "homo-genius" speech community', in A. Livia and K. Hall
    (eds), *Queerly Phrased: Language, Gender, and Sexuality*, 181–201, New York:
    Oxford University Press.
Bateson, G. (1935), 'Culture, contact and schismogenesis', *Man*, 35: 178–83.
Bateson, G. (1971), 'Communication', in N. McQuown (ed.), *The Natural History
    of an Interview*, 177–99, Chicago: University of Chicago Microfilm Library
    Microfilm.
Bateson, G. (1972/2000), *Steps to an Ecology of Mind*, Chicago: University of
    Chicago Press.
Bauman, R. and Briggs, C. L. (1990), 'Poetics and performance as critical
    perspectives on language and social life', *Annual Review of Anthropology*,
    19: 59–88.
Baumann, G. (1996), *Contesting Culture: Discourses of Identity in Multi-Ethnic
    London*, Cambridge: Cambridge University Press.
Baynham, M. (2014), 'Identity: Brought about or brought along? Narrative as a
    privileged site for researching intercultural identities', in F. Dervin and K. Risager
    (eds), *Researching Identity and Interculturality*, 67–85, New York: Routledge.
Bérubé, A. (2010), *Coming Out Under Fire: The History of Gay Men and Women
    in World War II*, Chapel Hill: The University of North Carolina Press.
Bhatia, V. K. (1993), *Analysing Genre: Language Use in Professional Settings*,
    London: Longman.
Birdwhistell, R. L. (1952), *Introduction to Kinesics: An Annotation System for
    Analysis of Body Motion and Gesture*, Washington, DC: Department of State,
    Foreign Service Institute.
Blommaert, J. (2005), *Discourse: A Critical Introduction*, Cambridge: Cambridge
    University Press.
Blommaert, J. (2010), *The Sociolinguistics of Globalization*, Cambridge, UK; New
    York: Cambridge University Press.
Bloomfield, L. (1933), *Language*, Chicago: University of Chicago Press.
Bolinger, D. (1983), 'Intonation and Gesture', *American Speech*, 58 (2): 156–74.
Bourdieu, P. (1977), *Outline of a Theory of Practice*, translated by R. Nice,
    Cambridge: Cambridge University Press.
Bourdieu, P. (1991), *Language and Symbolic Power*, edited by J. B. Thompson,
    translated by G. Raymond and M. Adamson, Cambridge, MA: Harvard
    University Press.

Bourdieu, P. (1992), *The Logic of Practice*, translated by R. Nice, Stanford: Stanford University Press.

Briggs, C. L. (1988), *Competence in Performance: The Creativity of Tradition in Mexicano Verbal Art*, Philadelphia: University of Pennsylvania Press.

Briggs, C. L. and Bauman, R. (1992), 'Genre, intertextuality, and social power', *Journal of Linguistic Anthropology*, 2 (2): 131–72.

Brown, P. and Levinson, S. C. (1987), *Politeness: Some Universals in Language Usage*, Cambridge, UK: New York: Cambridge University Press.

Bruner, J. (1987), *Actual Minds, Possible Worlds*, Cambridge, MA: Harvard University Press.

Bucholtz, M. (1999a), 'Bad examples: Transgression and progress in language and gender studies', in M. Bucholtz, A. C. Liang and L. A. Sutton (eds), *Reinventing Identities: The Gendered Self in Discourse*, 3–24, New York: Oxford University Press.

Bucholtz, M. (1999b), '"Why be normal?": Language and identity practices in a community of nerd girls', *Language in Society*, 28: 203–23.

Bucholtz, M. and Hall, K. (2005), 'Identity and interaction: A sociocultural linguistic approach', *Discourse Studies*, 7: 585–614.

Burke, K. (1969), *A Grammar of Motives*, Berkeley, CA: University of California Press.

Butler, J. (1990/2006), *Gender Trouble: Feminism and the Subversion of Identity*, 2nd edn, New York: Routledge.

Butler, J. (1993a), *Bodies that Matter: On the Discursive Limits of 'Sex'*, New York: Psychology Press.

Butler, J. (1993b), 'Imitation and gender insubordination', in H. Abelove, M. A. Barale and D. A. Halperin (eds), *The Lesbian and Gay Studies Reader*, 307–20, New York: Routlege.

Butler, J. (1993c), 'Endangered/endangering: Schematic racism and white paranoia', in R. Gooding-Williams (ed.), *Reading Rodney King/Reading Urban Uprising*, 15–22, New York: Psychology Press.

Button, G. (1990), 'Going up a blind alley: Conflating conversation analysis and computational modelling', in P. Luff, N. Gilbert and D. Frohlich (eds), *Computers and Conversation*, 67–90, London: Academic Press.

Cain, C. (1991), 'Personal stories: Identity acquisition and self-understanding in alcoholics anonymous', *Ethos*, 19 (2): 210–53.

Cameron, D. (2001), *Working with Spoken Discourse*, Thousand Oaks, CA: Sage.

Channell, J. (1997), '"I just called to say I love you": Love and desire on the telephone', in K. Harvey and C. Shalom (eds), *Language and Desire: Encoding Sex, Romance, and Intimacy*, 143–69, London; New York: Psychology Press.

Chirrey, D. A. (2003), '"I hereby come out": What sort of speech act is coming out?', *Journal of Sociolinguistics*, 7 (1): 24–37.

Chomsky, N. (1965), *Aspects of the Theory of Syntax*, Cambridge, MA: MIT Press.

Chow, W. S. (2000), *Tongzhi: Politics of Same-Sex Eroticism in Chinese Societies*, New York: Routledge.

Chun, E. W. (2001), 'The construction of white, black, and Korean American identities through African American vernacular English', *Journal of Linguistic Anthropology*, 11 (1): 52–64.

Cicourel, A. V. (1992), 'The interpenetration of communicative contexts: Examples from medical encounters', in A. Duranti and C. Goodwin (eds), *Rethinking*

Context: Language as an Interactive Phenomenon, 291–310, Cambridge: Cambridge University Press.

Clark, H. H. (1992), *Arenas of Language Use*, Chicago: University of Chicago Press.

Clark, K. and Holquist, M. (1984), *Mikhail Bakhtin*, Cambridge, MA: Harvard University Press.

Cole, M. (1998), *Cultural Psychology: A Once and Future Discipline*, Cambridge, MA: The Belknap Press.

Coleman, E. (1982), 'Developmental stages of the coming out process', *Journal of Homosexuality*, 7 (2–3): 31–43.

Collins, R. (1981), 'On the microfoundations of macrosociology', *American Journal of Sociology*, 86 (5): 984–1014.

Cook, G. (2011), 'Discourse analysis', in J. Simpson (ed.), *The Routledge Handbook of Applied Linguistics*, 431–44, London; New York: Routledge.

Coupland, N. (2001), 'Dialect stylization in radio talk', *Language in Society*, 30 (3): 345–75.

Croteau, J. M. (1996), 'Research on the work experiences of lesbian, gay and bisexual people; an integrative review of methodology and findings', *Journal of Vocational Behavior*, 48: 195–209.

Davies, B. and Harré, R. (1990), 'Positioning: The discursive construction of selves', *Journal for the Theory of Social Behaviour*, 20 (1): 43–63.

de Certeau, M. (1984), *The Practice of Everyday Life*, Berkeley, CA: University of California Press.

De Fina, A. (2015), 'Enregistered and emergent identities in narrative', in F. Dervin and K. Risager (eds), *Researching Identity and Interculurality*, 46–66, New York; London: Routledge.

Derrida, J. (1984), *Margins of Philosophy*, translated by A. Bass, Chicago: University of Chicago Press.

Duranti, A. (1983), 'Samoan speechmaking across social events: One genre in and out of a "fono"', *Language in Society*, 12 (1): 1–22.

Eckert, P. (2008), 'Communities of practice', in J. L. Mey (ed.), *Concise Encyclopedia of Pragmatics*, 109–12, Oxford: Elsevier Science.

Eckert, P. and McConnell-Ginet, S. (1992), 'Think practically and look locally: Language and gender as community-based practice', *Annual Review of Anthropology*, 21: 461–90.

Enfield, N. J. (2013), *Relationship Thinking: Agency, Enchrony, and Human Sociality*, New York: Oxford University Press.

Erikson, E. H. (1950), *Childhood and Society*, New York: W. W. Norton & Company.

Erikson, E. H. (1968), *Identity: Youth and Crisis*, New York: W. W. Norton & Company.

Erikson, E. H. (1975), *Life History and the Historical Moment*, New York: W. W. Norton & Company.

Erickson, F. (1986), 'Money tree, lasagna bush, salt and pepper: Social construction of cohesion in a conversation among Italian-Americans', in D. Tannen (ed.), *Analyzing Discourse: Text and Talk: Georgetown University Round Table on Languages and Linguistics 1981*, 43–70, Washington, DC: Georgetown University Press.

Erickson, F. (1990), 'The social construction of discourse coherence in a family dinner table conversation', in B. Dorval (ed.), *Conversational Organization and its Development*, 207–38, Norwood, NJ: Ablex.

Erickson, F. (2004), *Talk and Social Theory: Ecologies of Speaking and Listening in Everyday Life*, Cambridge: Polity Press.

Erickson, F. and Schultz, J. (1982), *The Counselor as Gatekeeper: Social Interaction in Inverviews*, New York: Academic Press.

Everett, D. L. (2012), *Language: The Cultural Tool*, New York: Vintage.

Fairclough, N. (1992), *Discourse and Social Change*, Oxford: Polity Press.

Firth, J. R. (1937), *The Tongues of Men*, Oxford: Oxford University Press.

Foucault, M. (1969), *The Archeology of Knowledge*, translated by A. M. S. Smith, New York: Random House.

Foucault, M. (1971), 'Orders of discourse', *Social Science Information*, 10 (2): 7–30.

Foucault, M. (1976), *The History of Sexuality, Vol. 1: An Introduction*, translated by R. Hurley, New York: Vintage.

Frobenius, M. (2014), 'Audience design in monologues: How bloggers involve their viewers', *Journal of Pragmatics*, 72: 59–72.

Gal, S. and Irvine, J. (1995), 'The boundaries of languages and disciplines', *Social Research*, 62: 967–1001.

Garfinkel, H. (1967), *Studies in Ethnomethodology*, Englewood Cliffs, NJ: Prentice Hall.

Garfinkel, H. (2002), *Ethnomethodology's Program: Working out Durkheim's Aphorism*, Boulder, CO: Rowman & Littlefield.

Gee, J. P. (2011), *An Introduction to Discourse Analysis: Theory and Method*, 3rd edn, New York: Routledge.

Gee, J. P. (2012), *Social Linguistics and Literacies: Ideology in Discourses*, 4th edn, London; New York: Routledge.

Gee, J. P. (2014a), 'Tools of inquiry and discourses', in N. Coupland and A. Jaworski (eds), *A Discourse Reader*, 143–53, London: Routledge.

Gee, J. P. (2014b), *Unified Discourse Analysis: Language, Reality, Virtual Worlds and Video Games*, Abingdon, Oxon: Routledge.

Gee, J. P. and Green, J. L. (1998), 'Discourse analysis, learning and social practice: A methodological study', *Review of Research in Education*, 23: 119–69.

Gershon, I. (2012), *The Breakup 2.0: Disconnecting Over New Media*, Ithaca: Cornell University Press.

Gibson, J. J. (1986), *The Ecological Approach to Visual Perception*, Boston: Psychology Press.

Giddens, A. (1986), *The Constitution of Society: Outline of the Theory of Structuration*, Berkeley: University of California Press.

Giddens, A. (1991), *Modernity and Self-Identity: Self and Society in the Late Modern Age*, Cambridge: Polity Press.

Goffman, E. (1959), *The Presentation of Self in Everyday Life*, New York: Doubleday.

Goffman, E. (1963), *Stigma: Notes on the Management of Spoiled Identity*, Englewood Cliffs, NJ: Prentice Hall.

Goffman, E. (1964), 'The neglected situation', *American Anthropologist*, 66: 133–6.

Goffman, E. (1966), *Behavior in Public Places: Notes on the Social Organization of Gatherings*, New York: The Free Press.

Goffman, E. (1967), *Interaction Ritual*, Chicago: Aldine Publishing Co.

Goffman, E. (1971), *Relations in Public*, New York: Basic books.

Goffman, E. (1974), *Frame Analysis: An Essay on the Organization of Experience*, New York: Harper and Row.

Goffman, E. (1981), *Forms of Talk*, Oxford: Blackwell.

Goffman, E. (1983a), 'The interaction order: American Sociological Association, 1982 Presidential Address', *American Sociological Review*, 48 (1): 1–17.

Goffman, E. (1983b), 'Felicity's condition', *American Journal of Sociology*, 89 (1): 1–53.

Goodwin, C. (1980), 'Restarts, pauses, and the achievement of a state of mutual Gaze at turn beginning', *Sociological Inquiry* 50: 272–302.

Goodwin, C. (1981), *Conversational Organization: Interaction Between Speakers and Hearers*, New York: Academic Press.

Goodwin, C. (1984), 'Notes on story structure and the organization of participation', in J. Maxwell Atkinson and John Heritage (eds), *Structures of Social Action*, 225–46, Cambridge: Cambridge University Press.

Goodwin, C. (1994), 'Professional vision', *American Anthropologist*, 96 (3): 606–33.

Goodwin, C. and Duranti, A. (1992), 'Rethinking context: An introduction', in A. Duranti and C. Goodwin (eds), *Rethinking Context: Language as an Interactive Phenomenon*, 1–42, Cambridge, UK; New York: Cambridge University Press.

Grice, H. P. (1957/89), *Studies in the Way of Words*, Cambridge, MA: Harvard University Press.

Griffin, P. (1992), 'From hiding out to coming out: Empowering lesbian and gay educators', in K. Harbeck (ed.), *Coming Out of the Classroom Closet*, 167–96, New York: Harrington Park Press.

Gumperz, J. J. (1972), *Language in Social Groups*, Stanford, CA: Stanford University Press.

Gumperz, J. J. (1982), *Discourse Strategies*, Cambridge: Cambridge University Press.

Gumperz, J. J. (ed.) (1982), *Language and Social Identity*, Cambridge: Cambridge University Press.

Gumperz, J. J. and Hymes, D. H. (1964), *The Ethnography of Communication*, Washington, DC: American Anthropological Association.

Hacking, I. (1975), *Why Does Language Matter to Philosophy?*, Cambridge: Cambridge University Press.

Haddington, P. (2006), 'The organization of gaze and assessments as resources for stance taking', *Text and Talk*, 26 (3): 281–328.

Hall, E. T. (1966/90), *The Hidden Dimension*, New York: Anchor.

Hall, S. (1996), 'Who needs identity?', in S. Hall and P. du Gay (eds), *Questions of Cultural Identity*, 1–17, London; Thousand Oaks, CA: Sage.

Halliday, M. A. K. (1973), *Explorations in the Functions of Language*, New York: Elsevier.

Halliday, M. A. K. (1978), *Language as Social Semiotic: The Social Interpretation of Language and Meaning*, London: Edward Arnold.

Hanks, W. F. (1996), *Language and Communicative Practices*, Boulder, CO: Westview Press.

Hanks, W. F. (2001), 'Indexicality', in A. Duranti (ed.), *Key Terms in Language and Culture*, 119–21, Oxford: Blackwell.

Harley, D. and Fitzpatrick, G. (2009), 'Creating a conversational context through video blogging: A case study of Geriatric 1927', *Computers in Human Behavior*, 25 (3): 679–89.

Harré, R. (1983), 'Identity projects', in G. M. Breakwell (ed.), *Threatened Identities*, 31–51, New York: Wiley.

Harris, R. (1981/2002), *The Language Myth in Western Culture*, New York: Psychology Press.

Harris, R. (1996), *Signs, Language, and Communication: Integrational and Segregational Approaches*, New York: Psychology Press.

Harris, Z. (1952), 'Discourse analysis', *Language*, 28 (1): 1–30.

Haviland, J. B. (2007), 'Master speakers, master gesturers: A string quartet master class', in S. Duncan, E. Levy and J. Cassell (eds), *Gesture and the Dynamic Dimension of Language: Essays in Honor of David McNeill*, 147–72, Philadelphia: John Benjamins.

Haviland, J. B. (2009), 'Cultural and social dimension of spoken discourse', in J. L. Mey (ed.), *Concise Encyclopedia of Pragmatics*, 170–3, Oxford: Elsevier Science.

Haynes, D. (2013), Answering Bakhtin. The I.B. Taurus Blog. Retrieved from http://theibtaurisblog.com/2013/05/01/answering-bakhtin/.

Heritage, J. and Atkinson, M. (1984), 'Introduction', in M. Atkinson and J. Heritage (eds), *Structures in Social Action: Studies in Conversation Analysis*, 1–15, Cambridge: Cambridge University Press.

Heritage, J. and Clayman, S. (2010), *Talk in Action*, Malden, MA; Oxford: Wiley-Blackwell.

Hockett, C. F. (1960), 'The origin of speech', *Scientific American*, 203: 88–111.

Hoenisch, S. (8 May 2006), A Wittgensteinian approach to discourse analysis. Retrieved from http://www.criticism.com/da/lw_da.html.

Holland, D. and Lave, J. (2001), 'History in person: An introduction', in D. Holland and J. Lave (eds), *History in Person: Enduring Struggles, Contentious Practice, Intimate Identities*, 3–33, Santa Fe, NM: School of American Research Press.

Holmes, J. (1988), 'Paying compliments: A sex-preferential politeness strategy', *Journal of Pragmatics*, 12 (4): 445–65.

Hughes, R. (2011), *Teaching and Researching: Speaking*, 2nd edn, Harlow, UK: Pearson Education.

Humphreys, K. (2000), 'Community narratives and personal stories in Alcoholics Anonymous', *Journal of Community Psychology*, 28 (5): 495–506.

Hutchby, I. (2001), *Conversation and Technology: From the Telephone to the Internet*, Cambridge: Polity Press.

Hutchby, I. and Wooffitt, R. (2008), *Conversation Analysis*, Cambridge: Polity Press.

Hymes, D. (1971), 'Competence and performance in linguistic theory', in R. Huxley and E. Ingram (eds), *Language Acquisition: Models and Methods*, New York: Academic Press.

Hymes, D. (1974), *Foundations in Sociolinguistics: An Ethnographic Approach*, Philadelphia: University of Pennsylvania Press.

Hymes, D. H. (1996), *Ethnography, Linguistics, Narrative Inequality: Toward An Understanding of Voice*, London: Taylor & Francis.

Iedema, R. (2001), 'Resemiotization', *Semiotica*, 137 (1–4): 23–39.

Innis, H. A. (1951), *The Bias of Communication*, Toronto: University of Toronto Press.

Johnstone, B. (2007), 'Linking identity and dialect through stancetaking', in R. Englebretson (ed.), *Stancetaking in Discourse: Subjectivity in Interaction*, 49–68, Amsterdam: John Benjamins.

Johnstone, B. (2009), 'Pittsburghese shirts: Commodification and the enregisterment of an urban dialect', *American Speech*, 84 (2): 157–75.

Johnstone, B., Andrus, J. and Danielson, A. E. (2006), 'Mobility, indexicality, and the enregisterment of "Pittsburghese"', *Journal of English Linguistics*, 34 (2): 77–104.

Johnstone, B. and Kiesling, S. F. (2008), 'Indexicality and experience: Exploring the meanings of /aw/-monophthongization in Pittsburgh', *Journal of Sociolinguistics*, 12 (1): 5–33.

Jones, R. H. (2002a), 'Mediated action and sexual risk: Discourses of sexuality and AIDS in the People's Republic of China', Unpublished PhD diss., Sydney: Macquarie University.

Jones, R. H. (2002b), 'A walk in the park: Frames and positions in AIDS prevention outreach among gay men in China', *Journal of Sociolinguistics*, 6 (4): 575–88.

Jones, R. H. (2004), 'The problem of context in computer mediated communication', in R. Scollon and P. LeVine (eds), *Discourse and Technology: Multimodal Discourse Analysis*, 20–33, Washington, DC: Georgetown University Press.

Jones, R. H. (2005), 'Sites of engagement as sites of attention: Time, space and culture in electronic discourse', in S. Norris and R. Jones (eds), *Discourse in Action: Introducing Mediated Discourse Analysis*, 44–54, London: Routledge.

Jones, R. H. (2008b), 'The role of text in televideo cybersex', *Text & Talk*, 28 (4): 453–73.

Jones, R. H. (2011), 'Sport and re/creation: What skateboarders can teach us about learning', *Sport, Education and Society*, 16 (5): 593–611.

Jones, R. H. (2012), *Discourse Analysis: A Resource Book for Students*, Milton Park, Abingdon, Oxon; New York, NY: Routledge.

Jones, R. H. (2013), *Health and Risk Communication: An Applied Linguistic Perspective*, London: Routledge.

Jones, R. H. (2015), 'Generic intertextuality in online social activism: The case of the It Gets Better project', *Language in Society*, 44: 317–39.

Juzwik, M. (2004), 'Towards an ethics of answerability: Reconsidering dialogism in sociocultural literacy research', *College Composition and Communication*, 55 (3): 536–67.

Kang, M. A. (1998), 'Triadic participation in organizational meeting interaction', *Issues in Applied Linguistics*, 9 (2): 139–50.

Katriel, T. (1999), 'Rethinking the terms of social interaction', *Research on Language and Social Interaction*, 32: 95–101.

Kendon, A. (1967), 'Some functions of gaze direction in social interaction', *Acta Psychologica*, 26: 22–63.

Kendon, A. (1970), 'Movement coordination in social interaction', *Acta Psychologica*, 32: 1–25.

Kendon, A. (1975), 'Gesticulation, speech and the gesture theory of language', *Research on Language and Social Interaction*, 27 (3): 175–200.

Kendon, A. (1990), *Conducting Interaction: Patterns of Behavior in Focused Encounters*, Cambridge: Cambridge University Press.

Kendon, A. and Ferber, A. (1973), 'A description of some human greetings', in R. P. Michael and J. H. Crook (eds), *Comparative Behaviour and Ecology of Primates*, 591–668, London: Academic Press.

Kiesling, S. F. (2012), 'Ethnography of speaking', in C. B. Paulston, S. F. Kiesling and E. S. Rangel (eds), *The Handbook of Intercultural Discourse and Communication*, 77–89, New York: John Wiley & Sons, Ltd.

Kimmel, M. (2001), 'Masculinity as homophobia: Fear, shame, and silence in the construction of gender identity', in S. Whitehead and F. Barrett (eds), *The Masculinities Reader*, 266–87, Cambridge: Polity Press.

Kitzinger, C. (2000), 'Doing feminist conversation analysis', *Feminism & Psychology*, 10 (2): 163–93.

Kitzinger, C. and Frith, H. (1999), 'Just say no? The use of conversation analysis in developing a feminist perspective on sexual refusal', *Discourse & Society*, 10 (3): 293–316.

Knobel, M. and Lankshear, C. (2015), 'Language, creativity and remix culture', in R. H. Jones (ed.), *Routledge Handbook of Language and Creativity*, 398–414, London: Routledge.

Kress, G. R. (2009), *Multimodality: A Social Semiotic Approach to Contemporary Communication*, London; New York: Routledge.

Kress, G. R. and van Leeuwen, T. (1996), *Reading Images: The Grammar of Visual Design*, London: Routledge.

Kristeva, J. (1986), 'Word, dialogue, and the novel', in T. Moi (ed.), *The Kristeva Reader*, 35–61, New York: Columbia University Press.

Kulick, D. (2003a), 'Language and desire', in J. Holmes and M. Meyerhoff (eds), *Handbook of Language and Gender*, 119–41, Oxford: Blackwell.

Kulick, D. (2003b), 'No', *Language and Communication*, 23: 139–51.

Labov, W. (1972a), 'The study of language in its social context', in P. Giglioli (ed.), *Language and Social Context*, 283–307, Harmondsworth: Penguin.

Labov, W. (1972b), *Sociolinguistic Patterns*, Philadelphia: University of Pennsylvania Press.

Labov, W. and Fanshel, D. (1977), *Therapeutic Discourse: Psychotherapy as Conversation*, New York: Academic Press.

Labov, W. and Waletzky, J. (1967), 'Narrative analysis: Oral versions of personal experience', in I. Helm (ed.), *Essays on the Verbal and Visual Arts*, 12–44, Proceedings of the 1966 Annual Spring Meeting of the American Ethnological Society. Seattle, WA: University of Washington Press.

Lanier, J. (2011), *You Are Not a Gadget: A Manifesto*, New York: Vintage.

Lave, J. and Wenger, E. (1991), *Situated Learning: Legitimate Peripheral Participation*, Cambridge: Cambridge University Press.

Leap, W. (1999), 'Language, socialization, and silence in Gay adolescence', in M. Bucholtz, A. C. Liang and L. A. Sutton (eds), *Reinventing Identities: The Gendered Self in Discourse*, 259–72, New York: Oxford University Press.

Leech, G. N. (1983), *Principles of Pragmatics*, London: Longman.

Lemke, J. L. (1999), 'Typological and topological meaning in diagnostic discourse', *Discourse Processes*, 27 (2): 173–85.

Lemke, J. L. (2000), 'Opening up closure: Semiotics across scales', *Annals of the New York Academy of Sciences*, 901 (1): 100–11.

le Page, R. B. and Tabouret-Keller, A. (1985), *Acts of Identity: Creole-Based Approaches to Language and Ethnicity*, Cambridge, UK; New York: Cambridge University Press.

Levinson, S. C. (1983), *Pragmatics*, Cambridge: Cambridge University Press.

Liang, A. C. (1997), 'The creation of coherence in coming out stories', in A. Livia and K. Hall (eds), *Queerly Phrased: Language, Gender, and Sexuality*, 287–309, New York: Oxford University Press.

Liang, A. C. (1999), 'Conversationally implicating lesbian and gay identity', in M. Bucholtz, A. C. Liang and L. A. Sutton (eds), *Reinventing Identities: The Gendered Self in Discourse*, 293–310, New York: Oxford University Press.

Liddicoat, A. J. (2004), 'The projectability of turn constructional units and the role of prediction in listening', *Discourse Studies*, 6 (4): 449–69.

Liu, J. P. and Ding, N. F. (2005), 'Reticent poetics, queer politics', *Inter-Asia Cultural Studies*, 6 (1): 30–55.

Lucy, J. (1993a), 'General Introduction', in J. Lucy (ed.), *Reflexive Language*, 1–4, New York: Cambridge University Press.

Lucy, J. (1993b), 'Reflexive language in the human disciplines', in J. Lucy (ed.), *Reflexive Language*, 9–31, New York: Cambridge University Press.

Luke, A. (1996), 'Series editor's introduction', in D. H. Hymes (ed.), *Ethnography, Linguistics, Narrative Inequality: Toward an Understanding of Voice*, i–ix, London: Taylor & Francis.

Lyman, P. (1998), 'The fraternal bond as a joking relationship: A case study of the role of sexist jokes in male group bonding', in M. Kimmel and M. Messner (eds), *Men's Lives*, 171–93, Boston, MA: Allyn and Bacon.

Lyotard, J.-F. (1979), *The Postmodern Condition*, Manchester: Manchester University Press.

Malinowski, B. (1923), 'The problem of meaning in primitive languages', in C. K. Ogden and I. A. Richards (eds), *The Meaning of Meaning: A Study of Influence of Language Upon Thought and of the Science of Symbolism*, 296–336, New York: Harcourt, Brace and World.

Malinowski, B. (1935), *Coral Gardens and Their Magic*, London: Allen & Unwin.

Malone, M. (1997), *Worlds of Talk: The Presentation of Self in Everyday Conversation*, Cambridge: Polity Press.

Mason, D. (2011), 'Queer youth, mobility, and the narratives of It Gets Better', in *Queer Issues in the Study of Education and Culture III*, 12–17, Retrieved from http://www.ismss.ualberta.ca/sites/dev.ismss.ualberta.ca/files/QSEC2011.pdf#page=13.

Martínez-Cabeza, M. A. (2009), 'Dangerous words: Threats, perlocutions and strategic actions', in W. Oleksy and P. Stalmaszczyk (eds), *Cognitive Approaches to Language and Linguistic Data: Studies in Honor of Barbara Lewandowska-Tomaszczyk*, 269–84, Frankfurt: Peter Lang.

Maynard, D. W. (2003), *Bad News, Good News: Conversational Order in Everyday Talk and Clinical Settings*, Chicago: University Of Chicago Press.

McLuhan, M. (1964/2001), *Understanding Media: The Extensions of Man*, London: Routledge.

McNeill, D. (2005), *Gesture and Thought*, Chicago: University of Chicago Press.

Mehan, H. (1993), 'Beneath the skin and between the ears: A case study in the politics of representation', in S. Chaiklin and J. Lave (eds), *Understanding Practice: Perspectives on Activity and Context*, 241–68, Cambridge: Cambridge University Press.

Mey, J. (2013), 'A brief sketch of the historical development of pragmatics', in K. Allen (ed.), *The Oxford Handbook of the History of Linguistics*, 588–611, Oxford: Oxford University Press.

Meyrowitz, J. (1985), *No Sense of Place: The Impact of Electronic Media on Social Behavior*, Oxford; New York: Oxford University Press.

Mondada, L. (2012), 'Talking and driving: Multiactivity in the car', *Semiotica*, 191: 223–56.

Morgan, M. (2006), 'Speech community', in A. Duranti (ed.), *A Companion to Linguistic Anthropology*, 3–22, Malden, MA: Blackwell Publishing.

Mori, J. (2003), 'The construction of interculturality: A study of initial encounters between Japanese and American Students', *Research on Language and Social Interaction*, 36 (2): 143–84.

Morson, G. S. (2009), 'Addressivity', in J. L. Mey (ed.), *Concise Encyclopedia of Pragmatics*, 13–16, Oxford: Elsevier.

Müller, C. (2003), 'Forms and uses of the palm up open hand', in C. Müller and R. Posner (eds), *The Semantics and Pragmatics of Everyday Gestures. The Berlin Conference*, 234–56, Berlin: Weidler.

Nevile, M. (2012), 'Interaction as distraction in driving: A body of evidence', *Semiotica*, 191: 169–96.

Nielsen, G. M. (2012), *Norms of Answerability, The Social Theory Between Bakhtin and Habermas*, Albany: SUNY Press.

Nishizaka, A. (1995), 'The interactive constitution of interculturality: How to be a Japanese with words', *Human Studies*, 18: 301–26.

Norris, S. (2004), *Analyzing Multimodal Interaction: A Methodological Framework*, London: Routledge.

Norris, S. and Jones, R. (eds) (2005), *Discourse in Action: Introducing Mediated Discourse Analysis*, London: Routledge.

Ochs, E. (1993), 'Indexing gender', in A. Duranti and C. Goodwin (eds), *Rethinking Context: Language as an Interactive Phenomenon*, 335–58, Cambridge: Cambridge University Press.

Ochs, E. and Capps, L. (2009), *Living Narrative: Creating Lives in Everyday Storytelling*, Cambridge, MA: Harvard University Press.

Orne, J. (2011), 'You will always have to "out" yourself: Reconsidering coming out through strategic outness', *Sexualities*, 14 (6): 681–703.

Pascoe, C. J. (2005), '"Dude, you're a fag": Adolescent masculinity and the fag discourse', *Sexualities*, 8 (3): 329–46.

Pillet-Shore, D. (2012), 'Greeting: Displaying stance through prosodic recipient design', *Research on Language and Social Interaction*, 45 (4): 375–98.

Pomerantz, A. (1984), 'Agreeing and disagreeing with assessments: Some features of preferred and dispreferred turn shapes', in J. M. Atkinson and J. Heritage (eds), *Structures of Social Action*, 57–101, Cambridge: Cambridge University Press.

Puckett, A. (2000), *Seldom ask, Never Tell: Labor and Discourse in Appalachia*, Oxford; New York: Oxford University Press, 2001.

Rampton, B. (1995), *Crossing: Language and Ethnicity among Adolescents*, London; New York: Addison Wesley Publishing Company.

Rampton, B. (2008), *Language in Late Modernity: Interaction in an Urban School*, Cambridge: Cambridge University Press.

Rasmussen, M. L. (2004), 'The problem of coming out', *Theory Into Practice*, 43 (2): 144–50.

Rawls, A. W. (1987), 'The interaction order sui generis: Goffman's contribution to social theory', *Sociological Theory*, 5: 136–49.

Raymond, G. and Sidnell, J. (2014), 'Conversation analysis', in A. Jaworski and N. Coupland (eds), *The Discourse Reader*, 2nd edn, 249–63, London; New York: Routledge.

Ruesch, J. and Bateson, G. (1951), *Communication: The Social Matrix of Psychiatry*, New York: W. W. Norton & Company.

Sacks, H. (1972), 'On the analyzability of stories by children', in J. J. Gumperz and D. Hymes (eds), *Directions in Sociolinguistics: The Ethnography of Communication*, 325–45, New York: Holt, Rinehart and Winston.

Sacks, H. (1984), 'On doing "being ordinary"', in M. Atkinson and J. Heritage (eds), *Structures of Social Action*, 413–29, Cambridge: Cambridge University Press.

Sacks, H. (1992a), *Lectures on Conversation Vol. 1*, edited by G. Jefferson and E. A. Schegloff, Oxford: Wiley-Blackwell.

Sacks, H. (1992b), *Lectures on Conversation Vol. 2*, edited by G. Jefferson and E. A. Schegloff, Oxford: Wiley-Blackwell.

Sacks, H., Schegloff, E. and Jefferson, G. (1974), 'A simplest systematics for the organization of turn-taking for conversation', *Language,* 50: 696–735.

Samra-Fredericks, D. (2010), 'Researching everyday practice: The ethnomethodological contribution', in D. Golsorkhi, L. Rouleau, D. Seidl and E. Vaara (eds), *Cambridge Handbook of Strategy as Practice*, 230–42, Cambridge: Cambridge University Press.

Saussure, F. de (1916/59), *Course in General Linguistics*, New York: Philosophical Library.

Savage, D. and Miller, T. (2011), *It Gets Better: Coming Out, Overcoming Bullying, and Creating a Life Worth Living*, New York: Penguin.

Schank, R. C. and Abelson, R. P. (1977), *Scripts, Plans, Goals, and Understanding: An Inquiry into Human Knowledge Structures*, New York: Psychology Press.

Schegloff, E. A. (1968), 'Sequencing in conversational openings', *American Anthropologist*, 70 (6): 1075–95.

Schegloff, E. A. (1972), 'Notes on conversational practise: Formulating place', in D. Sudnow (ed.), *Studies in Social Interaction,* 75–119, New York: Free Press.

Schegloff, E. A. (1980), 'Preliminaries to preliminaries: "Can I ask you a question?"', *Sociological Inquiry*, 50 (3–4): 104–52.

Schegloff, E. A. (1992), 'Introduction', in H. Sacks (ed.), *Lectures on Conversation*, vol. 1, ix–lxii, Oxford: Blackwell.

Schegloff, E. A. (2007), *Sequence Organization in Interaction: A Primer in Conversation Analysis*, Cambridge: Cambridge University Press.

Schegloff, E. A. and Sacks, H. (1973), 'Opening up closings', *Semiotica*, 8 (4): 289–327.

Schieffelin, B. B., Woolard, K. A. and Kroskrity, P. V. (eds) (1998), *Language Ideologies : Practice and Theory*, New York: Oxford University Press.

Schiffrin, D. (1988), *Discourse Markers*, Cambridge: Cambridge University Press.

Schiffrin, D. (1996), 'Narrative as self-portrait: Sociolinguistic constructions of identity', *Language in Society*, 25 (2): 167–203.

Schober, M. F. and Brennan, S. E. (2003), 'Processes of interactive spoken discourse: The role of the partner', in A. C. Graesser, M. A. Gernsbacher and S. R. Goldman (eds), *Handbook of Discourse Processes*, 123–64, Mahwah, NJ: Lawrence Erlbaum Associates.

Scollon, R. (1998), *Mediated Discourse as Social Interaction: A Study of News Discourse*, London: Longman.

Scollon, R. (2001), *Mediated Discourse: The Nexus of Practice*, London: Routledge.

Scollon, R. (2002), 'Intercultural communication as mediated discourse', Unpublished manuscript, Washington, DC: Georgetown University.

Scollon, R. (2008), 'Discourse itineraries: Nine processes of resemiotization', in V. K. Bhatia, J. Flowerdew and R. H. Jones (eds), *Advances in Discourse Studies*, 233–44, London: Routledge.

Scollon, R. and Scollon, S. W. (1981), *Narrative, Literacy, and Face in Interethnic Communication*, Norwood, NJ: Ablex Publishing Corporation.

Scollon, R. and Scollon, S. W. (2004), *Nexus Analysis: Discourse and the Emerging Internet*, London: Routledge.

Scollon, R., Scollon, S. W. and Jones, R. H. (2012), *Intercultural Communication: A Discourse Approach*, 3rd edn, Chichester: Wiley-Blackwell.

Scollon, R., Tsang, W. K., Li, D., Yung, V. and Jones, R. (1998), 'Voice, appropriation and discourse representation in a student writing task', *Linguistics and Education*, 9 (3): 227–50.

Searle, J. R. (1969), *Speech Acts: An Essay in the Philosophy of Language*, Cambridge: Cambridge University Press.

Shepard, B. (2009), *Queer Political Performance and Protest*, New York: Routledge.

Shuy, R. (1996), *Language Crimes: The Use and Abuse of Language Evidence in the Courtroom*, Oxford: Wiley-Blackwell.

Silverstein, M. (1992), 'The indeterminacy of contextualization: When is enough enough?', in A. DiLuzio and P. Auer (eds), *The Contextualization of Language*, 550–75, Amsterdam: Benjimins.

Silverstein, M. (1993), 'Metapragmatic discourse and metapragmatic function', in J. Lucy (ed.), *Reflexive Language*, 33–38, New York: Cambridge University Press.

Silverstein, M. (1998), 'Contemporary transformations of local linguistic communities', *Annual Review of Anthropology*, 27: 401–26.

Silverstein, M. (2003), 'Indexical order and the dialectics of sociolinguistic life', *Language and Communication*, 23 (3–4): 193–229.

Silverstein, M. and Urban, G. (eds) (1996), *Natural Histories of Discourse*, Chicago: University of Chicago Press.

Simons, H. W. (1995), 'Arguing about the ethics of past actions: An analysis of a taped conversation about a taped conversation', *Argumentation*, 9 (1): 225–50.

Sinclair, J. M. and Coulthard, R. M. (1975), *Towards an Analysis of Discourse: The English used by Teachers and Pupils*, London: Oxford University Press.

Sindoni, M. G. (2013), *Spoken and Written Discourse in Online Interactions: A Multimodal Approach*, New York; London: Routledge.

Skinner, B. F. (1957/91), *Verbal Behavior*, Acton, MA: Copley Publishing Group.

Solove, D. J. (2007), *The Future of Reputation: Gossip, Rumor, and Privacy on the Internet*, New Haven: Yale University Press.

Sperber, D. and Wilson, D. (1996), *Relevance: Communication and Cognition*, 2nd edn, Oxford and Cambridge, MA: Wiley-Blackwell.

Spivak, G. (1987), *In Other Worlds: Essays in Cultural Politics*, London: Taylor and Francis.

Stivers, T., Enfield, N. J., Brown, P., Englert, C., Hayashi, M., Heinemann, T., Hoymann, G., Rossano, F., de Ruiter, J. P., Yoon, K. E. and Levinson, S. C. (2009), 'Universals and cultural variation in turn-taking in conversation', *Proceedings of the National Academy of Sciences*, 106 (26): 10587–92.

Stivers, T. and Heritage, J. (2001), 'Breaking the sequential mould: Narrative and other methods of answering "more than the question" during medical history taking', *Text*, 21 (1): 151–85.

Streeck, J. (1983), *Social Order in Child Communication: A Study in Microethnography*, Amsterdam: Benjamins.

Streeck, J. and Mehus, S. (2005), 'Microethnography: The study of practices', in K. L. Fitch and R. E. Sanders (eds), *Handbook of Language and Social Interaction*, 381–404, Mahwah, NJ: Lawrence Erlbaum.

Suchman, L. A. (2007), *Human-Machine Reconfigurations: Plans and Situated Actions*, 2nd edn, Cambridge, UK; New York: Cambridge University Press.

Swales, J. (1990), *Genre Analysis: English in Academic and Research Settings*, Cambridge: Cambridge University Press.

Swidler, A. (1986), 'Culture in action: Symbols and strategies', *American Sociological Review*, 51 (2): 273–86.

Tannen, D. (1984), 'The pragmatics of cross-cultural communication', *Applied Linguistics*, 5 (3): 189–95.

Tannen, D. (1992), *That's Not What I Meant!: How Conversational Style Makes or Breaks Relationships*, New York: Ballantine.

Tannen, D. (ed.) (1993), *Framing in Discourse*, New York: Oxford University Press.

Tannen, D. (2005), *Conversational Style: Analyzing Talk among Friends*, 2nd edn, New York: Oxford University Press.

ten Have, P. (1990), 'Methodological issues in conversation analysis', *Bulletin de Méthodologie Sociologique*, Nr. 27 (June): 23–51.

ten Have, P. (2007), *Doing Conversation Analysis*, London; Thousand Oaks, CA: Sage.

Terasaki, A. K. (2000), 'Pre-announcement sequences in conversation', in G. H. Lerner (ed.), *Conversation Analysis: Studies From the First Generation*, 171–223, Amsterdam: John Benjamins.

Thomas, J. (1983), 'Cross-cultural pragmatic failure', *Applied Linguistics*, 4 (2): 91–112.

Thomas, J. (1995), *Meaning in Interaction: An Introduction to Pragmatics*, London; New York: Routledge.

Trudgill, P. (1974), *The Social Differentiation of English in Norwich*, Cambridge: Cambridge University Press.

Urban, G. (1996), *Metaphysical Community*, Austin: University of Texas Press.

van Leeuwen, T. (1996), 'The representation of social actors', in C. R. Caldas-Coulthard and M. Coulthard (eds), *Texts and Practices: Readings in Critical Discourse Analysis*, 32–70, London: Routledge.

van Leeuwen, T. and Wodak, R. (1999), 'Legitimizing immigration control: A discourse-historical analysis', *Discourse Studies*, 1 (1): 83–118.

Voloshinov, V. N. (1973), *Marxism and the Philosophy of Language*, translated by L. Matejka and I. R. Titunik, New York: Seminar Press.

Vygotsky, L. S. (1962), *Thought and Language*, translated by E. Hanfmann and G. Vakar, Cambridge, MA: MIT Press.

Vygotsky, L. S. (1981), 'The instrumental method in psychology', in J. V. Wertsch (ed.), *The Concept of Activity in Soviet Psychology*, 134–43, Armonk, NY: M. E. Sharpe.

Wertsch, J. V. (1991), *Voices of the Mind: A Sociocultural Approach to Mediated Action*, Cambridge, MA: Harvard University Press.

Wertsch, J. V. (1994), 'The primacy of mediated action in sociocultural studies', *Mind, Culture and Activity*, 1 (4): 202–8.

Wertsch, J. V. (1998a), *Mind as Action*, New York: Oxford University Press.

Wertsch, J. V. (1998b), 'Vygotsky and Bakhtin on community', unpublished manuscript, St. Louis, MO: Washington University.

Widdowson, H. G. (1996), *Linguistics*, Oxford: Oxford University Press.

Wieder, D. L. and Pratt, S. (1990), 'On being a recognizable Indian among Indians', in D. Carbaugh (ed.), *Cultural Communication and Intercultural Contact*, 45–64, Hillside, NJ: Lawrence Erlbaum.

Wilkinson, S. and Kitzinger, C. (2011), 'Conversation analysis', in K. Hyland and B. Paltridge (eds), *Continuum Companion to Discourse Analysis*, 22–37, London: Contiuum.

Wittgenstein, L. (1958/69), *Philosophical Investigations*, translated by G. E. M. Anscombe, London: Blackwell.

Wodak, R. (1996), *Disorders of Discourse*, London: Longman.

Wodak, R. (2001), 'The discourse historical approach', in R. Wodak and M. Meyer (eds), *Methods of Critical Discourse Analysis*, 63–94, London: Sage.

Wortham, S. (2003), 'Accomplishing identity in participant-denoting discourse', *Journal of Linguistic Anthropology*, 13 (2): 189–210.

Wortham, S. and Reyes, A. (2015), *Discourse Analysis Beyond the Speech Event*, London: Routledge.

Yancy, G. and Butler, J. (12 January 2015), 'Interview: What's wrong with "all lives matter?"', *New York Times*. Retrieved from http://opinionator.blogs.nytimes.com/2015/01/12/whats-wrong-with-all-lives-matter/?_r=0.

Zimmerman, D. (1998), 'Identity, context and interaction', in C. Antaki and G. Widdicombe (eds), *Identities in Talk*, 87–106, London: Sage.

Index